STANDARDS INTO PRACTICE

SCHOOL-BASED ROLES

Innovation Configuration maps for
Standards for Professional Learning

MetLife Foundation

MetLife Foundation supported the revision and publication of
Standards for Professional Learning and related resources.

Co-authors: Joellen Killion, Shirley Hord, Patricia Roy, Jacqueline Kennedy, Stephanie Hirsh.

Editors: Tracy Crow, Rebecca Bender.

Designers: David McCoy, Kitty Black.

Reference citation for this book:

Learning Forward. (2012). *Standards into practice: School-based roles. Innovation Configuration maps for Standards for Professional Learning.* Oxford, OH: Author.

Printed in the United States of America
Item #B544
ISBN: 978-1-936630-06-6

Learning Forward
504 S. Locust St.
Oxford, OH 45056
513-523-6029
800-727-7288
Fax: 513-523-0638
Email: office@learningforward.org
www.learningforward.org

About MetLife Foundation

MetLife Foundation is committed to building a secure future for individuals and communities worldwide through a focus on empowering older adults, preparing young people, and building livable communities. In education, MetLife Foundation seeks to strengthen public schools through effective teaching and collaborative leadership, and to prepare students for access to and success in higher education, particularly during the crucial first year. The foundation's grant making is informed by findings from the annual *MetLife Survey of the American Teacher*. More information is available at www.metlife.org.

Contents

Foreword

When we introduced the first revision of the NSDC Standards for Staff Development in 2001, we thought we were finished with our most important work. We had defined effective professional development; with that people had what they needed to transform adult learning. Over the years, we heard how much educators appreciated our efforts, yet we saw little change in most individual and organizational actions related to professional development. While some educators moved toward adopting the standards into policy, they didn't know how to hold others accountable or support them in implementing the standards. We recognized that merely telling people about the elements that constituted effective professional development was not enough. We determined that we needed to provide a vision. Equipped with a vision for translating the standards into precise actions, each individual with responsibility for professional learning would have a roadmap for implementing the standards with fidelity.

Building on the long-standing Concerns-Based Adoption Model, we developed Innovation Configuration (IC) maps for the standards for 11 different educator roles. These Innovation Configuration maps create specific descriptions of what different educators do when they are implementing the standards. In addition, the IC maps provide detailed steps for progressing along the pathway from one's current set of behaviors to those that are described as ideal. IC maps address the concern that the standards do not provide educators the guidance they need to transform their professional learning to align with the standards.

Many people have used the first edition of the IC maps to guide planning, implementation, monitoring, and evaluation of professional learning. The maps add value to each phase of professional learning. They provide a resource for reflecting on and strengthening one's practice with explicit criteria. The IC maps guide movement to the highest level of implementation to increase the effectiveness and results of professional learning. They stimulate conversations and action planning for those who support educators implementing standards. The IC maps also serve as a diagnostic tool to assess the effectiveness of professional learning to improve results.

Over the years, we have had too many false starts in professional learning. When we introduced the revised Standards for Professional Learning in 2011, we included a standard focused specifically on implementation to address the reality that too much professional learning fails to achieve its intended outcome. Great planning with no follow-through is the primary reason that professional learning falls short. Frequently, early earnest efforts for reform are followed with insufficient commitment for strategic and substantive support over time to achieve implementation with fidelity. Energy, effort, and resources for professional learning subside too soon. The IC maps provide guidance for strengthening the effectiveness and results of professional learning for both educators and results.

Many have contributed to the development of the IC maps for school-based roles for the new standards. We are grateful to all who have contributed to this work with a special appreciation to Shirley Hord, Learning Forward's scholar laureate, Patricia Roy, senior consultant, Jacqueline Kennedy, associate director of strategy and development, and Joellen Killion, senior advisor. Gail Ritchie and Marie McElvoy-Parker, coaches in Fairfax County Public Schools, provided feedback on the IC maps. Through the development of the IC maps for school-based roles, many others have offered recommendations, suggestions, and feedback that helped shape the desired outcomes and variations for each standard.

We are particularly thankful to MetLife Foundation for its generous support of the standards revision process and the development of standards implementation resources, including the IC maps. The foundation's investment allows Learning Forward to create products and services to realize the vision described in the Standards for Professional Learning.

— *Stephanie Hirsh*
Executive Director, Learning Forward

Introduction

With the support and input of researchers, practitioners, and representatives of numerous professional associations and organizations, Learning Forward published a third iteration of *Standards for Professional Learning* in 2011, reflecting current research and practice in the field. These standards establish the core attributes of effective professional learning.

> Standards for Professional Learning enumerate the conditions, processes, and content of professional learning to support continuous improvement in leadership, teaching, and student learning. The standards stress that effective professional learning is embedded in a culture committed to continuous improvement and informed by data and research on student and educator learning (Learning Forward, 2011, p. 6).

The standards describe model professional learning and provide guidance to participants, facilitators, leaders, evaluators, and funders of professional learning.

> The Standards for Professional Learning describe the attributes of effective professional learning to guide the decisions and practices of all persons with responsibility to fund, regulate,

manage, conceive, organize, implement, and evaluate professional learning. [They] should closely study the standards and systematically use them as a template for organizing professional learning. However, the standards are also a consumers guide for all educators, describing what they should expect and demand of their professional learning, as well as their responsibilities to participate (Learning Forward, 2011, p. 14).

The seven new standards operate as a synergistic whole, working in unison to increase the effectiveness and results of professional learning.

> The standards are not, however, a workbook, tool kit, or technical assistance guide. They neither address every issue related to professional learning nor provide a road map for creating professional learning that is faithful to the standards. That is intentional. Using the standards to shape more effective professional learning will require study, thought, discussion, and planning (Learning Forward, 2011, p. 14).

All people and entities with either direct or indirect responsibility for students' education— teachers, principals, superintendents, support staff, parents, boards of education, state education agencies, independent consultants, intermediate service agencies, professional associations and organizations, and higher education institutions—could benefit from well-designed and effective professional learning. Yet helping potential users to understand more clearly just what the standards look like when they are in operation can be a challenge. Innovation Configuration (IC) maps (Hall & Hord, 2010; Hord, Rutherford, Huling-Austin, & Hall, 2006) offer a solution to this problem.

Essentially, IC maps identify and describe the major components of new practice—in this case, the new standards—in operation. This volume presents those IC maps with introductory material that explains the concept and use of innovation configuration and its application to staff development.

INNOVATION CONFIGURATION

Studies of the implementation of policies, programs, and processes have shown that innovations are typically applied in a variety of ways. Just because authorities mandate, experts request, or colleagues agree to adopt innovations does not guarantee fidelity of implementation. In other words, there is not a simple *yes* or *no* answer to the question "Is the literacy program, discipline policy, or set of Learning Forward standards implemented?" The answer lies somewhere along a continuum that indicates varying degrees and/or types of use of the innovation. The concept of innovation

configuration was born because individual users adapt or modify parts of new practices as they implement them. This concept of the adaptation of innovations led to the development of IC maps that describe an innovation's major components when the innovation is in use. The IC maps also describe how users alter these components while implementing them.

An IC map is a way to precisely define quality and measure fidelity. On the IC map (Table 1 on page 8), the most ideal way of implementing the components, or the desired outcome (the label used in the IC maps for the Learning Forward standards), is stated at the left end of the continuum, with decreasingly desirable levels or variations appearing along the continuum to the right. The number 1 or ideal variation of each desired outcome signifies the highest-quality implementation. The IC map, then, can be used to measure the degree to which an individual implementer is approaching the ideal variation by being faithful to the desired outcomes—achieving fidelity.

The IC map is created so as to describe an innovation *in operation*—that is, how individuals are actively using it. Therefore, the IC map:

- Uses active voice rather than passive;
- Has a subject of its statements that identifies who is doing the action; and
- Contains a rich array of action verbs—actions that can be observed.

To structure an IC map, major components or desired outcomes of the innovation are identified. The desired outcomes describe the salient behaviors of people in the designated role in relation to the innovation. Tables 1 and 2, for instance, show IC maps that describe what the teacher does related to the first key idea of Learning Forward's Learning Communities standard, **1.1, Engage in continuous improvement**. The two desired outcomes are:

Desired outcome 1.1.1: Develops capacity to apply the seven-step cycle of continuous improvement.

Desired outcome 1.1.2: Applies the cycle of continuous improvement with fidelity in professional learning.

For each desired outcome, the team of developers has written a continuum of behaviors, placing the most desirable levels of behavior on the left side of the continuum. The behaviors located on the right end are unacceptable behaviors associated with the desired outcome. When any implementer demonstrates behaviors to the right of Level 1, he or she seeks support and assistance to move toward Level 1. Depending on the size of the gap and the needed competencies, the time and type of support needed to move closer to Level 1 may vary.

Each continuum specifies the most significant factor(s) related to the desired outcome. Table 1 contains the variations for **Desired outcome 1.1.1 with the variations moving from ideal at Level 1 to least desirable at Level 6. In some instances, Levels 5 or 6 are blank because no additional variations exist.**

Table 1: Teacher Learning Community Desired Outcome 1.1.1

TEACHER / **Learning Communities**

1.1 Engage in continuous improvement					
Level 1	Level 2	Level 3	Level 4	Level 5	Level 6
Desired outcome 1.1.1: Develops capacity to apply the seven-step cycle of continuous improvement.					
• Develops knowledge and skills about the seven steps of the cycle of continuous improvement.	• Develops understanding of six of the seven steps of the cycle of continuous improvement.	• Develops understanding of five of the seven steps of the cycle of continuous improvement.	• Develops understanding of four or fewer steps of the seven steps of the cycle of continuous improvement.	• Fails to develop knowledge and skills about the cycle of continuous improvement.	

Table 2: Teacher Learning Community Desired Outcome 1.1.2

TEACHER / **Learning Communities**

1.1 Engage in continuous improvement					
Level 1	Level 2	Level 3	Level 4	Level 5	Level 6
Desired outcome 1.1.2: Applies the cycle of continuous improvement with fidelity in professional learning.					
• Employs the seven-step cycle of continuous improvement in individual, team, and schoolwide professional learning. • Maintains commitment to employ the cycle of continuous improvement in individual and team learning. • Supports colleagues in employing the cycle in individual and team learning.	• Employs six steps of the seven-step cycle of continuous improvement in individual, team, and schoolwide professional learning. • Maintains commitment to employ the cycle in individual and team learning.	• Employs five steps of the seven-step cycle of continuous improvement in individual and team professional learning.	• Employs four or fewer steps of the seven-step cycle of continuous improvement in individual and team professional learning.	• Employs four or fewer steps of the seven-step cycle of continuous improvement in individual professional learning.	• Fails to use the cycle of continuous improvement in professional learning.

The IC map, then, is an instrument that describes the innovation in action. It provides a mental image of the innovation and a "vision" toward which the user is moving. Thus, the IC map shares information needed to enable individuals in different roles to take the initial steps in implementing the innovation.

INNOVATION CONFIGURATIONS AND THE STANDARDS

IC maps for each of the seven standards provide educators with:

- A clear and richly descriptive vision of what the standards look like in action (in schools, districts, state departments, etc.—wherever professional learning occurs) in order to support the continuous learning of educators;

- A guide to design professional learning that explains not only what the standards look like in operation, but also how to implement them;

- A guide to create precise plans and access sufficient resources for implementing the standards in all professional learning and in the work of those who are responsible for all aspects of professional learning; and

- A tool to assess implementation of the standards.

IC maps have been created for 12 distinct roles in education that share responsibility for professional learning. These are presented in three volumes. Volume I includes the school-based roles—teachers, coaches/teacher leaders, principals, and school leadership teams. Volume II contains the district-based roles of central office, directors of professional learning, superintendents, and school boards. Volume III includes the external roles of external assistance providers, professional associations, institutes of higher education, and technical assistance providers.

For example, the Learning Communities standard states: "Professional learning that increases educator effectiveness and results for all students occurs within learning communities committed to continuous improvement, collective responsibility, and goal alignment." If teachers' role for the first key action area of the Learning Community standards appears in Tables 1 and 2, one might reasonably ask, What is the principal's role for this standard? What would the principal be doing relative to this standard in his or her school building? What vision of the principal's role might we imagine? To describe and specify the principal's role for the Learning Communities standard, seven desired outcomes were generated. In the set of desired outcomes that describe the principal's role for the Learning Communities standard, the first desired outcome (**1.1.1**) is **Develops own and others' capacity to apply the seven-step cycle of continuous improvement.** The ideal descriptor (Level 1) includes the following two actions:

- **Develops own knowledge and skills about the seven steps of the cycle of continuous improvement.**

- **Instructs staff and SLT about and models the seven steps of the cycle of continuous improvement.**

For the second Desired outcome (**1.1.2**), **Desired outcome 1.1.2: Applies the seven-step cycle of continuous improvement with fidelity to lead professional learning**, the principal's ideal variations are:

- **Models the application of the seven-step cycle in schoolwide decision making.**

- **Facilitates SLT and staff to apply the seven-step cycle of continuous improvement with fidelity in individual, team, and schoolwide professional learning.**

- **Provides SLT and staff coaching to clarify and support faithful use of the cycle.**

The ideal descriptor (Level 1) describes the expected actions, an important strategy for implementation of the standard, and reveals what the individual in the identified role will be doing as this specific professional learning standard is implemented.

UNIVERSAL APPLICATION OF THE STANDARDS AND IC MAPS TO PROFESSIONAL LEARNING

The IC maps apply to all forms of professional learning, whether it is focused on individuals, schools or teams, or program implementation. The standards make it clear that the purpose of professional learning is to increase educator effectiveness and results for all students. Like the standards, these IC maps apply to all forms of professional learning for all educators, the employees within an education system who directly or indirectly support student learning. A large portion of professional learning is designed to develop educators' knowledge, skills, dispositions, and practices to achieve district and school improvement goals.

In some cases, schools and individuals develop plans for professional learning that describe how and what individuals, teams, or whole faculties will learn to achieve the designated goals. For example, a school faculty and learning teams within a school engage in professional learning to improve both their individual and collective capacity to achieve school, team, and individual classroom improvement goals. This might be the case if a school has a goal of closing the achievement gap among various student groups by providing those who interact with students deeper understanding about various instructional strategies and ways to adapt the curriculum to meet the learning needs of ELL, special needs, or high-poverty students to ensure high levels of performance from all students. In other cases, selected educators engage in professional learning to implement new programs, practices, or systems. Teachers of science, coaches who support these teachers, and principals participate in professional learning when new science curriculum is introduced, for example, so that they learn about the curriculum, know how to use it to design instruction, develop the expertise to apply the curriculum in instruction, and build the capacity to support implementation of the new curriculum over time. Individual educators engage in professional learning to strengthen their performance, meet their individual development goals, pursue areas of interest, and advance their careers.

The IC maps apply to all professional learning, not just major initiatives that include professional learning for teachers. The standards apply regardless of which educators are learning, who is designing and facilitating the learning, where the learning occurs, or what the specific outcomes for professional learning are. When districts are developing, selecting, or purchasing professional learning to address individual learning needs of educators, the standards and IC maps apply. When teams of educators meet together in learning teams to improve their practice and student results, the standards and IC maps apply. When the school leadership team (SLT), coach, principal, or external assistance provider plans and facilitates professional learning, the standards and IC maps apply. When districts plan districtwide or support school-based professional learning, the standards and IC maps apply. When external assistance providers, professional associations, state departments or ministries of education, institutes of higher education, nonprofit organizations, professional associations, independent consultants, or for-profit universities or organizations provide professional learning, the standards and IC maps apply. The standards and

IC maps apply whether the professional learning occurs in real time, face-to-face, in a hybrid environment, or completely online.

CONSTRUCTION OF IC MAPS FOR THE STANDARDS

The IC maps were created using a process of drafting, revision, review, and calibration across roles. First, the authors studied the Standards for Professional Learning and research about how various roles contribute to effective professional learning. They identified the key actions for each standard embedded in the elaboration for each standard. The key actions were further described as desired outcome statements. The writing team articulated a continuum of actions in decreasing value, starting from the ideal on the left end of the continuum. Reviewers, who are practitioners serving in each role, provided feedback on the draft maps to the writing team. Each revision clarified the continuum of actions.

A matrix of all desired outcomes for all roles in each volume is organized into a Crosswalk at the end of each volume. The Crosswalk provides another way to express the holistic nature of the standards and the contributions each educator role makes to professional learning's effectiveness and results. The Crosswalk describes the system of supports necessary so that each role group receives assistance to accomplish its responsibilities related to professional learning. Each role has responsibilities and should expect support to fulfill essential tasks.

For instance, in the Crosswalk in the Resource standard's first key action, **3.1, Prioritize human, fiscal, material, technology, and time resources**, the first desired outcome is **3.1.1**. This stipulates that the principal **Defines resources for professional learning**. Teachers' roles in this arena are different, so their first desired outcome states

3.1.1. Contributes to definition of resources for professional learning. The coordination of all desired outcomes across role groups helps to enhance implementation by eliminating potential barriers and clarifying each implementer's responsibilities. The chart also clarifies the actions necessary to increase the probability that the desired outcomes will be achieved.

The idea behind the delineation of the responsibilities of each educator role is to promote systemic responsibility for professional learning, both from within and from outside, through the alignment of desired outcomes for all role groups. The interrelatedness of these outcomes is expressed in the matrix and confirmed by the Crosswalk. Used in conjunction with other standards implementation resources, such as the Standards Assessment Inventory, the Standards Facilitator Guide, the explanatory videos, and the standards document itself, those responsible for planning, implementing, or evaluating professional learning will have the resources necessary for full implementation of the standards for professional learning to achieve results for educators and students. Access these resources or information about them at www.learningforward.org/standards.

Principals and teachers might use the IC maps to guide in planning and implementing effective professional learning. They might use the IC maps to assess their own practices in professional learning. Subsequently, they can use the IC maps to plan improvements in professional learning by working toward the desired outcomes of the standards that they want to strengthen. Other volumes of the IC maps will delineate responsibilities for roles outside the school. *Standards in Practice: District-based Roles* describes what central office staff and local elected officials, central office staff, director of professional learning, superintendent, and school board, do to support professional learning. *Standards in Practice: External Roles* describes what technical assistance agencies, state/provincial departments of education, institutes of higher education, and professional associations do to support professional learning.

The IC maps provide clear pictures of Learning Forward's standards for professional learning in practice and guide educators in increasing the quality and results of professional learning. The ultimate goal of educator learning is a positive impact on student learning, and the standards clarify the attributes of the professional learning that produces that impact.

SCHOOL-BASED ROLES

Volume I includes four distinct school-based roles. Since the school is the primary site of learning for many educators, particularly those who most directly affect student results, this volume comes first. It is important to note that the IC maps include behaviors associated with professional learning and not all of the responsibilities of any given role. For example, the Teacher IC map describes the behaviors of teachers in relationship to professional learning, frequently described as one of the performance or practice standards of effective teachers. These IC maps do not describe any individual role comprehensively.

Teacher

The term *teacher* describes all educators who have immediate instructional contact with students. For example, the role of teacher includes those who serve either full time or for a portion of their time as classroom teachers, instructional aides, resource or instructional specialists (such as in special needs, technology, math, literacy, English language arts, etc.) who work directly with students, and tutors.

Other specialized staff are also included, such as social workers, counselors, school media specialists, librarians, and others, if their role includes some instruction to individual or small groups of students.

Coach

The term *coach* is used to describe all instructional support staff who work with teachers in schools. Not all coaches will have the title of coach, nor will all serve a single school. Some who fall into the role of coach might be district-based and serve multiple schools. Some might be called instructional facilitators, literacy specialists, math coaches, teacher leaders, instructional specialists, department- or grade-level lead teachers, master teachers, mentors, and so on. Those who are coaches hold some responsibility for providing support for implementation of professional learning within schools and classrooms. They work closely with principals to plan, facilitate, and support implementation of professional learning to achieve individual, team, school, and district goals.

School Leadership Team

A school leadership team is one of the decision-making teams within a school. This team is known by many different titles and has many different roles. Some have comprehensive responsibilities for school improvement, while others have more limited responsibility. This IC map encompasses the responsibilities this team has for decisions related to the ongoing planning, design, implementation, and/or evaluation of professional learning. Some school leadership teams include elected or appointed members of the instructional, support, and administrative staff as well as students (when appropriate) within a school. Occasionally, as required by certain regulations under which the school operates, school leadership teams may include parents or community members. The principal is a member of the leadership team and operates from a platform of shared leadership, engaging other stakeholders in decisions regarding professional learning. In the absence of a formal school leadership team, the principal assumes most of these responsibilities with input from members of the staff.

Principal

Educators who fall within the role of principal include those with primary leadership responsibility and authority within a place-based or online school or cluster of schools. This role includes principals, assistant principals, grade-level or house principals, deans, and others who are responsible for the overall success of a school, its staff, and its students. The role of principal may also apply to a school's administrative team. In some education systems, principals may have responsibilities that will be included in the second volume of district roles because they have both district and school responsibilities.

REFERENCES

Hall, G. & Hord, S. (2010). *Implementing change: Patterns, principles, and potholes* (3rd ed.). Upper Saddle River, NJ: Prentice Hall.

Hord, S., Rutherford, W., Huling-Austin, L., & Hall, G. (2006). *Taking charge of change.* Austin, TX: SEDL.

Learning Forward. (2011). *Standards for professional learning.* Oxford, OH: Author.

Professional learning that increases
educator effectiveness and results for
all students...

Standards for Professional Learning

The following pages include the standards and
their elaborations from *Standards for Professional
Learning*, published by Learning Forward (2011).

Standards for Professional Learning

LEARNING COMMUNITIES: Professional learning that increases educator effectiveness and results for all students occurs within learning communities committed to continuous improvement, collective responsibility, and goal alignment.

LEADERSHIP: Professional learning that increases educator effectiveness and results for all students requires skillful leaders who develop capacity, advocate, and create support systems for professional learning.

RESOURCES: Professional learning that increases educator effectiveness and results for all students requires prioritizing, monitoring, and coordinating resources for educator learning.

DATA: Professional learning that increases educator effectiveness and results for all students uses a variety of sources and types of student, educator, and system data to plan, assess, and evaluate professional learning.

LEARNING DESIGNS: Professional learning that increases educator effectiveness and results for all students integrates theories, research, and models of human learning to achieve its intended outcomes.

IMPLEMENTATION: Professional learning that increases educator effectiveness and results for all students applies research on change and sustains support for implementation of professional learning for long-term change.

OUTCOMES: Professional learning that increases educator effectiveness and results for all students aligns its outcomes with educator performance and student curriculum standards.

Professional learning that increases educator effectiveness and results for all students **occurs within learning communities committed to continuous improvement, collective responsibility, and goal alignment.**

LEARNING COMMUNITIES

LEADERSHIP

RESOURCES

DATA

Professional learning within communities requires continuous improvement, promotes collective responsibility, and supports alignment of individual, team, school, and school system goals. Learning communities convene regularly and frequently during the workday to engage in collaborative professional learning to strengthen their practice and increase student results. Learning community members are accountable to one another to achieve the shared goals of the school and school system and work in transparent, authentic settings that support their improvement.

ENGAGE IN CONTINUOUS IMPROVEMENT

Learning communities apply a cycle of continuous improvement to engage in inquiry, action research, data analysis, planning, implementation, reflection, and evaluation. Characteristics of each application of the cycle of continuous improvement are:

- The use of data to determine student and educator learning needs;
- Identification of shared goals for student and educator learning;
- Professional learning to extend educators' knowledge of content, content-specific pedagogy, how students learn, and management of classroom environments;
- Selection and implementation of appropriate evidence-based strategies to achieve student and educator learning goals;
- Application of the learning with local support at the work site;
- Use of evidence to monitor and refine implementation; and
- Evaluation of results.

DEVELOP COLLECTIVE RESPONSIBILITY

Learning communities share collective responsibility for the learning of all students within the school or school system. Collective responsibility brings together the entire education community, including members of the education workforce — teachers, support staff, school system staff, and administrators — as well as families, policy makers, and other stakeholders, to increase effective teaching in every classroom. Within learning communities, peer accountability rather than formal or administrative accountability ignites commitment to professional learning. Every student benefits from the strengths and expertise of every educator when communities of educators learn together and are supported by local communities whose members value education for all students.

Collective participation advances the goals of a whole school or team as well as those of individuals. Communities of caring, analytic, reflective, and inquiring educators collaborate to learn what is necessary to increase student learning. Within learning communities, members exchange feedback about their practice with one another, visit each other's classrooms or work settings, and share resources. Learning community members strive to refine their collaboration, communication, and relationship skills to work within and across both internal and external systems to support student learning. They develop norms of collaboration and relational trust and employ processes and structures that unleash expertise and strengthen capacity to analyze, plan, implement, support, and evaluate their practice.

While some professional learning occurs individually, particularly to address individual development goals, the more one educator's learning is shared and supported by others, the more quickly the culture of continuous improvement, collective

responsibility, and high expectations for students and educators grows. Collective responsibility and participation foster peer-to-peer support for learning and maintain a consistent focus on shared goals within and across communities. Technology facilitates and expands community interaction, learning, resource archiving and sharing, and knowledge construction and sharing. Some educators may meet with peers virtually in local or global communities to focus on individual, team, school, or school system improvement goals. Often supported through technology, cross-community communication within schools, across schools, and among school systems reinforces shared goals, promotes knowledge construction and sharing, strengthens coherence, taps educators' expertise, and increases access to and use of resources.

Communities of learners may be various sizes, include members with similar or different roles or responsibilities, and meet frequently face-to-face, virtually, or through a combination. Educators may be members of multiple learning communities. Some communities may include members who share common students, areas of responsibility, roles, interests, or goals. Learning communities tap internal and external expertise and resources to strengthen practice and student learning. Because the education system reaches out to include students, their families, community members, the education workforce, and public officials who share responsibility for student achievement, some learning communities may include representatives of these groups.

CREATE ALIGNMENT AND ACCOUNTABILITY

Professional learning that occurs within learning communities provides an ongoing system of support for continuous improvement and implementation of school and systemwide initiatives. To avoid fragmentation among learning communities and to strengthen their contribution to school and system goals, public officials and school system leaders create policies that establish formal accountability for results along with the support needed to achieve results. To be effective, these policies and supports align with an explicit vision and goals for successful learning communities. Learning communities align their goals with those of the school and school system, engage in continuous professional learning, and hold all members collectively accountable for results.

The professional learning that occurs within learning communities both supports and is supported by policy and governance, curriculum and instruction, human resources, and other functions within a school system. Learning communities bridge the knowing-doing gap by transforming macro-level learning — knowledge and skill development — into micro-level learning — the practices and refinements necessary for full implementation in the classroom or workplace. When professional learning occurs within a system driven by high expectations, shared goals, professionalism, and peer accountability, the outcome is deep change for individuals and systems.

RELATED RESEARCH

Bolam, R., McMahon, A., Stoll, L., Thomas, S., & Wallace, M. (with Greenwood, A., et al.). (2005, May). *Creating and sustaining effective professional learning communities* (Research Brief RB637). Nottingham, United Kingdom: Department for Education and Skills.

Hord, S.M. (Ed.). (2004). *Learning together, leading together: Changing schools through professional learning communities.* New York: Teachers College Press & NSDC.

Lieberman, A. & Miller, L. (Eds.) (2008). *Teachers in professional communities: Improving teaching and learning.* New York: Teachers College Press.

McLaughlin, M.W. & Talbert, J.E. (2001). *Professional communities and the work of high school teaching.* Chicago: University of Chicago Press.

Saunders, W.M., Goldenberg, C.N., & Gallimore, R. (2009, December). Increasing achievement by focusing grade-level teams on improving classroom learning: A prospective, quasi-experimental study of Title I schools. *American Educational Research Journal, 46*(4), 1006-1033.

NOTES

Professional learning that increases educator effectiveness and results for all students **requires skillful leaders who develop capacity, advocate, and create support systems for professional learning.**

LEARNING COMMUNITIES

DATA

RESOURCES

LEADERSHIP

Leaders throughout the pre-K-12 education community recognize effective professional learning as a key strategy for supporting significant school and school system improvements to increase results for all students. Whether they lead from classrooms, schools, school systems, technical assistance agencies, professional associations, universities, or public agencies, leaders develop their own and others' capacity to learn and lead professional learning, advocate for it, provide support systems, and distribute leadership and responsibility for its effectiveness and results.

DEVELOP CAPACITY FOR LEARNING AND LEADING

Leaders hold learning among their top priorities for students, staff, and themselves. Leaders recognize that universal high expectations for all students require ambitious improvements in curriculum, instruction, assessment, leadership practices, and support systems. These improvements require effective professional learning to expand educators' knowledge, skills, practices, and dispositions. All leaders demand effective professional learning focused on substantive results for themselves, their colleagues, and their students. Leaders artfully combine deep understanding of and cultural responsiveness to the community they serve with high expectations and support for results to achieve school and school system goals. They embed professional learning into the organization's vision by communicating that it is a core function for improvement and by establishing and maintaining a public and persistent focus on educator professional learning.

Leaders of professional learning are found at

the classroom, school, and system levels. They set the agenda for professional learning by aligning it to classroom, school, and school system goals for student and educator learning, using data to monitor and measure its effects on educator and student performance. They may facilitate professional learning, coach and supervise those who facilitate it, or do both. As facilitators of professional learning, they apply a body of technical knowledge and skills to plan, design, implement, and evaluate professional learning. As coaches and supervisors of those who facilitate professional learning, they develop expertise in others about effective professional learning, set high standards for their performance, and use data to give frequent, constructive feedback.

To engage in constructive conversations about the alignment of student and educator performance, leaders cultivate a culture based on the norms of high expectations, shared responsibility, mutual respect, and relational trust. They work collaboratively with others, such as school and system-based resource personnel and external technical assistance providers, so that all educators engage in effective job-embedded or external professional learning to meet individual, team, school, and system goals.

Systems that recognize and advance shared leadership promote leaders from all levels of the organizations. Leaders can hold formal roles, such as principal, instructional coach, or task force chair, for long periods of time or informal roles, such as voluntary mentor or spokesperson, for shorter

periods. All leaders share responsibility for student achievement among members of the school and community. Leaders hold themselves and others accountable for the quality and results of professional learning. Leaders work collaboratively with others to create a vision for academic success and set clear goals for student achievement based on educator and student learning data.

ADVOCATE FOR PROFESSIONAL LEARNING

Leaders clearly articulate the critical link between increased student learning and educator professional learning. As supporters of professional

learning, they apply understanding of organizational and human changes to design needed conditions, resources, and other supports for learning and change.

As advocates for professional learning, leaders make their own career-long learning visible to others. They participate in professional learning within and beyond their own work environment. Leaders consume information in multiple fields to enhance their leadership practice. Through learning, they clarify their values and beliefs and their influence on others and on the achievement of organizational goals. Their actions model attitudes and behavior they expect of all educators.

Leaders engage with all stakeholders — those within the education workforce, students, public officials who oversee schools, parent and community organizations, and the business community — to communicate the importance of professional learning. They engage parents and other caretakers in the education of their children and establish partnerships with key community organizations to promote the success of all students.

CREATE SUPPORT SYSTEMS AND STRUCTURES

Skillful leaders establish organizational systems and structures that support effective professional learning and ongoing continuous improvement. They equitably distribute resources to accomplish individual, team, school, and school system goals. Leaders actively engage with policy makers and decision makers so that resources, policies, annual calendars, daily schedules, and structures support professional learning to increase student achievement. Leaders create and align policies and guidelines to ensure effective professional learn-

ing within their school systems or schools. They work within national, regional, and local agencies to adopt standards, monitor implementation, and evaluate professional learning's effectiveness and results.

RELATED RESEARCH

Knapp, M.S., Copland, M.A., & Talbert, J.E. (2003, February). *Leading for learning: Reflective tools for school and district leaders.* Seattle, WA: Center for the Study of Teaching and Policy.

Leithwood, K., Louis, K.S., Anderson, S., & Wahlstrom, K. (2004). *How leadership influences student learning: A review of research for the Learning from Leadership Project.* New York: Wallace Foundation.

Spillane, J.P., Halverson, R., & Diamond, J.B. (2001, April). Investigating school leadership practice: A distributed perspective. *Educational Researcher, 30*(3), 23-27.

Waters, J.T., Marzano, R.J., & McNulty, B.A. (2003). *Balanced leadership: What 30 years of research tells us about the effect of leadership on student achievement.* Aurora, CO: McREL.

York-Barr, J. & Duke, K. (2004, Fall). What do we know about teacher leadership? Findings from two decades of scholarship. *Review of Educational Research, 74*(3), 255-316.

NOTES

Professional learning that increases educator effectiveness and results for all students **requires prioritizing, monitoring, and coordinating resources for educator learning.**

LEARNING COMMUNITIES

LEADERSHIP

RESOURCES

DATA

Effective professional learning requires human, fiscal, material, technology, and time resources to achieve student learning goals. How resources are allocated for professional learning can overcome inequities and achieve results for educators and students. The availability and allocation of resources for professional learning affect its quality and results. Understanding the resources associated with professional learning and actively and accurately tracking them facilitates better decisions about and increased quality and results of professional learning.

PRIORITIZE HUMAN, FISCAL, MATERIAL, TECHNOLOGY, AND TIME RESOURCES

Resources for professional learning include staff, materials, technology, and time, all dependent on available funding. How these resources are prioritized to align with identified professional learning needs affects access to, quality of, and effectiveness of educator learning experiences. Decisions about resources for professional learning require a thorough understanding of student and educator learning needs, clear commitment to ensure equity in resource allocation, and thoughtful consideration of priorities to achieve the intended outcomes for students and educators.

Staff costs are a significant portion of the resource investment in professional learning. Costs in this category include school and school system leaders and other specialized staff who facilitate or support school- or school system-based professional learning, such as instructional coaches, facilitators, and mentors, as well as salary costs for educators when professional learning occurs within their workday. The time leaders commit to professional learning, either their own or for those they supervise, is a cost factor because it is time these leaders are investing in professional learning; managing this time is another area of responsibility for leaders.

Time allocated for professional learning is another significant investment. Education systems worldwide have schedules that provide time in the school day for teacher collaboration and planning to increase student learning. Learning time for educators may extend into after-school meetings, summer extended learning experiences, and occasional times during the workday when students are not present.

Professional learning embedded into educators' workdays increases the opportunity for all educators to receive individual, team, or school-based support within the work setting to promote continuous improvement. Dedicated job-embedded learning time elevates the importance of continuous, career-long learning as a professional responsibility of all educators and aligns the focus of their learning to the identified needs of students they serve. Including substantive time for professional learning, 15% or more, within the workday shifts some costs for external professional learning to support job-embedded professional learning.

Technology and material resources for professional learning create opportunities to access information that enriches practice. Use of high-speed broadband, web-based and other technologies, professional journals and books, software, and a comprehensive learning management system is essential to support individual and collaborative professional learning. Access to just-in-time learning resources and participation in local or global communities or networks available to individuals or teams of edu-

cators during their workday expand opportunities for job-embedded professional learning.

Investments in professional learning outside the school or workplace supplement and advance job-embedded professional learning. To increase alignment and coherence between job-embedded and external professional learning, both must address the individual, school, and school system goals for educator and student learning.

When economic challenges emerge, schools and school systems often reduce investments in professional learning. In high-performing countries, professional learning is valued so highly as a key intervention to improve schools that reducing it is not an option. Top-performing businesses frequently increase training and development in challenging times. In lean times, professional learning is especially important to prepare members of the workforce for the changes they will experience, maintain and increase student achievement, develop flexibility to detect and adapt to new economic conditions and opportunities, and sustain employee morale, retention, commitment, and expertise.

MONITOR RESOURCES

Resources for professional learning come from many sources, including government allocations, public and private agencies, and educators themselves. Tracking and monitoring these resources is challenging, yet essential. Some costs, such as those for staff, registrations, consultants, materials, stipends for mentor teachers, and relief teachers, are relatively easy to track. Others, such as the portion of time educators are engaged in job-embedded professional learning and technology used for professional learning, are more difficult to monitor. Yet without a consistent and comprehensive process to track and monitor resources, it is difficult to evaluate the appropriateness or effectiveness of their allocation and use.

The level of funding for professional learning in schools varies tremendously. Some studies on professional learning in public schools have suggested that the investments range from less than 1% of total operating expenses to as high as 12%. In the highest-performing countries, investments in professional learning for educators, particularly teachers and principals, are much higher. Decisions about funding must specifically address inequities in learning needs and opportunities to learn and be given highest priority so that that all students and the educators who serve them have the resources to achieve at the highest levels.

COORDINATE RESOURCES

The coordination of resources for professional learning is essential to their appropriate and effective use. With funding for professional learning, school improvement, and other reform initiatives coming from multiple sources and for multiple purposes, ensuring alignment and effectiveness

in resource use is paramount to ensuring success. School and school system leaders are primarily responsible for coordinating resources. However, all educators have a shared responsibility to understand and contribute to decisions about and monitor the effectiveness of resources allocated for professional learning.

To make certain that resources invested in professional learning achieve their intended results, school system leaders regularly convene representatives of all stakeholders to examine and recommend changes to policies, regulations, and agreements related to professional learning.

RELATED RESEARCH

Abdal-Haqq, I. (1996). *Making time for teacher professional development.* Washington, DC: ERIC Clearinghouse on Teaching and Teacher Education. (ERIC Document Reproduction Service No. ED 400259)

Chambers, J.G., Lam, I., & Mahitivanichcha, K. (2008, September). *Examining context and challenges in measuring investment in professional development: A case study of six school districts in the Southwest region* (Issues & Answers Report, REL 2008-No. 037). Washington, DC: U.S. Department of Education, Institute of Education Sciences, National Center for Education Evaluation and Regional Assistance, Regional Educational Laboratory Southwest.

Haslam, M.B. (1997, Fall). How to rebuild a local professional development infrastructure. *NAS Getting Better by Design.* Arlington, VA: New American Schools.

Odden, A., Archibald, S., Fermanich, M., & Gallagher, H.A. (2002). A cost framework for professional development. *Journal of Education Finance, 28*(1), 51-74.

OECD. (2011). *Strong performers and successful reformers in education: Lessons from PISA for the United States.* Paris: OECD Publishing.

NOTES

Professional learning that increases educator effectiveness and results for all students **uses a variety of sources and types of student, educator, and system data to plan, assess, and evaluate professional learning.**

LEARNING COMMUNITIES

LEADERSHIP

RESOURCES

DATA

Data from multiple sources enrich decisions about professional learning that leads to increased results for every student. Multiple sources include both quantitative and qualitative data, such as common formative and summative assessments, performance assessments, observations, work samples, performance metrics, portfolios, and self-reports. The use of multiple sources of data offers a balanced and more comprehensive analysis of student, educator, and system performance than any single type or source of data can. However, data alone do little to inform decision making and increase effectiveness.

Thorough analysis and ongoing use are essential for data to inform decisions about professional learning, as is support in the effective analysis and use of data.

ANALYZE STUDENT, EDUCATOR, AND SYSTEM DATA

Data about students, educators, and systems are useful in defining individual, team, school, and system goals for professional learning. Probing questions guide data analysis to understand where students are in relationship to the expected curriculum standards and to identify the focus for educator professional learning. Student data include formal and informal assessments, achievement data such as grades and annual, benchmark, end-of-course, and daily classroom work, and classroom assessments. Other forms of data, such as those that cover demographics, engagement, attendance, student perceptions, behavior and discipline, participation in extracurricular programs, and post-graduation education, are useful in understanding student learning needs, particularly if they are analyzed by student characteristics.

Knowing student learning needs guides decisions about educator professional learning, yet student data alone are insufficient. A comprehensive understanding of educator learning needs is essential to planning meaningful professional learning. Sample data to consider for identifying goals for educator learning include preparation information, performance on various assessments, educator perceptions, classroom or work performance, student results, and individual professional learning goals.

Changes at the student and educator levels are best sustained when school and system-level learning occur simultaneously. School and system administrators also engage in data collection and analysis to determine changes in policy, procedures, fiscal resources, human resources, time, or technology, for example, needed to support school- and team-based learning. Administrators might analyze data about inputs, such as fiscal, personnel, and time allocation; outputs, such as frequency of participation, level of engagement, and type of communication; and outcomes, such as changes in educator practice and student achievement.

ASSESS PROGRESS

Data also are useful to monitor and assess progress against established benchmarks. At the classroom level, teachers use student data to assess the effectiveness of the application of their new learning. When teachers, for example, design assessments and scoring guides and engage in collaborative analysis of student work, they gain crucial

information about the effect of their learning on students. Evidence of ongoing increases in student learning is a powerful motivator for teachers during the inevitable setbacks that accompany complex change efforts.

At the school level, leadership teams use data to monitor implementation of professional learning and its effects on educator practice and student learning. Engaging teams of teacher leaders and

administrators in analyzing and interpreting data, for example, provides them a more holistic view of the complexity of school improvement and fosters collective responsibility and accountability for student results.

Frequent collection and use of data about inputs, outputs, and outcomes of professional learning reinforce the cycle of continuous improvement by allowing for ongoing adjustments in the learning process to increase results for students, educators, and systems. Ongoing data collection, analysis, and use, especially when done in teams, provide stakeholders with information that sustains momentum and informs continuous improvement.

EVALUATE PROFESSIONAL LEARNING

Those responsible for professional learning implement and maintain standards for professional learning and use the standards to monitor, assess, and evaluate it. Well-designed evaluation of professional learning provides information needed to increase its quality and effectiveness. Evaluation of professional learning also provides useful information for those who advocate for professional learning; those responsible for engaging in, planning, facilitating, or supporting professional learning; and those who want to know about the contribution of professional learning to student achievement.

Internal and external evaluators conduct evaluations of professional learning. Some professional learning, such as programs funded through grants or other special funding, requires formal, external evaluations. Whether or not an external evaluation is required, all professional learning should be evaluated on an ongoing basis for its effectiveness and results. For example, a school system might engage in a rigorous evaluation of its mentoring and induction program every three years and collect other output data annually for formative assessment.

Questions that guide the evaluation of professional learning address its worth, merit, and effects. Evaluation questions are designed based on the goals of professional learning and the various audiences interested in the evaluation. For example, federal policy makers might want to know if the investment in professional learning contributed to changes in student achievement. School system leaders may want to know if increasing time for

teacher collaboration and adding coaches result in changes in teacher practice and student learning. Teachers might want to know if the implementation of new instructional practices increased their effectiveness with certain types of students. Evaluators design a process to answer the evaluation questions, gather quantitative and qualitative data from various sources, analyze and interpret the data, form conclusions, and recommend future actions.

Evaluation of professional learning includes examination of data related to inputs, outputs, and outcomes. Evaluation of professional learning follows a rigorous process, international standards for evaluation, and a code of ethics for evaluators.

RELATED RESEARCH

Datnow, A. (1999, April). *How schools choose externally developed reform designs* (Report No. 35). Baltimore: Center for Research on the Education of Students Placed At Risk.

Desimone, L., Porter, A., Garet, M., Yoon, K.S., & Birman, B. (2002, Summer). Effects of professional development on teachers' instruction: Results from a three-year longitudinal study. *Educational Evaluation and Policy Analysis, 24*(2), 81-112.

Griffith, P.L., Kimmel, S.J., & Biscoe, B. (2010, Winter). Teacher professional development for at-risk preschoolers: Closing the achievement gap by closing the instruction gap. *Action in Teacher Education, 31*(4), 41-53.

Reeves, D.B. (2010). *Transforming professional development into student results.* Alexandria, VA: ASCD.

Torgesen, J., Meadows, J.G., & Howard, P. (n.d.). *Using student outcome data to help guide professional development and teacher support: Issues for Reading First and K-12 reading plans.* Tallahassee, FL: Florida Center for Reading Research.

NOTES

Professional learning that increases educator effectiveness and results for all students **integrates theories, research, and models of human learning to achieve its intended outcomes.**

DATA

LEARNING COMMUNITIES

LEADERSHIP

RESOURCES

Integrating theories, research, and models of human learning into the planning and design of professional learning contributes to its effectiveness. Several factors influence decisions about learning designs, including the goals of the learning, characteristics of the learners, their comfort with the learning process and one another, their familiarity with the content, the magnitude of the expected change, educators' work environment, and resources available to support learning. The design of professional learning affects its quality and effectiveness.

APPLY LEARNING THEORIES, RESEARCH, AND MODELS

Cognitive psychologists, neuroscientists, and educators have studied how learning occurs for nearly a century. The resulting theories, research, and models of human learning shape the underlying framework and assumptions educators use to plan and design professional learning. While multiple designs exist, many have common features, such as active engagement, modeling, reflection, metacognition, application, feedback, ongoing support, and formative and summative assessment, that support change in knowledge, skills, dispositions, and practice.

Professional learning occurs in face-to-face, online, and hybrid settings. Some professional learning focuses on individual learning, while other forms focus on team-based or whole-school learning. Most professional learning occurs as a part of the workday, while other forms occur outside the school day. Both formal and informal designs facilitate and organize educator learning. Some learning designs use structured processes such as courses or workshops. Others are more fluid to allow for adjustments in the learning process. Some learning designs require team members or external experts as facilitators, while others are individually organized. Learning designs use synchronous or asynchronous interactions, live or simulated models and experiences, and print and nonprint resources to present information, model skills and procedures, provide low-risk practice, and support transfer to the workplace.

Job-embedded learning designs engage individuals, pairs, or teams of educators in professional learning during the workday. Designs for job-embedded learning include analyzing student data, case studies, peer observation or visitations, simulations, co-teaching with peers or specialists, action research, peer and expert coaching, observing and analyzing demonstrations of practice, problem-based learning, inquiry into practice, student observation, study groups, data analysis, constructing and scoring assessments, examining student or educator work, lesson study, video clubs, professional reading, or book studies. Learners and facilitators of learning may weave together multiple designs within on-site, online, or hybrid learning to achieve identified goals and to differentiate learning designs to meet the unique needs of individual learners. Learning designs that occur during the workday and engage peers in learning facilitate ongoing communication about learning, develop a collaborative culture with peer accountability, foster professionalism, and support transfer of the learning to practice.

Technology is rapidly enhancing and extending opportunities for professional learning. It particularly facilitates access to, sharing, construction, and analysis of information to enhance practice. Technology exponentially increases possibilities for personalizing, differentiating, and deepening learning, especially for educators who have limited access to on-site professional learning or who are eager to reach beyond the boundaries of their own work setting to join local or global networks to enrich their learning.

SELECT LEARNING DESIGNS

When choosing designs for professional learning, educators consider multiple factors. The first is

the intended outcome, drawn from analysis of student and educator learning needs. Learning designs that engage adult learners in applying the processes they are expected to use facilitate the learning of those behaviors by making them more explicit. Effective designs for professional learning assist educators in moving beyond comprehension of the surface features of a new idea or practice to developing a more complete understanding of its purposes, critical attributes, meaning, and connection to other approaches. To increase student learning, educator learning provides many opportunities for educators to practice new learning with ongoing assessment, feedback, and coaching so the learning becomes fully integrated into routine behaviors.

Educators are responsible for taking an active role in selecting and constructing learning designs that facilitate their own and others' learning. They choose appropriate learning designs to achieve their individual, team, or school goals. Educators' learning characteristics and preferences also inform decisions about learning designs. Learners' backgrounds, experiences, beliefs, motivation, interests, cognitive processes, professional identity, and commitment to school and school system goals affect how educators approach professional learning and the effectiveness of various learning designs. Decisions about learning designs consider all phases of the learning process, from knowledge and skill acquisition to application, reflection, refinement, assessment, and evaluation. Learning designers consider how to build knowledge, develop skills, transform practice, challenge attitudes and beliefs, and inspire action.

PROMOTE ACTIVE ENGAGEMENT

Active engagement in professional learning promotes change in educator practice and student learning. Active engagement occurs when learners interact during the learning process with the content and with one another. Educator collaborative learning consistently produces strong, positive effects on achievement of learning outcomes. Active engagement respects adults as professionals and gives them significant voice and choice in shaping

their own learning. Through active engagement, educators construct personal meaning of their learning, are more committed to its success, and identify authentic applications for their learning. Active learning processes promote deep understanding of new learning and increase motivation to implement it. Active learning processes include discussion and dialogue, writing, demonstrations, inquiry, reflection, metacognition, co-construction of knowledge, practice with feedback, coaching, modeling, and problem solving. Through exploration of individual and collective experiences, learners actively construct, analyze, evaluate, and synthesize knowledge and practices.

RELATED RESEARCH

Croft, A., Coggshall, J.G., Dolan, M., & Powers, E. (with Killion, J.). (2010, April). *Job-embedded professional development: What it is, who's responsible, and how to get it done well* (Issue Brief). Washington, DC: National Comprehensive Center for Teacher Quality.

Dede, C. (Ed.) (2006). *Online professional development for teachers: Emerging models and methods.* Cambridge, MA: Harvard Education Press.

Garet, M.S., Porter, A., Desimone, L., Birman, B., & Yoon, K.S. (2001, Winter). What makes professional development effective? Results from a national sample of teachers. *American Educational Research Journal, 38*(4), 915-945.

Joyce, B. & Showers, B. (2002). *Student achievement through staff development.* Alexandria, VA: ASCD.

Penuel, W.R., Fishman, B.J., Yamaguchi, R., & Gallagher, L.P. (2007, December). What makes professional development effective? Strategies that foster curriculum implementation. *American Educational Research Journal, 44*(4), 921-958.

NOTES

Professional learning that increases educator effectiveness and results for all students **applies research on change and sustains support for implementation of professional learning for long-term change.**

The primary goals for professional learning are changes in educator practice and increases in student learning. This is a process that occurs over time and requires support for implementation to embed the new learning into practices. Those responsible for professional learning apply findings from change process research to support long-term change in practice by extending learning over time. They integrate a variety of supports for individuals, teams, and schools. Finally, they integrate constructive feedback and reflection to support continuous improvement in practice that allows educators to move along a continuum from novice to expert through application of their professional learning.

APPLY CHANGE RESEARCH

Effective professional learning integrates research about individual, organization, technical, and adaptive change through supporting and sustaining implementation for long-term change. Those responsible for professional learning, whether leaders, facilitators, or participants, commit to long-term change by setting clear goals and maintaining high expectations for implementation with fidelity. Drawing from multiple bodies of research about change, leaders provide and align resources, including time, staff, materials, and technology, to initiate and sustain implementation. Individuals, peers, coaches, and leaders use tools and metrics to gather evidence to monitor and assess implementation. Leaders and coaches model salient practices and maintain a sustained focus on the goals and strategies for achieving them. Leaders create and maintain a culture of support by encouraging stakeholders to use data to identify implementation challenges and engage them in identifying and recommending ongoing refinements to increase results. They engender community support for implementation by communicating incremental successes, reiterating goals, and honestly discussing the complexities of deep change.

Understanding how individuals and organizations respond to change and how various personal, cognitive, and work environment factors affect those experiencing change gives those leading, facilitating, or participating in professional learning the ability to differentiate support, tap educators' strengths and talents, and increase educator effectiveness and student learning.

SUSTAIN IMPLEMENTATION

Professional learning produces changes in educator practice and student learning when it sustains implementation support over time. Episodic, periodic, or occasional professional learning has little effect on educator practice or student learning because it rarely includes ongoing support or opportunities for extended learning to support implementation. Formal professional learning, such as online, on-site, or hybrid workshops, conferences, or courses, is useful to develop or expand knowledge and skills, share emerging ideas, and network learners with one another. To bridge the knowing-doing gap and integrate new ideas into practice, however, educators need three to five years of

ongoing implementation support that includes opportunities to deepen their understanding and address problems associated with practice.

Ongoing support for implementation of professional learning takes many forms and occurs at the implementation site. It may be formalized through ongoing workshops designed to deepen understanding and refine educator practice. It occurs through coaching, reflection, or reviewing results. It may occur individually, in pairs, or in collaborative learning teams when educators plan,

implement, analyze, reflect, and evaluate the integration of their professional learning into their practice. It occurs within learning communities that meet to learn or refine instructional strategies; plan lessons that integrate the new strategies; share experiences about implementing those lessons; analyze student work together to reflect on the results of use of the strategies; and assess their progress toward their defined goals. School- and system-based coaches provide extended learning opportunities, resources for implementation, demonstrations of the practices, and specific, personalized guidance. Peer support groups, study groups, peer observation, co-teaching, and co-planning are other examples of extended support. When educators work to resolve challenges related to integration of professional learning, they support and sustain implementation. Professional learning is a process of continuous improvement focused on achieving clearly defined student and educator learning goals rather than an event defined by a predetermined number of hours.

PROVIDE CONSTRUCTIVE FEEDBACK

Constructive feedback accelerates implementation by providing formative assessment through the learning and implementation process. It provides specific information to assess practice in relationship to established expectations and to adjust practice so that it more closely aligns with those expectations. Feedback from peers, coaches, supervisors, external experts, students, self, and others offers information for educators to use as they refine practices. Reflection is another form of feedback in which a learner engages in providing constructive feedback on his or her own or others' practices.

Effective feedback is based on clearly defined expected behaviors, acknowledges progress toward expectations, and provides guidance for achieving full implementation. Giving and receiving feedback about successes and improvements require skillfulness in clear, nonjudgmental communication based on evidence, commitment to continu-

ous improvement and shared goals, and trusting, respectful relationships between those giving and receiving feedback.

To add validity and reliability to the feedback process, educators develop and use common, clear expectations that define practice so that the feedback is focused, objective, relevant, valid, and purposeful. Educators consider and decide what evidence best demonstrates the expected practices and their results. Frequent feedback supports continuous improvement, whereas occasional feedback is often considered evaluative. Feedback about progress toward expected practices provides encouragement to sustain the desired changes over time. Tools that define expected behaviors facilitate data collection and open, honest feedback.

RELATED RESEARCH

Bandura, A. (1986). *Social foundations of thought and action: A social cognitive theory.* Englewood Cliffs, NJ: Prentice-Hall.

Fullan, M. (2007). *The new meaning of educational change* (4th ed.). New York: Teachers College Press.

Hall, G. & Hord, S. (2011). *Implementing change: Patterns, principles, and potholes* (3rd ed.). Boston: Allyn & Bacon.

Huberman, M. & Miles, M.B. (1984). *Innovation up close: How school improvement works.* New York: Plenum.

Supovitz, J.A. & Turner, H.M. (2000, November). The effects of professional development on science teaching practices and classroom culture. *Journal of Research in Science Teaching, 37*(9), 963-980.

NOTES

Professional learning that increases
educator effectiveness and results for all
students **aligns its outcomes with educator
performance and student curriculum standards.**

DATA

LEARNING COMMUNITIES

LEADERSHIP

RESOURCES

For all students to learn, educators and professional learning must be held to high standards. Professional learning that increases results for all students addresses the learning outcomes and performance expectations education systems designate for students and educators. When the content of professional learning integrates student curriculum and educator performance standards, the link between educator learning and student learning becomes explicit, increasing the likelihood that professional learning contributes to increased student learning. When systems increase the stakes for students by demanding high, equitable outcomes, the stakes for professional learning increase as well.

MEET PERFORMANCE STANDARDS

Educator performance standards typically de-lineate the knowledge, skills, practices, and dispositions of highly effective educators. Standards guide preparation, assessment, licensing, induction, practice, and evaluation. Frequently regulated by government agencies, standards establish requirements for educator preparation, define expectations of an effective workforce, guide career-long professional learning of the education workforce, and set fair and reliable indicators of effectiveness for measuring educator performance.

Teacher standards specify what teachers need to know and do to deliver on the promise of an effective, equitable education for every student. Typical areas included in teacher standards are knowledge, skills, and dispositions related to content knowledge; pedagogy; pedagogical content knowledge; assessment; understanding how students learn; understanding how students' cognitive, social, emotional, and physical development influences their learning; engaging students with diverse cultures, language, gender, socioeconomic conditions, and exceptionalities; engaging families and communities in student learning; creating learning environments; professional growth and development; and professional collaboration.

Standards for school and system leaders, like teacher standards, describe what effective leaders know and do so that every student and educator performs at high levels. Whether for teacher leaders or school or school system administrators, these standards delineate specific expectations for preparation, assessment, licensure, professional learning, practice, and evaluation of those engaged in leadership roles within a school or school system. Typical areas covered in leader standards include establishing a vision and strategic plan for effective learning; leading learning of students and staff; developing workplace culture to support learning; engaging in their own professional learning; managing facilities, workforce, operations, and resources; establishing effective relationships and communication systems; managing change; sharing leadership with others; engaging staff and families in decision making; understanding and responding to the diverse needs of students and communities; understanding and responding to cultural, political, social, legal, and financial contexts; and securing individual, team, school, and whole system accountability for student success.

Standards for other members of the education workforce delineate the unique knowledge, skills, qualities, and dispositions required of those in specialized roles. These roles include school nurses, guidance counselors, librarians, instructional coaches, resource personnel, classroom assistants, and other instructional and noninstructional staff who are vital to schools and school systems. Standards for advanced or specialized certification guide professional learning for those who seek career advancement or differentiated roles.

ADDRESS LEARNING OUTCOMES

Student learning outcomes define equitable expectations for all students to achieve at high levels and hold educators responsible for implementing appropriate strategies to support student learning. Learning for educators that focuses on

student learning outcomes has a positive effect on changing educator practice and increasing student achievement. Whether the learning outcomes are developed locally or nationally and are defined in content standards, courses of study, curriculum, or curricular programs, these learning outcomes serve as the core content for educator professional learning to support effective implementation and results. With student learning outcomes as the focus, professional learning deepens educators' content knowledge, pedagogical content knowledge, and understanding of how students learn the specific discipline. Using student learning outcomes as its outcomes, professional learning can model and engage educators in practices they are expected to implement within their classrooms and workplaces.

BUILD COHERENCE

Coherence requires that professional learning builds on what educators have already learned; focuses on learning outcomes and pedagogy aligned with national or local curriculum and assessments for educator and student learning; aligns with educator performance standards; and supports educators in developing sustained, ongoing professional communication with other educators who are engaged in similar changes in their practice. Any single professional learning activity is more likely to be effective in improving educator performance and student learning if it builds on earlier professional learning and is followed up with later, more advanced work to become a part of a coherent set

of opportunities for ongoing professional learning. Coherence also ensures that professional learning is a part of a seamless process that begins in the preparation program and continues throughout an educator's career and aligns tightly with the expectations for effectiveness defined in performance standards and student learning outcomes.

RELATED RESEARCH

Blank, R.K., de las Alas, N., & Smith, C. (2007, February). *Analysis of the quality of professional development programs for mathematics and science teachers: Findings from a cross-state study.* Washington, DC: Council of Chief State School Officers.

Borko, H. (2004, November). Professional development and teacher learning: Mapping the terrain. *Educational Researcher, 33*(8), 3-15.

Cohen, D. & Hill, H. (2000). Instructional policy and classroom performance: The mathematics reform in California. *Teachers College Record, 102*(2), 294-343.

Kennedy, M. (1998, March). Education reform and subject matter knowledge. *Journal of Research in Science Teaching, 35*(3), 249-263.

Shulman, L.S. (2000, January-February). Teacher development: Roles of domain expertise and pedagogical knowledge. *Journal of Applied Developmental Psychology, 21*(1), 129-135.

NOTES

Innovation Configuration Maps

TEACHER

- **LEARNING COMMUNITIES**
- **LEADERSHIP**
- **RESOURCES**
- **DATA**
- **LEARNING DESIGNS**
- **IMPLEMENTATION**
- **OUTCOMES**

1.1 Engage in continuous improvement

Level 1	Level 2	Level 3	Level 4	Level 5	Level 6
Desired outcome 1.1.1: Develops capacity to apply the seven-step cycle of continuous improvement. *					
• Develops knowledge and skills about the seven steps of the cycle of continuous improvement.	• Develops understanding of six of the seven steps of the cycle of continuous improvement.	• Develops understanding of five of the seven steps of the cycle of continuous improvement.	• Develops understanding of four or fewer steps of the seven steps of the cycle of continuous improvement.	• Fails to develop knowledge and skills about the cycle of continuous improvement.	
Desired outcome 1.1.2: Applies the cycle of continuous improvement with fidelity in professional learning.					
• Employs the seven-step cycle of continuous improvement in individual, team, and schoolwide professional learning. • Maintains commitment to employ the cycle of continuous improvement in individual and team learning. • Supports colleagues in employing the cycle in individual and team learning.	• Employs six steps of the seven-step cycle of continuous improvement in individual, team, and schoolwide professional learning. • Maintains commitment to employ the cycle in individual and team learning.	• Employs five steps of the seven-step cycle of continuous improvement in individual and team professional learning.	• Employs four or fewer steps of the seven-step cycle of continuous improvement in individual and team professional learning.	• Employs four or fewer steps of the seven-step cycle of continuous improvement in individual professional learning.	• Fails to use the cycle of continuous improvement in professional learning.

*See the Appendix (p. 262) for an explanation of this concept.

1.2 Develop collective responsibility

Level 1	Level 2	Level 3	Level 4	Level 5	Level 6
Desired outcome 1.2.1: Advances collective responsibility.					
• Contributes, with colleagues, to the development of shared assumptions about and a shared definition of collective responsibility. • Shares evidence of collective responsibility. • Challenges, with principal and colleagues, practices and assumptions that create barriers to collective responsibility. • Takes action, with principal and colleagues, to overcome barriers to collective responsibility.	• Contributes to the development of shared assumptions about and a shared definition of collective responsibility. • Contributes to efforts to identify and overcome barriers to collective responsibility.	• Contributes to shared assumptions about and a definition of collective responsibility.	• States personal assumptions about and a definition of collective responsibility.	• Fails to address collective responsibility.	
Desired outcome 1.2.2: Engages with colleagues to meet the needs of all students.					
• Engages with colleagues in conversations about the impact of individual and collective professional learning on student achievement. • Engages in individual, team, and schoolwide professional learning to address the learning needs of all students.	• Engages with colleagues in conversations about the impact of individual and collective professional learning on student achievement. • Engages in individual, team, or schoolwide professional learning to address the learning needs of all students.	• Studies data with colleagues about the needs of students outside their individual classrooms. • Engages with colleagues in individual professional learning to address the learning needs of all students.	• Invites colleagues to participate in professional learning to address the needs of students outside their individual classrooms.	• Focuses attention only on learning needs of students in individual classrooms.	

1.2 Develop collective responsibility

Desired outcome 1.2.3: Models collective responsibility by participating in learning communities.

Level 1	Level 2	Level 3	Level 4	Level 5	Level 6
• Participates routinely in one or more ongoing learning communities within and beyond the school. • Shares with colleagues own learning as a member of learning communities.	• Participates routinely in one or more school-based learning communities. • Shares with colleagues own learning as a member of learning communities.	• Participates routinely in one school-based learning community.	• Participates occasionally in a school-based learning community.	• Fails to participate in a learning community.	

1.3 Create alignment and accountability

Desired outcome 1.3.1: Aligns professional learning with school goals.

Level 1	Level 2	Level 3	Level 4	Level 5	Level 6
• Engages in discussion with colleagues to develop understanding of school and system goals and strategies to align individual, team, and school goals and plans for professional learning. • Aligns individual and team professional learning goals with school goals.	• Engages in discussion with colleagues to develop understanding of school and system goals and strategies to align individual, team, and school goals and plans for professional learning. • Aligns individual professional learning goals with school goals.	• Establishes individual professional learning goals and strategies that align with school goals and strategies.	• Adopts school professional learning goals as own goals.	• Contributes to development of school professional learning goals and strategies without consideration of system goals and strategies.	• Fails to align individual professional learning goals with school goals.

2.1 Develop capacity for learning and leading

Level 1	Level 2	Level 3	Level 4	Level 5	Level 6
Desired outcome 2.1.1: Commits to continuous professional learning.					
• Assesses current leadership knowledge, skills, and dispositions and identifies strengths and needs. • Adopts ambitious improvement goals in curriculum, instruction, assessment, and leadership practices. • Adopts a disposition of curiosity and problem solving when confronted with student learning challenges. • Adopts collaborative learning as the primary approach to solving individual, team, and schoolwide challenges related to student learning. • Engages in a variety of professional learning throughout career. • Reflects on experiences with professional learning to identify effective practices, designs, and outcomes.	• Assesses current leadership knowledge, skills, and dispositions and identifies strengths and needs. • Adopts ambitious improvement goals in curriculum, instruction, assessment, and leadership practices. • Adopts collaborative learning as the primary approach to solving individual, team, and schoolwide challenges related to student learning. • Engages in a variety of professional learning throughout career. • Reflects on experiences with professional learning to identify effective practices, designs, and outcomes.	• Adopts ambitious improvement goals in curriculum, instruction, assessment, and leadership practices. • Adopts collaborative learning as the primary approach to solving individual and team challenges related to student learning. • Engages in professional learning throughout career. • Identifies effective practices, designs, and outcomes related to student learning.	• Accepts improvements in curriculum, instruction, assessment, and leadership practices. • Engages in professional learning related to specific improvement efforts.	• Disregards improvements in curriculum, instruction, assessment, and leadership practices. • Attends professional learning when required.	

2.1 Develop capacity for learning and leading

	Level 1	Level 2	Level 3	Level 4	Level 5	Level 6
Desired outcome 2.1.2: Develops capacity for leadership of professional learning.	• Analyzes own strengths and needs related to leadership. • Participates in an ongoing leadership development experience. • Establishes professional learning goal to develop and implement leadership skills, and practices. • Practices leadership skills in multiple settings within the school and teams.	• Participates in an ongoing leadership development experience. • Establishes professional learning goal to develop and implement leadership knowledge, skills, and practices. • Practices leadership skills in multiple settings within the school and teams.	• Participates in an ongoing leadership development experience.	• Participates in discrete leadership development experiences.	• Fails to participate in ongoing leadership development experiences.	
Desired outcome 2.1.3: Understands and uses the Standards for Professional Learning in decisions about professional learning.	• Studies, with colleagues, the Standards for Professional Learning to apply key ideas. • Accesses and uses new research and information about effective professional learning on an ongoing basis. • Applies the seven Standards for Professional Learning in individual, team, and schoolwide professional learning.	• Studies, with colleagues, the Standards for Professional Learning to apply key ideas. • Applies the seven Standards for Professional Learning in individual and team professional learning.	• Studies the Standards for Professional Learning to understand their ideas. • Applies five of the Standards for Professional Learning in individual or team professional learning.	• Names the Standards for Professional Learning.	• Makes decisions about professional learning without reference to the Standards for Professional Learning.	

2.1 Develop capacity for learning and leading

Desired outcome 2.1.4: Serves as a leader in professional learning.

Level 1	Level 2	Level 3	Level 4	Level 5	Level 6
• Takes an active role in planning, implementing, and evaluating individual, team, and schoolwide professional learning. • Applies leadership knowledge and skills in at least two learning teams within and beyond the school. • Participates in coaching related to leadership development. • Seeks opportunities and serves as a formal or informal leader of professional learning within and beyond the school (e.g., mentor, facilitator of learning team, schoolwide learning facilitator, resource provider, member of school or district professional learning team or other task force, member of SLT, etc.). • Participates in a learning community focused on leadership development. • Reflects on leadership experiences to refine and expand knowledge, skills, dispositions, and practices. • Helps develop guidelines that support formal or informal teacher leadership within the school and district.	• Takes an active role in planning, implementing, and evaluating individual and team professional learning. • Identifies practices, experiences, and designs of ineffective professional learning. • Applies leadership knowledge and skills in one or more learning teams within and beyond the school. • Seeks opportunities and serves as a formal or informal leader of professional learning within the school (e.g., mentor, facilitator of learning team, schoolwide learning facilitator, resource provider, member of school or district professional learning team or other task force, member of SLT, etc.). • Reflects on leadership experiences to refine and expand knowledge, skills, dispositions, and practices. • Helps develop guidelines that support formal or informal teacher leadership within the school and district.	• Takes an active role in planning, implementing, and evaluating individual and team professional learning. • Applies leadership knowledge and skills within a learning team in the school. • Seeks opportunities and serves as a formal or informal leader of professional learning within the school (e.g., mentor, facilitator of learning team, schoolwide learning facilitator, resource provider, member of school or district professional learning team or other task force, member of SLT, etc.).	• Recognizes responsibility for the results of individual professional learning. • Applies leadership knowledge and skills in a learning team within the school.	• Serves as a member of a school or district committee.	• Fails to serve as a formal or informal teacher leader within or beyond the school.

2.2 Advocate for professional learning

Level 1	Level 2	Level 3	Level 4	Level 5	Level 6
Desired outcome 2.2.1: Articulates the link between student learning and professional learning.					
• Explains the indelible connection between professional learning and student achievement to staff, students, parents, system leaders, public officials, and community members and partners. • Provides multiple examples of the link between individual, team, and schoolwide professional learning and student learning.	• Explains the indelible connection between professional learning and student achievement to staff, students, and parents. • Provides multiple examples of the link between individual, team, and schoolwide professional learning and student learning.	• Explains the indelible connection between professional learning and student achievement to staff and students. • Provides multiple examples of the link between individual, team, and schoolwide professional learning and student learning.	• Describes the connection between professional learning and student learning.	• Fails to explain the connection between professional learning and student learning.	

2.2 Advocate for professional learning

	Level 1	Level 2	Level 3	Level 4	Level 5	Level 6
Desired outcome 2.2.2: Advocates high-quality professional learning.						
	• Promotes high-quality professional learning with colleagues, students, parents, system leaders, colleagues, public officials, and community members and partners. • Advocates district- and school-based conditions and procedures to support effective individual, team, and schoolwide professional learning. • Develops and shares succinct messages about the role of professional learning in student learning with colleagues, students, parents, system leaders, colleagues, public officials, and community members and partners. • Supports collaborative professional learning when challenged by peers, students, parents, or community members. • Reports positive experiences and results from professional learning in internal and external communication vehicles. • Challenges practices, experiences, and designs of ineffective professional learning and advocates improvements.	• Promotes high-quality professional learning with colleagues, students, parents, system leaders, and colleagues. • Advocates school-based conditions and procedures to support effective individual and team professional learning. • Develops and shares succinct messages about the role of professional learning in student learning with colleagues, parents, and students. • Supports collaborative professional learning when challenged by peers and parents. • Reports positive experiences and results from professional learning in internal communication vehicles.	• Promotes high-quality professional learning with colleagues and system leaders. • Advocates school-based conditions and procedures to support effective individual and team professional learning. • Supports collaborative professional learning when challenged by peers. • Reports positive experiences and results from professional learning in internal communication vehicles.	• Promotes high-quality professional learning with colleagues.	• Fails to promote high-quality professional learning for staff.	

2.3 Create support systems and structures

	Level 1	Level 2	Level 3	Level 4	Level 5	Level 6
Desired outcome 2.3.1: Contributes to systems and structures for effective professional learning.						
	• Establishes, with colleagues and principal, school-based conditions for effective individual, team, and schoolwide professional learning (e.g., resources, policies, annual calendars, schedules, procedures, and structures). • Supports colleagues in understanding and establishing conditions for effective schoolwide professional learning. • Creates, with colleagues, conditions to support effective schoolwide and team professional learning. • Solves problems, with principal and colleagues, related to implementing conditions for effective professional learning.	• Collaborates with principal to establish school conditions for effective professional learning (e.g., resources, policies, annual calendars, schedules, procedures, and structures). • Creates, with colleagues, conditions to support effective team learning. • Solves problems, with principal, related to establishing conditions for effective professional learning.	• Advocates school conditions for effective professional learning (e.g., resources, policies, annual calendars, schedules, pro- cedures, and structures). • Creates, with colleagues, conditions to support effective team learning.	• Fails to contribute to establishing conditions for effective team and schoolwide professional learning.		

2.3 Create support systems and structures

Desired outcome 2.3.2: Develops capacity for skillful collaboration.

Level 1	Level 2	Level 3	Level 4	Level 5	Level 6
• Develops, with colleagues, the knowledge and skills to learn and work collaboratively. • Encourages colleagues to use collaboration to achieve individual, team, and schoolwide professional learning goals. • Develops, with colleagues, the capacity to resolve conflict. • Confronts assumptions and practices that create barriers to collective responsibility. • Practices skillful collaboration within schoolwide and team professional learning. • Seeks from and provides to colleagues feedback on collaboration skills.	• Develops, with colleagues, the knowledge and skills to learn and work collaboratively. • Encourages colleagues to use collaboration to achieve individual, team, and schoolwide professional learning goals. • Develops, with colleagues, the capacity to resolve conflict. • Practices skillful collaboration within schoolwide and team professional learning.	• Develops, with colleagues, the knowledge and skills to learn and work collaboratively. • Encourages colleagues to use collaboration to achieve individual, team, and schoolwide professional learning goals. • Practices skillful collaboration within team professional learning.	• Encourages colleagues to use collaboration to achieve individual, team, and schoolwide professional learning goals.	• Presumes staff uses collaboration to achieve individual, team, and schoolwide professional learning goals.	

2.3 Create support systems and structures

Desired outcome 2.3.3: Contributes to the development and maintenance of a collaborative culture.

Level 1	Level 2	Level 3	Level 4	Level 5	Level 6
• Develops and applies research-based knowledge and skills about collaborative cultures to support schoolwide and team learning and collaborative work.	• Develops and applies research-based knowledge and skills about collaborative cultures to support team learning and collaborative work.	• Models collaboration in interactions with colleagues, principal, and other school leaders.	• Models collaboration in interactions with colleagues, principal, and other school leaders.	• Accepts the current school culture without making efforts to improve it.	
• Models collaboration in interactions with colleagues, students, parents, community members, and system leaders.	• Models collaboration in interactions with colleagues, principal, and other school leaders.	• Assesses, with principal, the current culture to make improvements.	• Assesses, with principal, the current culture to make improvements.		
• Assesses, with principal and colleagues, the current culture to make improvements.	• Assesses, with principal, the current culture to make improvements.	• Contributes to the development of the social architecture of a collaborative culture that includes norms for individual, team, and schoolwide interactions; high expectations; and mutual respect.			
• Contributes to the development of the social architecture of a collaborative culture that includes norms for individual, team, and schoolwide interactions; high expectations; collective responsibility for high levels of learning for all students; mutual respect; and relational trust.	• Contributes to the development of the social architecture of a collaborative culture that includes norms for individual, team, and schoolwide interactions; high expectations; collective responsibility for high levels of learning for all students; and mutual respect.	• Works with colleagues to sustain a collaborative culture within learning teams.			
• Works with colleagues to sustain a collaborative culture within learning teams.	• Works with colleagues to sustain a collaborative culture within learning teams.				
• Confronts assumptions and practices that inhibit collaboration.					
• Identifies and addresses, with principal and colleagues, barriers to collaboration.					

3.1 Prioritize human, fiscal, material, technology, and time resources

Level 1	Level 2	Level 3	Level 4	Level 5	Level 6
Desired outcome 3.1.1: Contributes to definition of resources for professional learning.					
• Works, with principal and colleagues, to develop a shared definition of resources for professional learning. • Suggests resources for professional learning that include staff, materials, technology, funding, and time.	• Works, with principal and colleagues, to develop a shared definition of resources for professional learning. • Suggests resources for professional learning that include staff, materials, technology, funding, and time.	• Suggests resources for professional learning that include materials, technology, funding, and time.	• Suggests resources for professional learning that include funding and time.	• Suggests funding as the only resource for professional learning.	• Fails to define resources for professional learning.
Desired outcome 3.1.2: Recommends resources to align professional learning with high-priority student and educator learning needs.					
• Contributes to the criteria for resource allocation for professional learning based on high-priority student learning needs and individual, team, and schoolwide educator learning needs. • Recommends resources for individual, team, and schoolwide professional learning to achieve high-priority student and educator learning goals.	• Contributes to the criteria for resource allocation for professional learning based on high-priority student learning needs and individual and team educator learning needs. • Recommends resources for individual and team professional learning to achieve high-priority student and educator learning goals.	• Participates in decision making about prioritized learning needs. • Recommends resources for individual and team professional learning to achieve high-priority student and educator learning goals.	• Recommends distribution of available resources for professional learning based on individual educator requests.	• Fails to recommend resources for professional learning.	

3.1 Prioritize human, fiscal, material, technology, and time resources

Desired outcome 3.1.3: Selects appropriate resources for professional learning.

Level 1	Level 2	Level 3	Level 4	Level 5	Level 6
• Develops capacity to discriminate among available resources to select, access, use, and share resources. • Identifies available internal and external resources to meet high-priority student and educator learning needs. • Selects and uses appropriate professional learning resources that align with high-priority educator learning needs. • Uses data and research to explain the resources selected for individual and team professional learning.	• Develops capacity to discriminate among available resources to select, access, use, and share resources. • Identifies available internal resources to meet high-priority student and educator learning needs. • Selects and uses appropriate professional learning resources that align with high-priority educator learning needs. • Explains the resources selected for individual and team professional learning.	• Identifies available internal resources to meet high-priority student and educator learning needs. • Selects and uses appropriate professional learning resources that align with high-priority educator learning needs. • Explains the resources selected for individual and team professional learning.	• Identifies available internal resources to meet high-priority student and educator learning needs. • Selects professional learning resources without analysis.	• Selects professional learning resources without analysis.	• Fails to select appropriate resources for professional learning.

www.learningforward.org   800-727-7288

3.2 Monitor resources

	Level 1	Level 2	Level 3	Level 4	Level 5	Level 6
Desired outcome 3.2.1: Monitors effectiveness of the use of resources for professional learning.						
	• Establishes criteria for effective individual and team professional learning resources. • Tracks and monitors use of professional learning resources. • Uses the data to analyze the effectiveness of selected professional learning resources. • Provides feedback on the effectiveness of individual, team, and schoolwide professional learning resources. • Recommends changes to increase the effectiveness of professional learning resources.	• Establishes criteria for effective individual and team professional learning resources. • Tracks and monitors use of professional learning resources. • Uses the data to analyze the effectiveness of selected professional learning resources. • Provides feedback on the effectiveness of individual and team professional learning resources.	• Tracks and monitors use of professional learning resources. • Uses the data to analyze the effectiveness of selected professional learning resources. • Provides feedback on the effectiveness of individual and team professional learning resources.	• Provides feedback on the effectiveness of individual and team professional learning resources.	• Fails to monitor the effectiveness of professional learning resources.	

3.3 Coordinate resources

Desired outcome 3.3.1: Implements a comprehensive resource plan for professional learning.

Level 1	Level 2	Level 3	Level 4	Level 5	Level 6
• Supports the implementation of the professional learning resource plan to achieve high-priority student and educator learning goals. • Shares resources with colleagues to increase their effectiveness.	• Reads the professional learning resource plan to achieve high-priority student and educator learning goals. • Shares resources with colleagues to increase their effectiveness.	• Shares resources with colleagues to increase their effectiveness.	• Fails to implement the resource plan.		

4.1 Analyze student, educator, and system data

Desired outcome 4.1.1: Develops capacity to analyze and interpret data.

Level 1	Level 2	Level 3	Level 4	Level 5	Level 6
• Develops, with colleagues, knowledge and skills to access, organize, and display data. • Develops, with colleagues, knowledge and skills to analyze and interpret data from multiple sources (e.g, norm-referenced tests, student work samples, student portfolios, and school system-designed tests) to make team, grade-level, department, and individual decisions about professional learning.	• Develops knowledge and skills to access, organize, and display data. • Develops knowledge and skills to analyze and interpret data from multiple sources (e.g., norm-referenced tests, student work samples, student portfolios, and school system-designed tests) to make team, grade-level, department, and individual decisions about professional learning.	• Develops knowledge and skills to access, organize, and display data. • Develops knowledge and skills to analyze and interpret data from multiple sources (e.g., norm-referenced tests, student work samples, student portfolios, and school system-designed tests) to make individual decisions about professional learning.	• Develops knowledge and skills to access, organize, and display data to make individual decisions about professional learning.	• Fails to develop knowledge and skills to analyze and interpret data.	

4.1 Analyze student, educator, and system data

Desired outcome 4.1.2: Analyzes and interprets multiple sources of student data to determine professional learning needs.

Level 1	Level 2	Level 3	Level 4	Level 5	Level 6
• Analyzes, with colleagues, qualitative and quantitative student data from four or more sources to make predictions, observations, and inferences about the data. • Interprets, with staff and SLT, qualitative and quantitative student data from four or more sources to decipher trends, patterns, outliers, and root causes within the data. • Supports colleagues to independently identify findings, trends, patterns, outliers, and root causes from four or more sources of student data.	• Analyzes, with staff and SLT, qualitative and quantitative student data from 3 sources to make predictions, observations, and inferences about the data. • Interprets, with staff and SLT, qualitative and quantitative student data from three sources to decipher trends, patterns, outliers, and root causes within the data.	• Analyzes, with staff and SLT, qualitative and quantitative student data from two sources to make predictions, observations, and inferences about the data. • Interprets, with staff and SLT, qualitative and quantitative student data from two sources to decipher trends, patterns, outliers, and root causes within the data.	• Analyzes one source of student data.	• Accepts results of student data analysis from principal, coach, SLT, or others.	• Fails to analyze student data to determine professional learning needs.

4.1 Analyze student, educator, and system data

Desired outcome 4.1.3: Analyzes and interprets educator data to determine professional learning needs.

Level 1	Level 2	Level 3	Level 4	Level 5	Level 6
• Analyzes, with colleagues, qualitative and quantitative educator data from four or more sources to make predictions, observations, and inferences about the data. • Interprets, with staff and SLT, qualitative and quantitative educator data from four or more sources to decipher trends, patterns, outliers, and root causes within the data. • Supports colleagues to independently identify findings, trends, patterns, outliers, and root causes from four or more sources of educator data.	• Analyzes, with staff and SLT, qualitative and quantitative educator data from three sources to make predictions, observations, and inferences about the data. • Interprets, with staff and SLT, qualitative and quantitative educator data from three sources to decipher trends, patterns, outliers, and root causes within the data.	• Analyzes, with staff and SLT, qualitative and quantitative educator data from two sources to make predictions, observations, and inferences about the data. • Interprets, with staff and SLT, qualitative and quantitative educator data from two sources to decipher trends, patterns, outliers, and root causes within the data.	• Analyzes one source of educator data.	• Accepts results of educator data analysis from principal, coach, SLT, or others.	• Fails to engage in analyzing educator data.

4.1 Analyze student, educator, and system data

Level 1	Level 2	Level 3	Level 4	Level 5	Level 6
Desired outcome 4.1.4: Analyzes and interprets school data to determine professional learning needs.					
• Analyzes, with colleagues, qualitative and quantitative school data from four or more sources to make predictions, observations, and inferences about the data. • Interprets, with staff and SLT, qualitative and quantitative school data from four or more sources to decipher trends, patterns, outliers, and root causes within the data. • Supports colleagues to independently identify findings, trends, patterns, outliers, and root causes from four or more sources of school data.	• Analyzes, with staff and SLT, qualitative and quantitative school data from three sources to make predictions, observations, and inferences about the data. • Interprets, with staff and SLT, qualitative and quantitative school data from three sources to decipher trends, patterns, outliers, and root causes within the data.	• Analyzes, with staff and SLT, qualitative and quantitative school data from two sources to make predictions, observations, and inferences about the data. • Interprets, with staff and SLT, qualitative and quantitative school data from two sources to decipher trends, patterns, outliers, and root causes within the data.	• Analyzes one source of school data.	• Accepts results of school data analysis from principal, coach, SLT, or others.	• Fails to engage in analyzing school data.
Desired outcome 4.1.5: Uses analyzed data to determine professional learning needs.					
• Uses, with colleagues, analyzed data to identify needs for individual and team professional learning.	• Uses, with colleagues, analyzed data to identify needs for individual or team professional learning.	• Uses analyzed data to identify needs for individual or team professional learning.	• Identifies needs for individual and team professional learning.	• Fails to use student, educator, or school data to identify needs for individual and team professional learning.	

4.2 Assess progress

Desired outcome 4.2.1: Determines formative data to assess progress toward professional learning benchmarks and goals.

Level 1	Level 2	Level 3	Level 4	Level 5	Level 6
• Establishes, with principal and colleagues, benchmarks to assess progress toward individual, team, and schoolwide professional learning goals. • Establishes monthly, with principal and colleagues, qualitative and quantitative formative data to assess progress toward individual, team, and schoolwide professional learning benchmarks and goals.	• Establishes, with principal and colleagues, benchmarks to assess progress toward individual and team professional learning goals. • Establishes quarterly, with principal and colleagues, qualitative and quantitative formative data to assess progress toward individual and team professional learning benchmarks and goals.	• Establishes, with principal and colleagues, benchmarks to assess progress toward individual and team professional learning goals. • Establishes semiannually, with principal and colleagues, qualitative and quantitative formative data to assess progress toward individual and team professional learning benchmarks and goals.	• Identifies annually either qualitative or quantitative data to assess progress toward individual professional learning benchmarks and goals.	• Fails to identify data to assess progress toward individual or team professional learning benchmarks and goals.	

4.2 Assess progress

	Level 1	Level 2	Level 3	Level 4	Level 5	Level 6
Desired outcome 4.2.2: Collects, analyzes, and uses data to continuously assess progress toward professional learning benchmarks and goals.	• Uses, with colleagues, analyzed data to identify enhancers of and barriers to progress. • Engages with colleagues in problem solving to address identified barriers to achieving professional learning benchmarks and goals. • Makes, with colleagues, data-based, in-process adjustments in individual and team professional learning (i.e., learning designs, coaching activities, and timeframes). • Celebrates with colleagues progress toward professional learning benchmarks and goals.	• Uses, with colleagues, analyzed data to identify enhancers of and barriers to progress. • Engages with colleagues in problem solving to address identified barriers to achieving professional learning benchmarks and goals. • Makes, with colleagues, data-based, in-process adjustments in individual and team professional learning (i.e., learning designs, coaching activities, and timeframes).	• Uses analyzed data to identify enhancers of and barriers to progress. • Solves problems that create barriers to achieving professional learning benchmarks and goals. • Makes data-based, in-process adjustments in individual professional learning (i.e., learning designs, coaching activities, and timeframes).	• Uses analyzed data to identify enhancers of and barriers to progress.	• Fails to use data to assess progress toward professional learning benchmarks and goals.	
Desired outcome 4.2.3: Uses analysis of progress to make adjustments in professional learning.	• Uses analyzed data related to student learning and changes in classroom practice to adjust and refine schoolwide, team, and individual professional learning.	• Uses analyzed data related to student learning and changes in classroom practice to adjust and refine schoolwide and team professional learning.	• Uses analyzed data related to student learning and changes in classroom practice to adjust and refine schoolwide professional learning.	• Uses analyzed data related to student learning and changes in classroom practice to adjust and refine schoolwide professional learning.	• Disregards any data to adjust or refine professional learning.	• Fails to use analysis of progress to adjust and refine professional learning.

4.3 Evaluate professional learning

Level 1	Level 2	Level 3	Level 4	Level 5	Level 6
Desired outcome 4.3.1: Contributes to the development of an evaluation plan for professional learning.					
• Contributes to the development of a theory of change, logic model, and evaluation framework to evaluate schoolwide and team professional learning.	• Contributes to the development of a theory of change and evaluation framework to evaluate team professional learning.	• Contributes to the development of an evaluation framework to evaluate team professional learning.	• Contributes to the identification of data sources and data collection methods to evaluate individual professional learning.	• Identifies data collection methods to evaluate individual and team professional learning.	• Fails to contribute to the evaluation of professional learning.
Desired outcome 4.3.2: Uses a variety of formative and summative data to evaluate the effectiveness and results of professional learning.					
• Collects, with colleagues, student data (e.g, test scores, benchmark results, student surveys, interviews, etc.) and classroom observations to measure changes in student learning and behaviors associated with professional learning. • Collects, with colleagues, data about changes in teacher knowledge, skills, and dispositions associated with professional learning. • Collects, with colleagues, educator data (e.g, staff surveys, interviews, self-reports, and observations) to assess changes in classroom practices associated with professional learning. • Collects, with colleagues, data to assess changes in school culture and organizational structures, policies, and processes associated with professional learning.	• Collects, with colleagues, student data (e.g., test scores, benchmark results, student surveys, interviews, etc.) and classroom observations to determine changes in student learning associated with professional learning. • Collects, with colleagues, data about changes in teacher knowledge, skills, and dispositions associated with professional learning. • Collects with colleagues educator data (e.g., staff surveys, interviews, self-reports, and observations) to identify changes in classroom practices associate with professional learning.	• Collects, with colleagues, student data (e.g., test scores, benchmark results, student surveys, interviews, etc.) and classroom observations to determine changes in student learning associated with professional learning. • Collects, with colleagues, data about changes in teacher knowledge, skills, and dispositions associated with professional learning.	• Collects, with colleagues, student data (e.g., test scores, benchmark results, student surveys, interviews, etc.) and classroom observations to determine changes in student learning associated with professional learning.	• Fails to contribute to the evaluation of the effectiveness and results of professional learning.	

4.3 Evaluate professional learning

Desired outcome 4.3.3: Uses data to evaluate the effectiveness of professional learning designs, content, and duration.

Level 1	Level 2	Level 3	Level 4	Level 5	Level 6
• Identifies, with colleagues, data to evaluate the effectiveness of learning designs to develop knowledge, skills, dispositions, and practices. • Engages in individual and team reflection about attainment of professional learning goals. • Analyzes and interprets, with colleagues, data about collaboration, learning, and results. • Forms conclusions, with colleagues, about the design, content, and duration of professional learning.	• Identifies, with colleagues, data to evaluate the effectiveness of learning designs to develop knowledge, skills, dispositions, and practices. • Analyzes and interprets, with colleagues, data about collaboration, learning, and results. • Forms conclusions, with colleagues, about the design, content, and duration of professional learning.	• Identifies, with colleagues, data to evaluate the effectiveness of learning designs to develop knowledge, skills, and practices. • Analyzes and interprets data about collaboration, learning, and results. • Forms conclusions about the design, content, and duration of professional learning.	• Identifies data to evaluate the effectiveness of individual professional learning designs, content, and duration.	• Fails to evaluate the effectiveness of individual and team professional learning designs, content, and duration.	

5.1 Apply learning theories, research, and models

Desired outcome 5.1.1: Develops a knowledge base about theories, research, and models of adult learning.

Level 1	Level 2	Level 3	Level 4	Level 5	Level 6
• Studies, with colleagues, research, theories, and models of adult learning. • Discusses, with colleagues, how the theories, models, and research apply to individual, team, and schoolwide professional learning. • Contributes to a collection of resources on educator learning for personal individual, team, and whole staff use. • Accesses school resources on educator professional learning for individual and team use.	• Studies, with SLT, research, theories, and models of adult learning. • Discusses, with colleagues, how the theories, models, and research apply to individual, team, and schoolwide professional learning. • Accesses the school's resources on educator professional learning for individual and team use.	• Studies research, theories, and models of adult learning. • Explains how the research, theories, and models apply to own professional learning.	• Reads periodically resources about research, theories, and models related to educator learning.	• Accesses resources about educator learning.	• Fails to add to knowledge base about learning theories, research, and models.

5.1 Apply learning theories, research, and models

Desired outcome 5.1.2: Develops a knowledge base about multiple designs for professional learning. *

Level 1	Level 2	Level 3	Level 4	Level 5	Level 6
• Develops, with colleagues and principal, knowledge about, skills to facilitate, and expertise to implement 10 or more learning designs. • Identifies and discusses essential features of high-quality learning designs (e.g., active engagement, reflection, metacognition, ongoing support, formative assessment). • Discusses with colleagues the appropriateness of 8 to 10 learning designs for team-based learning.	• Develops, with principal, knowledge about, skills to facilitate, and expertise to implement six to nine learning designs. • Identifies and discusses essential features of high-quality learning designs (e.g., active engagement, reflection, metacognition, ongoing support, formative assessment). • Discusses with colleagues the appropriateness of six to nine learning designs for team-based learning.	• Develops knowledge about, skills to facilitate, and expertise to implement five learning designs. • Identifies and discusses essential features of high-quality learning designs (e.g., active engagement, reflection, metacognition, ongoing support, formative assessment). • Discusses with colleagues the appropriateness of five learning designs for team-based learning.	• Develops knowledge about, skills to facilitate, and expertise to implement three to four learning designs.	• Develops knowledge about, skills to facilitate, and expertise to implement fewer than three learning designs.	• Fails to develop knowledge about multiple designs for professional learning.

*See the Appendix (p. 262) for an explanation of this concept.

5.2 Select learning designs

Level 1	Level 2	Level 3	Level 4	Level 5	Level 6
Desired outcome 5.2.1: Acquires and shares knowledge about the multiple factors influencing the selection of learning designs. *					
• Develops knowledge about factors that influence how adults learn. • Contributes to identification of factors influencing individual, team, and schoolwide professional learning. • Identifies factors that influence individual and team professional learning.	• Develops knowledge about factors that influence how adults learn. • Contributes to identification of factors influencing schoolwide professional learning. • Identifies factors that influence individual and team professional learning.	• Develops knowledge about factors that influence how adults learn. • Identifies factors that influence individual and team professional learning.	• Acquires knowledge about factors that influence how adults learn.	• Fails to acquire knowledge about multiple factors influencing the selection of learning designs.	
Desired outcome 5.2.2: Applies knowledge to the selection of appropriate learning designs.					
• Identifies essential features in high-quality professional learning to achieve individual and team learning goals (e.g., active engagement, reflection, metacognition, ongoing support, etc.). • Reviews multiple in-person, blended, and online learning designs to select the ones most appropriate to achieve individual and team learning goals. • Supports colleagues to select appropriate individual and team learning designs.	• Identifies essential features in high-quality professional learning to achieve individual and team learning goals (e.g., active engagement, reflection, metacognition, ongoing support, etc.). • Reviews multiple in-person, blended, and online learning designs to select the ones most appropriate to achieve individual and team learning goals.	• Reviews in-person, blended, and online learning designs to select the ones most appropriate to achieve individual and team learning goals.	• Reviews in-person, blended, and online learning designs to select the one most appropriate to achieve individual and team learning goals.	• Fails to select appropriate learning designs for individual and team professional learning.	

*See the Appendix (p. 262) for an explanation of this concept.

5.2 Select learning designs

Desired outcome 5.2.3: Uses appropriate technology to enhance and extend professional learning.

Level 1	Level 2	Level 3	Level 4	Level 5	Level 6
• Uses technology to personalize professional learning. • Employs technology to deepen and expand opportunities for professional learning (e.g., subject-area networks, online coursework, action research studies, or sharing lesson plans). • Uses technology to participate in international, national, regional, and local collegial learning networks.	• Uses technology to personalize professional learning. • Employs technology to deepen and expand opportunities for professional learning (e.g. subject-area networks, online coursework, action research studies, or sharing lesson plans). • Uses technology to participate in national, regional, and local collegial learning networks.	• Uses technology to personalize professional learning. • Uses technology to participate in national, regional, and local collegial learning networks.	• Uses technology to personalize professional learning.	• Fails to use technology for professional learning.	

5.2 Select learning designs

Desired outcome 5.2.4: Implements appropriate learning designs.

Level 1	Level 2	Level 3	Level 4	Level 5	Level 6
• Engages in a variety of in-person, blended, and online learning designs to address all phases of the learning process (i.e., build knowledge; develop skills; address dispositions; and support implementation, reflection, and refinement). • Uses appropriate in-person, blended, and online learning designs during individual and team professional learning. • Recommends to and supports colleagues to implement appropriate in-person, blended, and online learning designs. • Analyzes, with principal and other learning facilitators, the interaction between learning designs used and the results achieved.	• Engages in a variety of in-person, blended, and online learning designs to address all phases of the learning process (i.e., build knowledge; develop skills; address dispositions; and support implementation, reflection, and refinement). • Uses appropriate in-person, blended, and online learning designs during individual and team professional learning. • Supports colleagues to implement appropriate in-person, blended, and online learning designs. • Recommends to and supports learning teams to use appropriate learning designs.	• Engages in a variety of in-person, blended, and online learning designs to address all phases of the learning process (i.e., build knowledge; develop skills; address dispositions; and support implementation, reflection, and refinement). • Uses appropriate in-person, blended, and online learning designs during individual and team professional learning.	• Engages in a variety of in-person, blended, and online learning designs to address all phases of the learning process (i.e., build knowledge; develop skills; address dispositions; and support implementation, reflection, and refinement).	• Identifies in-person, blended, and online learning designs that address building-knowledge and developing-skills phases of the learning process.	• Fails to implement appropriate in-person, blended, and online learning designs for individual and team professional learning.

5.2 Select learning designs

Desired outcome 5.2.5: Aligns professional learning designs with desired changes in classroom instruction.

	Level 1	Level 2	Level 3	Level 4	Level 5	Level 6
	• Identifies, with colleagues and principal, the changes in classroom instruction required to achieve professional learning goals. • Selects designs for individual and team professional learning that model and align with desired changes in instructional practice. • Implements the learning designs with fidelity. • Analyzes, with colleagues and coach, the effectiveness of the selected learning designs to produce changes in classroom practice.	• Identifies, with colleagues and principal, the changes in classroom instruction desired to achieve professional learning goals. • Selects designs for individual and team professional learning that model and align with the desired changes in instructional practice. • Implements the learning designs with fidelity.	• Identifies changes in classroom instruction desired to achieve professional learning goals. • Selects designs for individual and team professional learning that model and align with the desired changes in instructional practice. • Implements the learning designs with fidelity.	• Selects designs for individual professional learning that model and align with the desired changes in instructional practice.	• Fails to align professional learning designs with desired changes in classroom instruction.	

5.3 Promote active engagement

Level 1	Level 2	Level 3	Level 4	Level 5	Level 6
Desired outcome 5.3.1: Engages with colleagues during professional learning.					
• Engages actively in individual, team, and schoolwide professional learning. • Elicits colleagues' participation in and contribution to discussions in team and schoolwide professional learning. • Models and shares strategies and protocols for active engagement in team and schoolwide professional learning. • Uses, with principal and colleagues, assessment results to improve opportunities for and effectiveness of active engagement.	• Engages actively in individual, team, and schoolwide professional learning. • Elicits colleagues' participation in and contribution to discussions in team and schoolwide professional learning. • Models and shares strategies and protocols for active engagement in team professional learning.	• Engages actively in individual and team professional learning. • Elicits colleagues' participation in and contribution to discussions in team professional learning.	• Engages actively in individual and team professional learning.	• Fails to model and promote active engagement in team and schoolwide professional learning.	

5.3 Promote active engagement

Desired outcome 5.3.2: Supports colleagues to engage actively in professional learning.

Level 1	Level 2	Level 3	Level 4	Level 5	Level 6
• Establishes, with principal and colleagues, an expectation that schoolwide professional learning integrates active engagement strategies and protocols. • Recommends to and supports colleagues to use active engagement strategies and protocols. • Commits to using strategies for active engagement in professional learning. • Supports colleagues in holding each other accountable for active participation in team and schoolwide learning.	• Establishes, with principal and colleagues, an expectation that schoolwide professional learning integrates active engagement strategies and protocols. • Recommends to and supports colleagues to use active engagement strategies and protocols. • Supports colleagues in holding each other accountable for active participation in team and schoolwide learning.	• Recommends that schoolwide professional learning integrates active engagement strategies and protocols. • Recommends to colleagues strategies and protocols for active engagement. • Supports colleagues in holding each other accountable for active participation in team and schoolwide learning.	• Recommends that schoolwide professional learning integrates active engagement strategies and protocols.	• Fails to support active engagement in professional learning.	

6.1 Apply change research

Desired outcome 6.1.1: Develops capacity to apply research on change to support implementation of professional learning. *

Level 1	Level 2	Level 3	Level 4	Level 5	Level 6
• Reviews, with colleagues, research studies and examples of exemplary change practices (IC maps, SoC, LoU, RPLIM, PDSA, etc.) to develop own understanding of and skills needed to facilitate the change process. • Participates in additional professional learning about the change process to address opportunities and problems of practice. • Develops and applies, with principal and colleagues, knowledge and skills needed to participate in the change process.	• Reviews, with colleagues, research studies and examples of exemplary change practices (IC maps, SoC, LoU, RPLIM, PDSA, etc.) to develop own understanding of and skills needed to facilitate the change process. • Participates in additional professional learning about the change process to address opportunities and problems of practice. • Discusses, with colleagues, information to increase understanding of the change process.	• Reviews research studies and examples of exemplary practice (IC maps, SoC, LoU, RPLIM, PDSA, etc.) to develop own understanding of and skills needed to facilitate the change process. • Participates in additional professional learning about the change process to address opportunities and problems of practice.	• Reads articles, papers, and reports about the change process.	• Fails to engage in ongoing professional learning about the change process.	

*See the Appendix (p. 262) for an explanation of this concept.

6.1 Apply change research

	Level 1	Level 2	Level 3	Level 4	Level 5	Level 6
Desired outcome 6.1.2: Applies research on change when making decisions about professional learning.	• Uses, with principal and colleagues, change research to inform decisions related to individual and team professional learning. • Adopts patience and perseverance to support colleagues throughout the change process. • Interacts with colleagues frequently to respond to concerns related to implementation. • Recognizes privately and publicly colleagues' implementation efforts and accomplishments.	• Uses, with principal, change research to inform decisions related to individual and team professional learning. • Adopts patience and perseverance to support others throughout the change process. • Interacts occasionally with colleagues to respond to concerns related to implementation. • Recognizes privately colleagues' implementation efforts and accomplishments.	• Uses change research to inform individual and team decisions related to implementation. • Recognizes privately individual and team implementation efforts and accomplishments.	• Uses change research to make decisions about individual implementation.	• Fails to apply change research to plans and actions to support implementation of professional learning.	
Desired outcome 6.1.3: Monitors implementation of professional learning.	• Develops, with principal and colleagues, guides/tools (e.g., IC maps) to clarify expectations for implementation. • Uses guides/tools to support team implementation of professional learning. • Meets with principal and colleagues to use guides/tools to assess and refine individual and team implementation.	• Uses guides/tools to support team implementation of professional learning. • Meets with principal to use guides/tools to assess and refine individual and team implementation.	• Identifies individual progress using implementation guides/tools.	• States intention to implement professional learning.	• Fails to monitor implementation of individual professional learning.	

6.2 Sustain implementation

Desired outcome 6.2.1: Participates in differentiated support for implementation of professional learning.

Level 1	Level 2	Level 3	Level 4	Level 5	Level 6
• Demonstrates efficacy related to implementation of professional learning. • Selects opportunities for professional learning that are consistent with own needs to support and improve implementation. • Requests support for own personal needs for supporting and improving implementation. • Uses in-person, blended, and technology-enhanced support for implementation. • Determines, with colleagues, how to support and improve each other's implementation.	• Selects opportunities for professional learning that are consistent with own needs to support and improve implementation. • Requests support for own personal needs for supporting and improving implementation. • Uses in-person, blended, or technology-enhanced support for implementation. • Determines, with colleagues, how to support and improve each other's implementation.	• Selects opportunities for professional learning that are consistent with own needs to support and improve implementation. • Requests support for own personal needs for supporting and improving implementation. • Uses in-person, blended, or technology-enhanced support for implementation.	• Fails to participate in differentiated support for implementation.		

6.2 Sustain implementation

		Level 1	Level 2	Level 3	Level 4	Level 5	Level 6
		Desired outcome 6.2.2: Continues support to reach high-fidelity implementation of professional learning.					
		• Contributes to a plan for continuous support for three to five years for implementation of professional learning. • Advocates support for implementation of professional learning that adjusts with the maturity and fidelity of implementation. • Provides colleagues with continued support to facilitate their implementation. • Recommends that colleagues seek continued support at least weekly to refine and improve implementation.	• Contributes to a plan for continuous support for over two years for implementation of professional learning. • Advocates support for implementation of professional learning that adjusts with the maturity and fidelity of implementation. • Recommends that colleagues seek continued support at least biweekly to refine and improve implementation.	• Contributes to a plan for ongoing support over one year for implementation of professional learning. • Recommends that colleagues seek continued support at least monthly to refine and improve implementation.	• Contributes to a plan for occasional support for implementation of professional learning.	• Fails to access support to reach high-fidelity implementation of professional learning.	

6.3 Provide constructive feedback

Level 1	Level 2	Level 3	Level 4	Level 5	Level 6
Desired outcome 6.3.1: Develops capacity to give and receive constructive feedback.					
• Develops, with colleagues, research-based knowledge and skills to give and receive constructive feedback. • Supports colleagues' knowledge and skills to give and receive constructive feedback. • Contributes to risk-free opportunities for individuals and teams to practice giving and receiving feedback. • Models giving and receiving constructive feedback. • Provides to and seeks from individuals and teams feedback on use of constructive feedback.	• Develops, with colleagues, research-based knowledge and skills to give and receive constructive feedback. • Contributes to risk-free opportunities for individuals and teams to practice giving and receiving feedback. • Models giving and receiving constructive feedback. • Provides to and seeks from individuals and teams feedback on use of constructive feedback.	• Develops knowledge and skills to give and receive constructive feedback. • Models giving and receiving constructive feedback.	• Develops knowledge and skills to give and receive constructive feedback.	• Fails to develop knowledge and skills to give and receive constructive feedback.	

6.3 Provide constructive feedback

Desired outcome 6.3.2: Gives and receives constructive feedback to accelerate and refine implementation of professional learning.

Level 1	Level 2	Level 3	Level 4	Level 5	Level 6
• Reflects daily individually on implementation of professional learning. • Provides to and seeks from individuals and teams constructive feedback on implementation weekly using varied tools and strategies. • Analyzes and shares with colleagues feedback data monthly about implementation to improve individual, team, and schoolwide support.	• Reflects weekly individually on implementation of professional learning. • Provides to and seeks from individuals and teams constructive feedback on implementation monthly using varied tools and strategies. • Analyzes and shares with colleagues feedback data quarterly about implementation to improve individual, team, and schoolwide support.	• Reflects monthly individually on implementation of professional learning. • Provides to and seeks from colleagues constructive feedback on implementation quarterly using varied tools and strategies. • Analyzes and shares with colleagues feedback data quarterly about implementation to improve team and schoolwide support.	• Reflects semiannually individually on implementation of professional learning. • Analyzes and shares with colleagues feedback data semiannually about implementation to improve team and schoolwide support.	• Reflects annually individually on implementation of professional learning. • Analyzes and shares with colleagues feedback data annually about implementation to improve team and schoolwide support.	• Fails to seek and provide input on implementation of professional learning.

7.1 Meet performance standards

Desired outcome 7.1.1: Uses educator performance standards to identify professional learning needs.

Level 1	Level 2	Level 3	Level 4	Level 5	Level 6
• Analyzes performance standards with colleagues to create shared meaning. • Engages in public and private reflection to assess current practices in relationship to educator performance standards to identify strengths and areas for growth. • Reviews formative and summative performance data to identify strengths and areas for growth. • Uses assessment results to develop personal professional learning goals. • Develops, with team members, team professional learning goals that integrate personal learning goals.	• Engages in public and private reflection to assess current practices in relationship to educator performance standards to identify strengths and areas for growth. • Reviews formative and summative performance data to identify strengths and areas for growth. • Uses assessment results to develop personal professional learning goals. • Develops, with team members, team professional learning goals that integrate personal learning goals.	• Assesses current practices in relationship to educator performance standards to identify strengths and areas for growth. • Reviews formative and summative performance data to identify strengths and areas for growth. • Uses assessment results to develop personal professional learning goals.	• Assesses current practices in relationship to educator performance standards to identify strengths and areas for growth.	• Assesses current practices in relationship to educator performance standards to identify strengths.	• Fails to identify needs for professional learning.

7.1 Meet performance standards

Level 1	Level 2	Level 3	Level 4	Level 5	Level 6
Desired outcome 7.1.2: Uses educator performance standards to make decisions about the content of professional learning.					
• Links areas for growth to educator performance standards to identify knowledge, skills, dispositions, and practices needed to attain individual, team, and schoolwide goals for professional learning. • Uses educator performance standards to identify the content of individual and team professional learning. • Supports colleagues in using educator performance standards to identify the content of professional learning. • Monitors the content of professional learning for alignment with educator performance standards.	• Links areas for growth to educator performance standards to identify knowledge, skills, and practices needed to attain individual and team goals for professional learning. • Uses educator performance standards to identify the content of individual and team professional learning. • Supports colleagues in using educator performance standards to identify the content of professional learning.	• Links areas for growth to educator performance standards to identify knowledge and skills needed to attain individual and team goals for professional learning. • Uses educator performance standards to identify the content of individual and team professional learning.	• Uses educator performance standards to identify the content of individual professional learning.	• Uses personal preference to identify content for professional learning.	• Identifies content for professional learning without analysis of educator performance standards.

7.1 Meet performance standards

		Level 1	Level 2	Level 3	Level 4	Level 5	Level 6
		Desired outcome 7.1.3: Engages in professional learning to meet teacher performance standards.					
		• Develops research-based knowledge about teacher role expectations, responsibilities, and performance standards. • Engages, with colleagues, in professional learning to develop teaching skills reflected in performance standards. • Practices teaching skills until mastery is achieved. • Engages in coaching, feedback, and reflection on own performance.	• Develops knowledge about teacher performance standards. • Engages, with colleagues, in professional learning to develop teaching skills reflected in performance standards. • Practices teaching skills until mastery is achieved. • Engages in coaching, feedback, and reflection on own performance.	• Studies teacher performance standards. • Engages in professional learning to develop teaching skills reflected in performance standards. • Practices teaching skills until mastery is achieved.	• Reads teacher performance standards.	• Fails to engage in professional learning related to performance standards.	

7.2 Address learning outcomes

Desired outcome 7.2.1: Uses student learning outcomes to identify professional learning needs.

Level 1	Level 2	Level 3	Level 4	Level 5	Level 6
• Analyzes student learning outcomes with colleagues to create shared meaning. • Engages in public and private reflection to assess current practices in relationship to student learning outcomes to identify strengths and areas for growth. • Reviews formative and summative student learning assessments to identify strengths and areas for growth. • Uses assessment results to develop individual professional learning goals. • Develops, with team members, team professional learning goals that integrate personal learning goals.	• Engages in public and private reflection to assess current practices in relationship to student learning outcomes to identify strengths and areas for growth. • Reviews formative and summative student learning assessments to identify strengths and areas for growth. • Uses assessment results to develop individual professional learning goals. • Develops, with team members, team professional learning goals that integrate personal learning goals.	• Assesses current practices in relationship to student learning outcomes to identify strengths and areas for growth. • Reviews formative and summative student learning assessments to identify strengths and areas for growth. • Uses assessment results to develop individual professional learning goals.	• Assesses current practices in relationship to student learning outcomes to identify strengths and areas for growth.	• Assesses current practices in relationship to student learning outcomes to identify strengths.	• Fails to use student learning outcomes to identify needs for professional learning.

TEACHER / Outcomes

7.2 Address learning outcomes

Level 1	Level 2	Level 3	Level 4	Level 5	Level 6
Desired outcome 7.2.2: Uses student learning outcomes to make decisions about the content of professional learning.					
• Links areas for growth to student learning outcomes to identify knowledge, skills, dispositions, and practices needed to attain individual and team professional learning goals. • Uses student learning outcomes to select the content of individual and team professional learning. • Supports colleagues to use student learning outcomes to identify the content of their professional learning. • Reviews the content of professional learning for alignment with student learning outcomes.	• Reviews student learning outcomes to identify knowledge, skills, and practices needed to attain schoolwide goals for professional learning. • Uses student learning outcomes to select the content of individual and team professional learning. • Supports teams in using student learning outcomes to identify the content of individual and team professional learning.	• Reviews student learning outcomes to identify knowledge and skills needed to attain schoolwide goals for professional learning. • Selects student learning outcomes that become the content of individual professional learning.	• Selects student learning outcomes that become the content of schoolwide professional learning.	• Uses personal preference to select content for professional learning.	• Identifies content for professional learning without reference to student learning outcomes.
Desired outcome 7.2.3: Engages in professional learning to increase student results.					
• Engages in professional learning with colleagues to develop content, pedagogy, and pedagogical content related to student learning outcomes. • Engages in coaching, feedback, and reflection on the effects of own performance on student learning.	• Engages in professional learning with colleagues to develop content, pedagogy, and pedagogical content related to student learning outcomes. • Reflects on the effects of own performance on student learning.	• Studies student learning outcomes. • Engages in professional learning to develop content and pedagogy to achieve student learning outcomes.	• Reads about student learning outcomes. • Engages in professional learning on instruction.	• Fails to engage in professional learning related to student learning outcomes.	

7.3 Build coherence

Desired outcome 7.3.1: Develops an understanding of the congruence between professional learning and other school and school system initiatives.

Level 1	Level 2	Level 3	Level 4	Level 5	Level 6
• Participates, with colleagues, in conversations to develop understanding of the relationships among school and school system processes and initiatives; the school improvement goals; individual, team, and schoolwide professional learning goals; and professional learning. • Transfers learning among multiple initiatives. • Communicates with colleagues about the application of professional learning to support multiple school processes and initiatives. • Aligns, with principal and colleagues, professional learning with school improvement goals and other school processes and initiatives.	• Participates, with colleagues, in conversations to develop understanding of the relationships among school and school system processes and initiatives; the school improvement goals; individual, team, and schoolwide professional learning goals; and professional learning. • Transfers learning among multiple initiatives. • Communicates with colleagues about the application of professional learning to support multiple school processes and initiatives.	• Participates, with colleagues, in conversations to develop understanding of the relationships among the school improvement goals, schoolwide professional learning goals, and professional learning.	• Seeks to understand the relationships among the school improvement goals, schoolwide professional learning goals, and professional learning.	• Fails to develop an understanding of the relationships among the school and school system processes and initiatives, the school improvement goals, schoolwide professional learning goals, and professional learning.	

Innovation Configuration Maps

COACH

- **LEARNING COMMUNITIES**
- **LEADERSHIP**
- **RESOURCES**
- **DATA**
- **LEARNING DESIGNS**
- **IMPLEMENTATION**
- **OUTCOMES**

1.1 Engage in continuous improvement

Level 1	Level 2	Level 3	Level 4	Level 5	Level 6
Desired outcome 1.1.1: Develops own and others' capacity to apply the seven-step cycle of continuous improvement. *					
• Develops own knowledge and skills about the seven steps of the cycle of continuous improvement. • Develops capacity of individuals, teams, and whole staff to use the cycle of continuous improvement. • Provides examples that illustrate the seven steps of the cycle.	• Develops own knowledge and skills about the cycle of continuous improvement. • Develops capacity of individuals and teams to use the cycle of continuous improvement. • Provides examples that illustrate the seven steps of the cycle.	• Develops own knowledge and skills about the seven steps of the cycle of continuous improvement. • Develops capacity of individuals to use the cycle of continuous improvement. • Provides examples that illustrate the seven steps of the cycle.	• Develops own knowledge about the cycle of continuous improvement.	• Fails to develop own and others' knowledge and skills about the cycle of continuous improvement.	
Desired outcome 1.1.2: Applies the cycle of continuous improvement with fidelity to facilitate professional learning.					
• Applies the seven-step cycle of continuous improvement in individual, team, and schoolwide professional learning. • Uses the cycle of continuous improvement to reflect on coaching services. • Facilitates faithful application of the cycle for individuals, teams, and whole staff use.	• Applies the seven-step cycle of continuous improvement in individual and team professional learning. • Facilitates faithful application of the cycle for individuals and teams.	• Applies the seven-step cycle of continuous improvement in individual or team professional learning. • Facilitates faithful application of the cycle for individuals or teams.	• Encourages teams to use the seven steps in the cycle.	• Fails to use the cycle of continuous improvement in professional learning.	

*See the Appendix (p. 262) for an explanation of this concept.

1.2 Develop collective responsibility

Level 1	Level 2	Level 3	Level 4	Level 5	Level 6
Desired outcome 1.2.1: Advances collective responsibility.					
• Develops, with colleagues, shared assumptions about and a shared definition of collective responsibility. • Facilitates colleagues as they engage in collaborative practice. • Challenges practices and assumptions that create barriers to collective responsibility. • Contributes to efforts to identify and overcome barriers to collective responsibility.	• Develops, with colleagues, shared assumptions about and a shared definition of collective responsibility. • Facilitates colleagues as they engage in collaborative practice. • Contributes to efforts to identify and overcome barriers to collective responsibility.	• Develops, with colleagues, shared assumptions about and a shared definition of collective responsibility. • Facilitates colleagues as they engage in collaborative practice. • Provides examples of collective responsibility in action.	• States personal assumptions about and a definition of collective responsibility.	• Fails to address collective responsibility.	
Desired outcome 1.2.2: Fosters engagement of all colleagues in meeting the needs of all students.					
• Engages colleagues in conversations about the impact of individual and collective professional learning on student achievement. • Engages colleagues in individual, team, and schoolwide professional learning to address the learning needs of all students.	• Engages colleagues in conversations about the impact of individual and collective professional learning on student achievement. • Meets with colleagues in individual and team professional learning to address the learning needs of all students.	• Shares data with colleagues about the needs of students outside of individual classrooms. • Meets with colleagues in individual professional learning to address the learning needs of all students.	• Invites colleagues to participate in professional learning to address the needs of students outside individual classrooms.	• Fails to engage colleagues in conversations about professional learning to address student learning needs.	

1.2 Develop collective responsibility

Desired outcome 1.2.3: Models collective responsibility by participating in learning communities.

Level 1	Level 2	Level 3	Level 4	Level 5	Level 6
• Participates routinely in a learning community of coaches. • Participates routinely in at least one school-based learning community. • Shares with colleagues own learning as a member of learning communities.	• Participates routinely in at least one school-based learning community. • Shares with colleagues own learning as a member of a learning community.	• Participates routinely in one school-based learning community.	• Participates occasionally in one or more learning communities.	• Fails to participate in learning communities.	

1.3 Create alignment and accountability

Desired outcome 1.3.1: Aligns professional learning with school goals.

Level 1	Level 2	Level 3	Level 4	Level 5	Level 6
• Develops own knowledge of school and system goals and strategies. • Aligns own professional learning goals with school goals. • Facilitates colleagues' discussions to clarify school and system goals. • Facilitates individuals and teams to set professional learning goals that align with school goals. • Reviews individual and team professional learning goals for alignment with school goals and strategies.	• Develops own knowledge of school and system goals and strategies. • Aligns own professional learning goals with school goals. • Facilitates colleagues' discussions to clarify school and system goals. • Facilitates individuals and teams to set professional learning goals that align with school goals. • Reviews individual or teams professional learning goals for alignment with school goals and strategies.	• Develops own knowledge of school and system goals and strategies. • Aligns own professional learning goals with school goals. • Facilitates individuals and teams to set professional learning goals that align with school goals.	• Encourages colleagues to develop individual and team professional learning goals that align with school goals.	• Fails to align professional learning goals with school goals.	

1.3 Create alignment and accountability

Level 1	Level 2	Level 3	Level 4	Level 5	Level 6
Desired outcome 1.3.2: Supports colleagues to use the cycle of continuous improvement to achieve professional learning goals.					
• Assesses the fidelity of own use of the cycle of continuous improvement. • Supports colleagues to apply the cycle of continuous improvement with fidelity. • Provides constructive feedback to individuals and teams to improve fidelity of implementation of the cycle. • Provides additional professional learning and support to refine implementation fidelity.	• Assesses the fidelity of own use of the cycle of continuous improvement. • Supports colleagues to apply the cycle of continuous improvement with fidelity. • Provides constructive feedback to teams and whole staff to improve fidelity of implementation of the cycle.	• Assesses the fidelity of own use of the cycle of continuous improvement. • Supports colleagues to apply the cycle of continuous improvement with fidelity. • Provides constructive feedback to whole staff to improve fidelity of implementation of the cycle.	• Assesses the fidelity of own use of the cycle of continuous improvement.	• Fails to assess the fidelity of implementation of the cycle of continuous improvement.	

2.1 Develop capacity for learning and leading

Level 1	Level 2	Level 3	Level 4	Level 5	Level 6
Desired outcome 2.1.1: Commits to continuous professional learning.					
• States publicly own professional learning goals. • Persists with own professional learning until achieving mastery. • Asks for constructive feedback from principal and colleagues. • Participates in and models professional learning that occurs over multiple years and includes hands-on and problem-based learning with multiple practice opportunities. • Participates in follow-up and coaching.	• States publicly own professional learning goals. • Persists with own professional learning until achieving mastery. • Participates in and models professional learning that occurs over multiple years and includes hands-on and problem-based learning with multiple practice opportunities. • Participates in follow-up and coaching.	• Participates in professional learning that occurs over a single year and includes hands-on and problem-based learning with multiple practice opportunities. • Participates in follow-up and coaching.	• Participates in a series of short-term learning activities on a variety of topics without ongoing support and assistance to promote implementation of new learning.	• Participates in a variety of disconnected learning activities (e.g. reads articles, attends professional conferences or workshops, participates in webinars, etc.) unrelated to own professional learning goals.	• Fails to participate in continuous professional learning.

2.1 Develop capacity for learning and leading

Level 1	Level 2	Level 3	Level 4	Level 5	Level 6
Desired outcome 2.1.2: Develops own and others' capacity for leadership of professional learning.					
• Develops own and colleagues' facilitation, relationship, and coaching skills to support professional learning. • Observes colleagues and provides feedback to them as they practice leadership skills. • Coaches colleagues as they serve as mentors, facilitators of collaborative learning teams, master teachers, or members of SLT. • Provides resources to colleagues as they serve as mentors, facilitators of collaborative learning teams, master teachers, or members of SLT. • Contributes to the establishment of school guidelines that support and protect teacher leadership practices.	• Develops own and colleagues' facilitation and relationship skills to support professional learning. • Coaches colleagues as they serve as mentors, facilitators of collaborative learning teams, master teachers, or members of SLT. • Provides resources to colleagues as they serve as mentors, facilitators of collaborative learning teams, master teachers, or members of SLT. • Contributes to the establishment of school guidelines that support and protect teacher leadership practices.	• Develops own and colleagues' facilitation and relationship skills to support professional learning. • Coaches colleagues as they serve as mentors, facilitators of collaborative learning teams, master teachers, or members of SLT. • Provides resources to colleagues as they serve as mentors, facilitators of collaborative learning teams, master teachers, or members of SLT.	• Develops own facilitation and relationship skills to support professional learning. • Provides resources to colleagues as they serve as mentors, facilitators of collaborative learning teams, master teachers, or members of SLT.	• Fails to develop own and colleagues' knowledge and skills to lead professional learning.	

2.1 Develop capacity for learning and leading

		Level 1	Level 2	Level 3	Level 4	Level 5	Level 6
Desired outcome 2.1.3: Understands and uses the Standards for Professional Learning in making decisions about professional learning.		• Studies the Standards for Professional Learning to apply key ideas. • Develops colleagues' understanding of the Standards for Professional Learning. • Accesses and uses new research and information about effective professional learning on an ongoing basis. • Applies the seven Standards for Professional Learning in facilitating individual, team, and schoolwide professional learning.	• Studies the Standards for Professional Learning to apply key ideas. • Accesses and uses new research and information about effective professional learning on an ongoing basis. • Applies the seven Standards for Professional Learning in facilitating individual, team, and schoolwide professional learning.	• Studies the Standards for Professional Learning to understand key ideas. • Applies five of the Standards for Professional Learning in facilitating individual, team, and schoolwide professional learning.	• Names the Standards for Professional Learning.	• Makes decisions about professional learning without reference to the Standards for Professional Learning.	

2.1 Develop capacity for learning and leading

Desired outcome 2.1.4: Serves as a leader of professional learning.

Level 1	Level 2	Level 3	Level 4	Level 5	Level 6
• Articulates the role of the coach related to professional learning. • Acknowledges responsibility for the quality and results of individual and team professional learning. • Articulates how decisions about professional learning are made and who is involved. • Shares leadership for professional learning with others, including principal, SLT, teams, coaches, and other learning facilitators. • Takes an active role in planning, implementing, and evaluating team and schoolwide professional learning. • Completes all of coach's responsibilities for professional learning.	• Articulates the role of the coach related to professional learning. • Acknowledges responsibility for the quality and results of individual and team professional learning. • Articulates how decisions about professional learning are made and who is involved. • Shares leadership for professional learning with principal. • Takes an active role in planning and implementing team and schoolwide professional learning. • Completes 75% of coach's responsibilities for professional learning.	• Articulates the role of the coach related to professional learning. • Acknowledges responsibility for the quality and results of individual and team professional learning. • Articulates how decisions about professional learning are made and who is involved. • Completes 50% of coach's responsibilities for professional learning.	• Articulates the role of the coach related to professional learning. • Completes less than 50% of coach's responsibilities for professional learning.	• Defers decision-making authority in professional learning to others.	

2.2 Advocate for professional learning

	Level 1	Level 2	Level 3	Level 4	Level 5	Level 6
Desired outcome 2.2.1: Articulates the link between student learning and professional learning.						
	• Explains the indelible connection between professional learning and student achievement to staff, students, parents, system leaders, public officials, and community members. • Provides multiple examples of the link between professional learning and student learning to staff, students, parents, system leaders, public officials, and community members and partners.	• Explains the indelible connection between professional learning and student achievement to staff, students, parents, system leaders, and community members. • Provides multiple examples of the link between professional learning and student learning to staff, students, parents, system leaders, and community members and partners.	• Explains the indelible connection between professional learning and student achievement to staff, parents, and system leaders. • Provides multiple examples of the link between professional learning and student learning to staff, parents, and system leaders.	• Describes the connection between professional learning and student learning.	• Fails to explain the connection between professional learning and student learning.	
Desired outcome 2.2.2: Advocates high-quality professional learning.						
	• Promotes high-quality professional learning with staff, students, parents, system leaders, colleagues, public officials, and community members and partners. • Advocates system- and school-based conditions to support effective individual, team, and school-wide professional learning. • Challenges practices, experiences, and designs of ineffective professional learning and advocates improvements.	• Promotes high-quality professional learning with staff, students, parents, system leaders, and colleagues. • Advocates system- and school-based conditions to support effective individual, team, and schoolwide professional learning.	• Promotes high-quality professional learning with staff and school system leaders. • Advocates school-based conditions to support effective individual, team, and schoolwide professional learning.	• Promotes high-quality professional learning with staff.	• Fails to promote high-quality professional learning for staff.	

2.3 Create support systems and structures

Level 1	Level 2	Level 3	Level 4	Level 5	Level 6

Desired outcome 2.3.1: Contributes to establishing systems and structures for effective professional learning.

Level 1	Level 2	Level 3	Level 4	Level 5	Level 6
• Establishes, with colleagues and principal, school-based conditions for effective individual, team, and schoolwide professional learning (e.g., resources, policies, annual calendars, schedules, procedures, and structures). • Supports colleagues in understanding and implementing conditions for effective individual and team professional learning. • Teaches multiple strategies for effective learning team meetings. • Teaches team members how to organize effective learning teams and how to identify content for meetings. • Solves problems, with colleagues and principal, related to establishing conditions for effective professional learning.	• Establishes, with colleagues and principal, school-based conditions for effective individual, team, and schoolwide professional learning (e.g., resources, policies, annual calendars, schedules, procedures, and structures). • Supports colleagues in understanding and implementing conditions for effective individual and team professional learning. • Shares with team members protocols for learning teams. • Recommends strategies for managing team meetings. • Facilitates conversations with learning team members about meeting organization, times, and content. • Solves problems, with principal, related to establishing conditions for effective professional learning.	• Establishes, with colleagues and principal, school-based conditions for effective individual, team, and schoolwide professional learning (e.g., resources, policies, annual calendars, schedules, procedures, and structures). • Supports colleagues in understanding and establishing conditions for effective individual and team professional learning. • Recommends strategies for managing team meetings.	• Supports colleagues in understanding and implementing conditions for effective individual and team professional learning.	• Fails to contribute to structures and systems to support professional learning.	

2.3 Create support systems and structures

Desired outcome 2.3.2: Prepares and supports colleagues to develop collaboration skills.

Level 1	Level 2	Level 3	Level 4	Level 5	Level 6
• Develops, with colleagues, the knowledge and skills to learn and work collaboratively. • Builds, with teams, a plan to support ongoing development of team collaboration skills. • Supports colleagues' understanding of the attributes of effective collaboration. • Provides information about team roles and meeting protocols for effective collaboration. • Models skillful facilitation for learning teams.	• Develops, with colleagues, the knowledge and skills to learn and work collaboratively. • Supports colleagues' understanding of the attributes of effective collaboration. • Provides information about team roles and meeting protocols for effective collaboration. • Models skillful facilitation for learning teams.	• Develops, with colleagues, the knowledge and skills to learn and work collaboratively. • Supports colleagues' understanding of the attributes of effective collaboration. • Provides information about team roles and meeting protocols for effective collaboration.	• Develops colleagues' knowledge about collaborative professional learning.	• Takes no responsibility for developing colleagues' collaboration skills.	

2.3 Create support systems and structures

Desired outcome 2.3.3: Contributes to the development and maintenance of a collaborative culture.

Level 1	Level 2	Level 3	Level 4	Level 5	Level 6
• Develops and applies research-based knowledge and skills about collaborative cultures to support team learning and collaborative work. • Assesses, with principal and colleagues, culture. • Models collaboration in interactions with colleagues, students, parents, and school leaders. • Contributes to the development of the social architecture of a collaborative culture that includes norms for individual, team, and schoolwide interactions; high expectations; collective responsibility; mutual respect; and relational trust. • Develops colleagues to serve as skilled facilitators who provide support during whole-school and learning team meetings. • Identifies and addresses, with principal and colleagues, assumptions and barriers to collaboration.	• Develops and applies research-based knowledge and skills about collaborative cultures to support team learning and collaborative work. • Assesses, with principal and colleagues, culture. • Models collaboration in interactions with colleagues, students, parents, and school leaders. • Contributes to the development of the social architecture of a collaborative culture that includes norms for individual, team, and schoolwide interactions; high expectations; collective responsibility; and mutual respect. • Develops colleagues to serve as skilled facilitators who provide support during schoolwide and team learning	• Assesses, with principal culture. • Models collaboration in interactions with colleagues, principal, and other school leaders. • Contributes to the development of the social architecture of a collaborative culture that includes norms for individual, team, and schoolwide interactions; high expectations; and mutual respect.	• Models collaboration in interactions with colleagues, principal, and other school leaders. • Assesses, with principal, current culture.	• Accepts the current school culture without making efforts to improve it.	

3.1 Prioritize human, fiscal, material, technology, and time resources

Level 1	Level 2	Level 3	Level 4	Level 5	Level 6
Desired outcome 3.1.1: Defines resources for professional learning.					
• Develops, with principal and colleagues, a shared definition of resources for professional learning. • Identifies resources for professional learning that include staff, materials, technology, funding, and time.	• Develops, with principal and colleagues, a shared definition of resources for professional learning. • Identifies resources for professional learning that include staff, materials, technology, funding, and time.	• Identifies resources for professional learning that include materials, technology, funding, and time.	• Describes the school's resources for professional learning.	• Fails to contribute to resources for professional learning.	

3.1 Prioritize human, fiscal, material, technology, and time resources

Desired outcome 3.1.2: Recommends resources to align professional learning with high-priority student and educator learning needs.

Level 1	Level 2	Level 3	Level 4	Level 5	Level 6
• Establishes, with principal and colleagues, criteria for resource allocation for professional learning based on high-priority student learning needs and individual, team, and schoolwide educator learning needs. • Recommends, with principal, SLT, and colleagues, resources to support individual, team, and schoolwide professional learning for high-priority student and educator learning needs. • Recommends internal and external resources to support individual, team, and schoolwide collaborative professional learning. • Gathers, with colleagues and principal, resources for individual, team, and schoolwide professional learning. • Shares information with colleagues about available resources for professional learning.	• Establishes, with principal and colleagues, criteria for resource allocation for professional learning based on high-priority student learning needs and individual, team, and schoolwide educator learning needs. • Recommends, with principal, resources to support individual and team professional learning for high-priority student and educator learning needs. • Recommends internal and external resources to support individual and team collaborative professional learning. • Gathers, with principal, resources for individual and team professional learning. • Shares information with colleagues about available resources for professional learning.	• Follows established criteria for resource allocation for professional learning based on high-priority student learning needs and schoolwide educator learning needs. • Recommends resources to support individual and team professional learning. • Recommends external resources to support individual and team collaborative professional learning. • Shares information with colleagues about available resources for professional learning.	• Recommends resources to support individual professional learning.	• Fails to recommend resources for professional learning.	

3.1 Prioritize human, fiscal, material, technology, and time resources

Level 1	Level 2	Level 3	Level 4	Level 5	Level 6
Desired outcome 3.1.3: Develops internal resources to support professional learning.					
• Develops and taps internal expertise of colleagues to support professional learning. • Builds capacity of colleagues to support each other's implementation of professional learning. • Facilitates ways to multiply the effects of resources allocated to professional learning. • Encourages others to conserve resources for professional learning.	• Develops and taps internal expertise of colleagues to support professional learning. • Builds internal capacity of staff to support the implementation of professional learning. • Facilitates ways to multiply the effects of resources allocated to professional learning.	• Taps internal expertise of colleagues to support professional learning. • Identifies ways to multiply the effects of resources allocated to professional learning.	• Fails to develop internal resources to support professional learning.		

COACH / Resources

3.1 Prioritize human, fiscal, material, technology, and time resources

Desired outcome 3.1.4: Recommends resources to support implementation of professional learning.

Level 1	Level 2	Level 3	Level 4	Level 5	Level 6
• Recognizes the need for long-term investment of resources for full implementation of professional learning. • Provides, with principal and colleagues, sufficient resources over multiple years to support full implementation of professional learning. • Sustains, with principal and colleagues, resources for support until full implementation of professional learning occurs. • Provides, with principal and colleagues, resources for differentiated support to all staff for full implementation. • Uses time to meet the differentiated needs of individuals and teams to support implementation of professional learning.	• Provides, with principal and colleagues, sufficient resources over multiple years to support full implementation of professional learning. • Provides, with principal and colleagues, resources for differentiated support to all staff for full implementation. • Uses time to meet the differentiated needs of individuals and teams to support implementation of professional learning.	• Recommends sufficient resources over multiple years to support full implementation of professional learning. • Provides, with colleagues, resources for differentiated support to all staff for full implementation.	• Recommends resources to support implementation of professional learning for one year.	• Fails to recommend resources to support implementation.	

3.1   Prioritize human, fiscal, material, technology, and time resources

	Level 1	Level 2	Level 3	Level 4	Level 5	Level 6
Desired outcome 3.1.5: Serves as a resource for professional learning.						
	• Delineates multiple ways to serve as a resource for individual, team, and schoolwide professional learning. • Develops expertise in areas related to schoolwide, individual, and team professional learning goals. • Shares expertise with individuals, teams, and whole staff to support professional learning. • Seeks feedback on the usefulness of resources recommended for professional learning.	• Delineates several ways to serve as a resource for individual and team professional learning. • Develops expertise in areas related to individual and team professional learning goals. • Shares expertise with individuals and teams to support professional learning. • Seeks feedback on the usefulness of resources recommended for professional learning.	• Describes how to serve as a resource for professional learning. • Develops expertise in areas related to professional learning goals. • Shares expertise with individuals and teams to support professional learning.	• Identifies services to provide to colleagues. • Develops expertise in areas related to professional learning goals.	• Fails to serve as a resource for professional learning.	

www.learningforward.org   800-727-7288

3.2 Monitor resources

Desired outcome 3.2.1: Monitors effectiveness of the use of resources for professional learning.

Level 1	Level 2	Level 3	Level 4	Level 5	Level 6
• Contributes to the tracking and monitoring of resources associated with professional learning to ensure equitable distribution of all resources. • Provides and seeks input on the effectiveness of resources for professional learning. • Tracks and reviews coaching data weekly to reflect on practice. • Uses, with principal, data to analyze the effectiveness of coaching and make needed adjustments. • Questions requests to divert time away from primary responsibilities. • Requests changes to coaching program and practice to improve effectiveness.	• Contributes to the tracking and monitoring of resources associated with professional learning to ensure equitable distribution of all resources. • Provides and seeks input on the effectiveness of resources for professional learning. • Tracks and reviews coaching data weekly to reflect on practice. • Uses, with principal, data to analyze the effectiveness of coaching and make needed adjustments. • Questions requests to divert time away from primary responsibilities.	• Contributes to the tracking and monitoring of resources associated with professional learning to ensure equitable distribution of all resources. • Provides and seeks input on the effectiveness of resources for professional learning. • Tracks and reviews coaching data weekly to reflect on practice. • Uses, with principal, data to analyze the effectiveness of coaching and make needed adjustments.	• Tracks and reviews coaching data weekly to reflect on practice. • Provides and seeks input on the effectiveness of resources used for professional learning.	• Tracks and reviews coaching data monthly to reflect on practice.	• Fails to monitor and/or track resources for professional learning.

3.3 Coordinate resources

Desired outcome 3.3.1: Contributes to a comprehensive resource plan for professional learning.

Level 1	Level 2	Level 3	Level 4	Level 5	Level 6
• Recommends ways to repurpose resources for high-priority professional learning needs. • Seeks and uses, with colleagues and principal, external resources for professional learning to enhance existing resources to achieve student learning goals. • Develops, with colleagues and principal, consensus about a multi-year resource plan for professional learning based on high-priority needs for student and educator learning. • Explains, using data and research, the role of coaching to support implementation of professional learning. • Supports the implementation of the professional learning resource plan to achieve high-priority student and educator learning goals. • Shares resources with colleagues to increase their effectiveness.	• Recommends ways to repurpose resources for high-priority professional learning needs. • Seeks and uses, with principal, external resources for professional learning to enhance existing resources to achieve student learning goals. • Contributes to the development of a multi-year resource plan for professional learning based on high-priority needs for student and educator learning. • Explains the role of coaching to support implementation of professional learning. • Supports the implementation of the professional learning resource plan to achieve high-priority student and educator learning goals. • Shares resources with colleagues to increase their effectiveness.	• Contributes to the development of a multi-year resource plan for professional learning based on high-priority needs for student and educator learning. • Supports the implementation of the professional learning resource plan to achieve high-priority student and educator learning goals. • Explains the role of coaching to support implementation of professional learning. • Recommends internal and external resources (people, materials, technology, etc.) to support individual and team professional learning. • Shares resources with colleagues to increase their effectiveness.	• Contributes to the development of a multi-year resource plan for professional learning based on high-priority needs for student and educator learning.	• Shares the annual budget for professional learning.	• Fails to develop and implement a resource plan for professional learning.

4.1 Analyze student, educator, and system data

Desired outcome 4.1.1: Develops own and colleagues' capacity to analyze and interpret data.

Level 1	Level 2	Level 3	Level 4	Level 5	Level 6
• Develops own, individual, and team knowledge and skills to access, organize, and display team, grade-level, department, and individual data. • Develops own, individual, and team knowledge and skills about how to analyze and interpret data from multiple sources (e.g., norm-referenced tests, student work samples, student portfolios, and school system–designed tests) to make team, grade-level, department, and individual decisions about professional learning.	• Develops own and team knowledge and skills to access, organize, and display team, grade-level, department, and individual data. • Develops own and team knowledge and skills about how to analyze and interpret data from multiple sources (e.g., norm-referenced tests, student work samples, student portfolios, and school system–designed tests) to make team, grade-level, department, and individual decisions about professional learning.	• Develops own knowledge and skills to access, organize, and display individual data. • Develops own knowledge and skills about how to analyze and interpret data from multiple sources (e.g., norm-referenced tests, student work samples, student portfolios, and school system–designed tests) to make individual decisions about professional learning.	• Develops own capacity to access, organize, and display.	• Fails to develop own and colleagues' capacity to analyze and interpret data.	

COACH / **Data**

4.1 Analyze student, educator, and system data

Desired outcome 4.1.2: Engages colleagues in analyzing and interpreting multiple sources of student data to determine professional learning needs.

Level 1	Level 2	Level 3	Level 4	Level 5	Level 6
• Facilitates data meetings with individuals and teams to analyze qualitative and quantitative student data from four or more sources to make predictions, observations, and inferences about the data. • Facilitates data meetings with individuals and teams to interpret qualitative and quantitative student data from four or more sources to decipher trends, patterns, outliers, and root causes within the data. • Supports colleagues to independently identify findings, trends, patterns, outliers, and root causes from four or more sources of student data.	• Facilitates data meetings with individuals and teams to analyze qualitative and quantitative student data from three sources to make predictions, observations, and inferences about the data. • Facilitates data meetings with individuals and teams to interpret qualitative and quantitative student data from three sources to decipher trends, patterns, outliers, and root causes within the data.	• Facilitates data meetings with individuals and teams to analyze qualitative and quantitative student data from two sources to make predictions, observations, and inferences about the data.	• Facilitates individual or team data meetings with individuals to analyze one source of student data.	• Presents the results of student data analysis to individuals, teams, or whole staff.	• Fails to engage staff in analyzing student data to determine student learning needs.

4.1 Analyze student, educator, and system data

Desired outcome 4.1.3: Engages colleagues in analyzing and interpreting multiple sources of educator data to determine professional learning needs.

Level 1	Level 2	Level 3	Level 4	Level 5	Level 6
• Facilitates data meetings with individuals and teams to analyze qualitative and quantitative educator data from four or more sources to make predictions, observations, and inferences about the data. • Facilitates data meetings with individuals and teams to interpret qualitative and quantitative educator data from four or more sources to decipher trends, patterns, outliers, and root causes within the data. • Supports colleagues to independently identify findings, trends, patterns, outliers, and root causes from four or more sources of educator data.	• Facilitates data meetings with individuals and teams to analyze qualitative and quantitative educator data from three sources to make predictions, observations, and inferences about the data. • Facilitates data meetings with individuals and teams to interpret qualitative and quantitative educator data from three sources to decipher trends, patterns, outliers, and root causes within the data.	• Facilitates data meetings with individuals and teams to analyze qualitative and quantitative educator data from two sources to make predictions, observations, and inferences about the data.	• Facilitates individual or team data meetings with individuals to analyze one source of educator data.	• Presents the results of educator data analysis to individuals, teams, or whole staff.	• Fails to engage staff in analyzing educator data to determine professional learning needs.

4.1 Analyze student, educator, and system data

Level 1	Level 2	Level 3	Level 4	Level 5	Level 6
Desired outcome 4.1.4: Engages colleagues in analyzing and interpreting multiple sources of school data to determine professional learning needs.					
• Facilitates data meetings with individuals and teams to analyze qualitative and quantitative school data from four or more sources to make predictions, observations, and inferences about the data. • Facilitates data meetings with individuals and teams to interpret qualitative and quantitative school data from four or more sources to decipher trends, patterns, outliers, and root causes within the data. • Supports colleagues to independently identify findings, trends, patterns, outliers, and root causes from four or more sources of school data.	• Facilitates data meetings with individuals and teams to analyze qualitative and quantitative school data from three sources to make predictions, observations, and inferences about the data. • Facilitates data meetings with individuals and teams to interpret qualitative and quantitative school data from three sources to decipher trends, patterns, outliers, and root causes within the data.	• Facilitates data meetings with individuals and teams to analyze qualitative and quantitative school data from two sources to make predictions, observations, and inferences about the data.	• Facilitates individual or team data meetings with individuals to analyze one source of school data.	• Presents results of school data analysis to individuals, teams, or whole staff.	• Fails to engage staff in analyzing school data to determine professional learning needs.

www.learningforward.org   800-727-7288

4.1 Analyze student, educator, and system data

Level 1	Level 2	Level 3	Level 4	Level 5	Level 6
Desired outcome 4.1.5: Supports colleagues to use analyzed data to determine professional learning needs.					
• Facilitates individuals and teams to use analyzed data to identify individual and team professional learning needs.	• Facilitates individuals and teams to use analyzed data to identify individual and team professional learning needs.	• Uses analyzed data to identify individual or team professional learning needs.	• Identifies needs for individual and team professional learning.	• Fails to use student, educator, or school data to identify needs for individual and team professional learning.	
Desired outcome 4.1.6: Supports colleagues in ongoing data analysis and interpretation to support continuous improvement.					
• Assists staff in gathering, analyzing, and interpreting classroom and team data to refine instructional strategies. • Meets with individuals and teams weekly to support analysis and interpretation of student, educator, and system data.	• Assists staff in gathering, analyzing, and interpreting classroom and team data to refine instructional strategies. • Meets with individuals and teams monthly to support analysis and interpretation of student, educator, and system data.	• Assists staff in gathering and analyzing classroom data to refine instructional strategies. • Meets with individuals and teams quarterly to support analysis and interpretation of student, educator, and system data.	• Meets with individuals and teams once or twice each school year to support analysis and interpretation of student data.	• Fails to support staff in ongoing data use and analysis.	

4.2 Assess progress

Level 1	Level 2	Level 3	Level 4	Level 5	Level 6
Desired outcome 4.2.1: Determines formative data to assess progress toward professional learning benchmarks and goals.					
• Identifies monthly, with individuals and teams, benchmarks to assess progress toward professional learning goals. • Identifies monthly, with individuals and teams, qualitative and quantitative formative data to measure progress toward professional learning benchmarks and goals.	• Identifies quarterly, with individuals and teams, benchmarks to assess progress toward professional learning goals. • Identifies quarterly, with individuals and teams, qualitative or quantitative formative data to measure progress toward professional learning benchmarks and goals.	• Identifies semiannually, with either individuals or teams, benchmarks to assess progress toward professional learning goals. • Identifies semiannually with either individuals or teams, qualitative or quantitative formative data to measure progress toward professional learning benchmarks and goals.	• Identifies annually for individuals or teams either qualitative or quantitative data to assess progress toward professional learning benchmarks and goals.	• Fails to identify data to assess progress toward professional learning benchmarks and goals.	
Desired outcome 4.2.2: Supports colleagues in collecting, analyzing, and using formative data to continuously assess progress toward professional learning benchmarks and goals.					
• Facilitates monthly individuals and teams to collect, analyze, and interpret formative data to assess progress toward individual and collective professional learning benchmarks and goals. • Facilitates monthly individuals and teams to use formative data to assess progress toward individual and collective professional learning benchmarks and goals.	• Facilitates quarterly individuals and teams to collect, analyze, and interpret formative data to assess progress toward individual and collective professional learning benchmarks and goals. • Facilitates quarterly individuals and teams to use formative data to assess progress toward individual and collective professional learning benchmarks and goals.	• Facilitates semiannually either individuals or teams to collect, analyze, and interpret formative data to assess progress toward individual and collective professional learning benchmarks and goals. • Facilitates semiannually either individuals or teams to use formative data to assess progress toward individual and collective professional learning benchmarks and goals.	• Facilitates annually either individuals or teams to collect, analyze, and interpret formative data to assess progress toward individual and collective professional learning benchmarks and goals.	• Fails to support colleagues to collect, analyze, and interpret formative data to assess progress toward professional learning benchmarks and goals.	

4.2 Assess progress

Desired outcome 4.2.3: Supports colleagues to use analysis of progress to make adjustments in professional learning.

Level 1	Level 2	Level 3	Level 4	Level 5	Level 6
• Facilitates individuals and teams to use analyzed data to identify enhancers of and barriers to progress. • Facilitates problem solving to address identified barriers to achieving professional learning benchmarks and goals. • Facilitates individuals and teams to make in-process, data-based adjustments in individual and team professional learning (i.e., learning designs, coaching activities, and timeframes). • Celebrates with individuals and teams progress toward professional learning benchmarks and goals.	• Facilitates individuals and teams to use analyzed data to identify enhancers of and barriers to progress. • Facilitates problem solving to address identified barriers to achieving benchmarks and goals for professional learning. • Facilitates individuals and teams to make in-process, data-based adjustments in individual and team professional learning (i.e., learning designs, coaching activities, and timeframes).	• Facilitates individuals and teams to use analyzed data to identify enhancers of and barriers to progress. • Solves problems that create barriers to achieving benchmarks and goals for professional learning. • Makes in-process, data-based adjustments in individual and team professional learning (i.e., learning designs, coaching activities, and timeframes).	• Uses analyzed data to identify enhancers of and barriers to progress.	• Fails to use analysis of progress to make needed adjustments in professional learning.	

4.3 Evaluate professional learning

Desired outcome 4.3.1: Contributes to the development of an evaluation plan for professional learning.

Level 1	Level 2	Level 3	Level 4	Level 5	Level 6
• Contributes to the development of a theory of change, logic model, and evaluation framework to evaluate schoolwide and team professional learning.	• Contributes to the development of a theory of change and evaluation framework to evaluate schoolwide and team professional learning.	• Contributes to the development of an evaluation framework to evaluate schoolwide and team professional learning.	• Contributes to the identification of data sources and data collection methods to evaluate schoolwide professional learning.	• Identifies data collection methods to evaluate schoolwide professional learning.	• Fails to contribute to the evaluation of professional learning.

4.3 Evaluate professional learning

Level 1	Level 2	Level 3	Level 4	Level 5	Level 6
Desired outcome 4.3.2: Uses a variety of formative and summative data to evaluate the effectiveness and results of professional learning.					
• Facilitates individuals and teams to collect student data (e.g., test scores, benchmark results, student surveys, interviews, etc.) and classroom observations to measure changes in student learning and behaviors associated with professional learning. • Facilitates individuals and teams to collect data to assess changes in teacher knowledge, skills, and dispositions associated with professional learning. • Facilitates individuals and teams to collect educator data (e.g., staff surveys, interviews, self-reports, and observations) to assess changes in classroom practices associated with professional learning. • Facilitates individuals and teams to collect data to assess changes in school culture and organizational structures, policies, and processes associated with professional learning.	• Facilitates individuals and teams to collect student data (e.g., test scores, benchmark results, student surveys, interviews, etc.) and classroom observations to measure changes in student learning associated with professional learning. • Facilitates individuals and teams to collect data to assess changes in teacher knowledge, skills, and dispositions associated with professional learning. • Facilitates individuals and teams to collect educator data (e.g., staff surveys, interviews, self-reports, and observations) to assess changes in classroom practices associated with professional learning.	• Facilitates individuals and teams to collect student data (e.g., test scores, benchmark results, student surveys, interviews, etc.) and classroom observations to measure changes in student learning associated with professional learning. • Facilitates individuals and teams to collect data to assess changes in teacher knowledge, skills, and dispositions associated with professional learning.	• Facilitates individuals and teams to collect student data (e.g., test scores, benchmark results, student surveys, interviews, etc.) and classroom observations to measure changes in student learning associated with professional learning.	• Fails to contribute to the evaluation of the effectiveness and results of professional learning.	

4.3 Evaluate professional learning

Desired outcome 4.3.3: Supports colleagues to use data to evaluate the effectiveness of professional learning designs, content, and duration.

Level 1	Level 2	Level 3	Level 4	Level 5	Level 6
• Facilitates individuals and teams to identify data to evaluate the effectiveness of learning designs to develop knowledge, skills, dispositions, and practices. • Facilitates individual and team reflection about attainment of professional learning goals. • Facilitates individuals and teams to analyze and interpret data about collaboration, learning, and results. • Facilitates individuals and teams to form conclusions about the design, content, and duration of professional learning.	• Facilitates individuals and teams to identify data to evaluate the effectiveness of learning designs to develop knowledge, skills, dispositions, and practices. • Facilitates individuals and teams to analyze and interpret data about collaboration, learning, and results. • Facilitates individuals and teams to form conclusions about the design, content, and duration of professional learning.	• Facilitates individuals and teams to identify data to evaluate the effectiveness of learning designs to develop knowledge, skills, and practices. • Facilitates individuals and teams to analyze and interpret data about collaboration, learning, and results. • Facilitates individuals and teams to form conclusions about the design, content, and duration of professional learning.	• Facilitates individuals or teams to identify data to evaluate the effectiveness of learning designs to develop knowledge and skills.	• Fails to support individuals or teams to evaluate the effectiveness of professional learning designs, content, and duration.	

4.3 Evaluate professional learning

Level 1	Level 2	Level 3	Level 4	Level 5	Level 6
Desired outcome 4.3.4: Supports colleagues to use evaluation results to improve individual and team professional learning.					
• Facilitates individuals, teams, and whole staff to use evaluation results regarding changes in knowledge, skills, dispositions, and practices to refine the design of individual and team professional learning. • Facilitates individuals, teams, and whole faculty to use evaluation results regarding changes in student learning to refine the design of individual and team professional learning.	• Facilitates individuals and teams to use evaluation results regarding changes in knowledge, skills, dispositions, and practices to refine the design of individual and team professional learning. • Facilitates individuals and teams to use evaluation results regarding changes in student learning to refine the design of individual and team professional learning.	• Facilitates individuals and teams to use evaluation results regarding changes in knowledge, skills, dispositions, and practices to refine the design of individual and team professional learning.	• Facilitates individuals and teams to use evaluation results regarding changes in knowledge and skills to refine the design of individual and team professional learning.	• Uses evaluation results to recommend changes in individual and team professional learning.	• Fails to use evaluation results to improve individual and team professional learning.
Desired outcome 4.3.5: Uses evaluation results to improve coaching.					
• Uses results (e.g., changes in teacher knowledge, skills, and practice and in student learning) to identify strengths and improvements in coaching. • Applies, with principal and/or supervisor, the findings to implement improvements in collaboration. • Enacts changes in coaching practice based on analyzed data.	• Uses results (e.g., changes in teacher knowledge, skills, and practice and in student learning) to identify strengths and improvements in coaching. • Applies, with principal and/or supervisor, the findings to implement improvements in collaboration.	• Uses results (e.g., changes in teacher knowledge, skills, and practice and in student learning) to identify strengths and improvements in coaching. • Develops a plan to implement improvements.	• Uses teacher feedback to identify strengths and improvements in coaching.	• Uses teacher feedback to identify coaching strengths.	• Fails to use evaluation data to improve coaching.

5.1 Apply learning theories, research, and models

	Level 1	Level 2	Level 3	Level 4	Level 5	Level 6
Desired outcome 5.1.1: Develops and shares a knowledge base about theories, research, and models of adult learning.	• Studies, with principal and colleagues, research, theories, and models of adult learning. • Engages others in developing knowledge and skills related to research, theories, and models of adult learning. • Contributes to a collection of resources on educator learning for personal, individual, team, and whole staff use.	• Studies, with principal, research, theories, and models of adult learning. • Engages others in developing knowledge and skills related to research, theories, and models of adult learning.	• Studies research, theories, and models of adult learning.	• Reads periodically resources about research, theories, and models related to educator learning.	• Accesses resources about educator learning.	• Fails to add to own or others' knowledge base about learning theories, research, and models.
Desired outcome 5.1.2: Builds colleagues' knowledge base about multiple designs for professional learning. *	• Develops knowledge about, skills to facilitate, and expertise to implement 12 or more learning designs. • Identifies and discusses essential features of high-quality learning designs (e.g., active engagement, reflection, metacognition, ongoing support, etc.). • Shares knowledge, skills, and practices associated with five or more learning designs with individuals, teams, and other learning facilitators. • Recommends learning designs to individuals, teams, and whole staff.	• Develops knowledge about, skills to facilitate, and expertise to implement 10 learning designs. • Identifies and discusses essential features of high-quality learning designs (e.g., active engagement, reflection, metacognition, ongoing support, etc.). • Shares knowledge, skills, and practices associated with four learning designs with individuals, teams, and other learning facilitators. • Recommends learning designs to individuals and teams.	• Develops knowledge about, skills to facilitate, and expertise to implement eight learning designs. • Identifies and discusses essential features of high-quality learning designs (e.g., active engagement, reflection, metacognition, ongoing support, etc.). • Recommends learning designs to individuals and teams.	• Develops knowledge about, skills to facilitate, and expertise to implement at least five learning designs.	• Develops knowledge about, skills to facilitate, and expertise to implement fewer than five learning designs.	• Fails to build colleagues' knowledge base about multiple designs for professional learning.

*See the Appendix (p. 262) for an explanation of this concept.

5.1 Apply learning theories, research, and models

Level 1	Level 2	Level 3	Level 4	Level 5	Level 6
Desired outcome 5.1.3: Implements multiple learning designs to facilitate professional learning.					
• Employs multiple job-embedded and formal learning designs to develop individual and team knowledge, skills, dispositions, and practices. • Adapts learning designs to align with learner needs and learning outcomes. • Builds capacity of team and other learning facilitators to use multiple learning designs by cofacilitating those designs. • Provides feedback to learning facilitators on the use of various learning designs.	• Employs multiple job-embedded and formal learning designs to develop individual and team knowledge, skills, dispositions, and practices. • Adapts learning designs to align with learner needs and learning outcomes. • Cofacilitates with team facilitators and other learning facilitators multiple learning designs to develop their independent use.	• Employs multiple job-embedded and formal learning designs to develop individual and team knowledge, skills, dispositions, and practices. • Adapts learning designs to align with learner needs and learning outcomes.	• Employs multiple learning designs to develop individual and team knowledge, skills, dispositions, and practices.	• Fails to employ multiple learning designs for all professional learning.	

5.2 Select learning designs

Desired outcome 5.2.1: Acquires and shares knowledge about the multiple factors influencing the selection of learning designs. *

Level 1	Level 2	Level 3	Level 4	Level 5	Level 6
• Clarifies the learning outcomes, including the knowledge, skills, dispositions, and practices, expected as a result of individual and team professional learning. • Develops knowledge about factors that influence how adults learn. • Shares knowledge about factors influencing adult learning with individuals and teams. • Identifies, with colleagues and principal, factors influencing the selection of the learning design. • Prioritizes, with colleagues, the factors most likely to influence the selection of learning designs. • Develops others' capacity to identify and determine which factors influence the selection of professional learning designs.	• Clarifies the learning outcomes, including the knowledge, skills, dispositions, and practices, expected as a result of individual and team professional learning. • Develops knowledge about factors that influence how adults learn. • Shares knowledge about factors influencing adult learning with individuals and teams. • Identifies factors influencing the selection of the learning designs.	• Clarifies the learning outcomes, including the knowledge, skills, dispositions, and practices, expected as a result of individual and team professional learning. • Develops knowledge about factors that influence how adults learn. • Identifies factors influencing the selection of learning designs.	• Acquires knowledge about factors that influence how adults learn. • Identifies factors influencing the selection of learning designs.	• Fails to acquire knowledge about the multiple factors influencing the selection of learning designs.	

*See the Appendix (p. 262) for an explanation of this concept.

5.2 Select learning designs

Level 1	Level 2	Level 3	Level 4	Level 5	Level 6
Desired outcome 5.2.2: Applies knowledge to the selection of appropriate learning designs.					
• Reviews, with colleagues, the factors influencing the current individual and team learning situation. • Weighs, with colleagues, which factors are more influential. • Selects, with colleagues, appropriate in-person, blended, and online learning designs for current learning needs. • Supports colleagues to select appropriate learning designs for individual, team, and schoolwide professional learning.	• Reviews the factors influencing the current individual and team learning situation with colleagues. • Weighs, with colleagues, which factors are more influential. • Selects, with colleagues, appropriate in-person, blended, and online learning designs for current learning needs.	• Reviews the factors influencing the current individual and team learning situation. • Weighs which factors are more influential. • Selects appropriate learning designs for current learning needs.	• Reviews the factors influencing the current individual and team learning situation. • Selects appropriate learning designs for current learning needs.	• Selects learning designs for current learning needs.	• Fails to consider critical factors when selecting learning designs.

5.2 Select learning designs

		Level 1	Level 2	Level 3	Level 4	Level 5	Level 6
		Desired outcome 5.2.3: Develops and shares knowledge about technology-enhanced learning designs.					
		• Develops, with colleagues, knowledge about available and emerging technology-enhanced learning designs for individual and team professional learning. • Shares knowledge about technology-enhanced learning designs with colleagues. • Establishes and applies, with principal and colleagues, criteria for selecting technology-enhanced professional learning designs. • Advocates the use of technology-enhanced learning designs to increase the efficiency and effectiveness of professional learning.	• Develops, with colleagues, knowledge about available technology-enhanced learning designs for individual and team professional learning. • Shares knowledge about technology-enhanced learning designs with colleagues. • Advocates the use of technology-enhanced learning designs to increase the efficiency and effectiveness of professional learning.	• Identifies and shares with individuals and teams available technology-enhanced learning designs for individual and team professional learning. • Establishes and applies criteria for selecting technology-enhanced professional learning designs.	• Identifies available technology-enhanced learning designs for individual and team professional learning.	• Fails to develop or share knowledge about technology-enhanced professional learning.	

5.2 Select learning designs

Desired outcome 5.2.4: Implements appropriate learning designs.

Level 1	Level 2	Level 3	Level 4	Level 5	Level 6
• Uses a variety of in-person, blended, and online learning designs to address all phases of the learning process (i.e., build knowledge; develop skills; address dispositions; and support implementation, reflection, and refinement).	• Uses a variety of in-person, blended, and online learning designs to address all phases of the learning process (i.e., build knowledge; develop skills; address dispositions; and support implementation, reflection, and refinement).	• Uses a variety of in-person, blended, and online learning designs to address all phases of the learning process (i.e., build knowledge; develop skills; address dispositions; and support implementation, reflection, and refinement).	• Uses a variety of in-person, blended, and online learning designs to address all phases of the learning process (i.e., build knowledge; develop skills; address dispositions; and support implementation, reflection, and refinement).	• Uses in-person, blended, and online learning designs that address building-knowledge and developing-skills phases of the learning process.	• Fails to implement appropriate learning designs for professional learning.
• Models appropriate in-person, blended, and online learning designs during schoolwide, individual, and team to enhance and differentiate professional learning.	• Models in-person, blended, and online appropriate learning designs during individual and team to enhance and differentiate professional learning.	• Models in-person, blended, and online appropriate learning designs and protocols during individual and team to enhance and differentiate professional learning.	• Recommends to colleagues appropriate job-embedded learning designs.		
• Supports colleagues to implement in-person, blended, and online appropriate learning designs.	• Supports colleagues to implement appropriate in-person, blended, and online job-embedded learning designs.	• Recommends to colleagues appropriate job-embedded learning designs.			
• Analyzes, with principal and other learning facilitators, the interaction of the learning designs used and the results achieved.					

5.2 Select learning designs

Desired outcome 5.2.5: Aligns professional learning designs with desired changes in classroom instruction.

Level 1	Level 2	Level 3	Level 4	Level 5	Level 6
• Identifies, with colleagues, the changes in classroom instruction required to achieve professional learning goals. • Selects in-person, blended, and online designs for individual and team professional learning that model and align with desired changes in instructional practice. • Implements the learning designs with fidelity. • Reflects, with individuals and teams, on the effectiveness of the learning designs to produce changes in classroom practice.	• Collaborates with colleagues to identify the changes in classroom instruction desired to achieve professional learning goals. • Selects in-person, blended, and online designs for individual and team professional learning that model and align with desired changes in instructional practice. • Implements the learning designs with fidelity.	• Identifies the changes in classroom instruction desired to achieve professional learning goals. • Selects in-person, blended, or online designs for individual and team professional learning that model and align with desired changes in instructional practice. • Implements the learning designs with fidelity.	• Selects in-person, blended, or online designs for individual and team professional learning that model and align with desired changes in instructional practice.	• Fails to align professional learning designs with desired changes in classroom instruction.	

5.3 Promote active engagement

Level 1	Level 2	Level 3	Level 4	Level 5	Level 6
Desired outcome 5.3.1: Models active engagement in professional learning.					
• Engages actively in team and schoolwide professional learning. • Models and shares strategies and protocols for active engagement in individual, team, and schoolwide professional learning. • Recommends self-assessment tools about active engagement. • Assesses, with colleagues, the effectiveness and frequency of active engagement to make improvements. • Elicits colleagues' participation in and contribution to discussions in individual, team, and schoolwide professional learning.	• Engages actively in team and schoolwide professional learning. • Models strategies and protocols for active engagement in individual, team, and schoolwide professional learning. • Recommends self-assessment tools about active engagement. • Elicits colleagues' participation in and contribution to discussions in individual, team, and schoolwide professional learning. • Assesses, with colleagues, the effectiveness and frequency of active engagement to make improvements.	• Engages actively in team and schoolwide professional learning. • Models strategies and protocols for active engagement in individual and team professional learning. • Elicits colleagues' participation in and contribution to discussions in individual, team, and schoolwide professional learning.	• Engages actively in team and schoolwide professional learning. • Elicits colleagues' participation in and contribution to discussions in individual, team, and schoolwide professional learning.	• Engages actively in team and schoolwide professional learning.	• Fails to model and share active engagement strategies and protocols in team and schoolwide professional learning.

5.3 Promote active engagement

Desired outcome 5.3.2: Supports colleagues to engage actively in professional learning.

Level 1	Level 2	Level 3	Level 4	Level 5	Level 6
• Establishes an expectation that individuals and teams participate actively in coach-facilitated professional learning. • Recommends to and supports colleagues to use multiple active engagement strategies in individual, team, and schoolwide professional learning. • Facilitates or cofacilitates collaborative interaction among team members during the learning process. • Assists learning teams to create norms that hold team members accountable for active engagement. • Identifies and addresses barriers to individual and team engagement. • Consults privately with colleagues who are unengaged in learning.	• Establishes an expectation that individuals and teams participate actively in coach-facilitated professional learning. • Recommends to and supports colleagues to use multiple active engagement strategies in individual, team, and schoolwide professional learning. • Facilitates or cofacilitates collaborative interaction among team members during the learning process. • Assists learning teams to create norms that hold team members accountable for active engagement. • Identifies and addresses barriers to individual and team engagement.	• Establishes an expectation that individuals and teams participate actively in coach-facilitated professional learning. • Recommends to and supports colleagues to use multiple active engagement strategies in individual, team, and schoolwide professional learning. • Facilitates or cofacilitates collaborative interaction among team members during the learning process.	• Facilitates collaborative interaction among team members during the learning process.	• Fails to support colleagues' active engagement in professional learning.	

5.3 Promote active engagement

Level 1	Level 2	Level 3	Level 4	Level 5	Level 6
Desired outcome 5.3.3: Incorporates strategies to promote active engagement in professional learning.					
• Employs multiple strategies to engage individuals, teams, and whole staff in professional learning. • Uses learning designs that engage learners in overt and covert cognition during learning. • Monitors engagement during individual and team professional learning • Adapts strategies to increase level of engagement.	• Employs multiple strategies to engage individuals and teams in professional learning. • Uses learning designs that engage learners in overt and covert cognition during learning. • Adapts strategies to increase level of engagement.	• Employs multiple strategies to engage individuals and teams in professional learning. • Uses learning designs that engage learners in overt and covert cognition during learning.	• Employs multiple strategies to engage individuals in professional learning.	• Employs one strategy to engage individuals in professional learning.	• Fails to incorporate strategies to promote active engagement in professional learning.

www.learningforward.org   800-727-7288

6.1 Apply change research

Level 1	Level 2	Level 3	Level 4	Level 5	Level 6
Desired outcome 6.1.1: Develops capacity to apply research on change to support implementation of professional learning. *					
• Reviews research studies and examples of exemplary change practices (IC maps, SoC, LoU, RPLIM, PDSA, etc.) to develop own understanding of and skills needed to facilitate the change process. • Participates in, with colleagues, additional professional learning about the change process to address opportunities and problems of practice. • Develops, with principal and colleagues, knowledge of and skills to lead and participate in the change process. • Demonstrates the value of research by sharing and citing relevant studies and reports when discussing change.	• Reviews research studies and examples of exemplary change practices (IC maps, SoC, LoU, RPLIM, PDSA, etc.) to develop own understanding of and skills needed to facilitate the change process. • Participates in, with colleagues, additional professional learning about the change process to address opportunities and problems of practice. • Discusses, with colleagues, information to increase understanding of the change process. • Demonstrates the value of research by sharing and citing relevant studies and reports when discussing change.	• Reviews research studies and examples of exemplary practice (IC maps, SoC, LoU, RPLIM, PDSA, etc.) to develop own understanding of and skills needed to facilitate the change process. • Participates in additional professional learning about the change process to address opportunities and problems of practice related to implementation.	• Reads articles, papers, and reports about the change process.	• Fails to engage in ongoing professional learning about the change process.	

*See the Appendix (p. 262) for an explanation of this concept.

6.1 Apply change research

	Level 1	Level 2	Level 3	Level 4	Level 5	Level 6
Desired outcome 6.1.2: Applies research on change to facilitate the implementation of professional learning.						
	• Uses change research to make decisions about implementation. • Addresses all phases of the learning process to support implementation of professional learning (i.e., build knowledge, develop skills, implementation, reflection, and refinement). • Adopts patience and perseverance to support colleagues throughout the change process. • Interacts with individuals and teams frequently to assess and respond to concerns related to implementation. • Recognizes privately and publicly individual, team, and schoolwide implementation efforts and accomplishments.	• Uses change research to make decisions about implementation. • Adopts patience and perseverance to support colleagues throughout the change process. • Interacts with individuals and teams frequently to assess and respond to concerns related to implementation. • Recognizes privately individual and team implementation efforts and accomplishments.	• Uses change research to make decisions about implementation. • Interacts with individuals and teams frequently to assess and respond to concerns related to implementation.	• Uses change research to make decisions about implementation.	• Fails to apply change research to plans and actions to support implementation of professional learning.	

6.1 Apply change research

Desired outcome 6.1.3: Supports monitoring of the progress of implementation of professional learning.

Level 1	Level 2	Level 3	Level 4	Level 5	Level 6
• Develops, with principal and colleagues, guides/tools (e.g., IC maps) to clarify expectations for implementation. • Uses guides/tools to support individual, team, and schoolwide use of professional learning. • Facilitates individual and team use of guides/tools to assess and refine implementation.	• Develops, with principal, guides/tools (e.g., IC maps) to clarify expectations for implementation. • Uses guides/tools to support individual and team use of professional learning.	• Uses guides/tools to support individual and team use of professional learning.	• Reinforces expectation for implementing professional learning.	• Fails to support monitoring of professional learning.	

6.2 Sustain implementation

Desired outcome 6.2.1: Differentiates support for implementation of professional learning.

Level 1	Level 2	Level 3	Level 4	Level 5	Level 6
• Demonstrates belief in colleagues' ability and willingness to be effective educators. • Elicits individual, team, and schoolwide needs based on assessment of implementation. • Uses the Standards for Professional Learning to guide the design and facilitation of ongoing professional learning to deepen understanding, enhance implementation, and refine practice. • Tailors classroom support to align with teachers' needs and concerns. • Employs multiple types of support to address each individual, team, and schoolwide need related to implementation. • Employs a variety of technology-enhanced implementation supports.	• Elicits individual, team, and schoolwide needs based on assessment of implementation. • Uses the Standards for Professional Learning to guide the design and facilitation of ongoing professional learning to deepen understanding, enhance implementation, and refine practice. • Tailors classroom support to align with teachers' needs and concerns. • Employs multiple types of support to address each individual, team, and schoolwide need related to implementation. • Employs a variety of technology-enhanced implementation supports.	• Uses the Standards for Professional Learning to guide the design and facilitation of ongoing professional learning to deepen understanding, enhance implementation, and refine practice. • Tailors classroom support to align with teachers' needs and concerns. • Employs multiple types of support to address each individual staff member's areas of need related to implementation.	• Provides implementation support to individuals and teams when requested.	• Provides implementation support to individuals when requested.	• Fails to provide differentiated support for implementation.

6.2 Sustain implementation

Desired outcome 6.2.2: Continues support to reach high-fidelity implementation of professional learning.

Level 1	Level 2	Level 3	Level 4	Level 5	Level 6
• Contributes to school-wide plan for continuous individual, team, and schoolwide support for three to five years for implementation of professional learning. • Adjusts individual and team support for implementation of professional learning with the maturity and fidelity of implementation. • Provides easily accessible in-person, blended, and technology-enhanced support that individuals, teams, and whole staff can access daily. • Reminds colleagues about expectations to access support at least weekly to refine and improve implementation.	• Contributes to school-wide plan for continuous support for two years for implementation of professional learning. • Adjusts support for implementation of professional learning with the maturity and fidelity of implementation. • Provides easily accessible in-person, blended, and technology-enhanced support that individuals and teams can access weekly. • Reminds colleagues about expectations to access support at least biweekly to refine and improve implementation.	• Contributes to school-wide plan for ongoing support for one year for implementation of professional learning. • Provides easily accessible in-person, blended, and technology-enhanced support that the whole staff can access monthly. • Reminds colleagues about expectations to access support at least monthly to refine and improve implementation.	• Provides easily accessible support that staff can access quarterly.	• Facilitates access to support for implementation.	• Fails to provide support for implementation of professional learning.

6.3 Provide constructive feedback

Level 1	Level 2	Level 3	Level 4	Level 5	Level 6
Desired outcome 6.3.1: Develops capacity to give and receive constructive feedback.					
• Develops, with colleagues, research-based knowledge and skills to give and receive constructive feedback. • Facilitates the development of colleagues' knowledge and skills to give and receive constructive feedback. • Facilitates risk-free opportunities for individuals and teams to practice giving and receiving feedback. • Models giving and receiving constructive feedback. • Provides to and seeks from individuals, teams, and whole staff feedback on use of constructive feedback.	• Develops, with colleagues, research-based knowledge and skills to give and receive constructive feedback. • Facilitates the development of colleagues' knowledge and skills to give constructive feedback. • Models giving and receiving constructive feedback. • Provides to and seeks from individuals and teams feedback on use of constructive feedback.	• Develops knowledge and skills to give and receive constructive feedback. • Models giving and receiving constructive feedback.	• Develops knowledge and skills to give and receive constructive feedback.	• Fails to develop own and colleagues' knowledge and skills to give and receive constructive feedback.	

www.learningforward.org   800-727-7288

6.3 Provide constructive feedback

Desired outcome 6.3.2: Gives and receives constructive feedback to accelerate and refine implementation of professional learning.

Level 1	Level 2	Level 3	Level 4	Level 5	Level 6
• Identifies and makes available, with principal, staff, and SLT, multiple in-person, blended, and technology-based strategies and tools (e.g., peer coaching, reviewing student work, lesson study, instructional rounds, peer observation, e-coaching, etc.) to give and receive feedback on implementation. • Provides to and seeks from individuals, teams, and whole staff constructive feedback on implementation weekly using varied tools and strategies. • Analyzes and shares, with principal, staff, and SLT, feedback data monthly about implementation.	• Identifies and makes available, with principal and SLT, multiple in-person, blended, and technology-based strategies and tools (e.g., peer coaching, reviewing student work, lesson study, instructional rounds, walk-throughs, peer observation, e-coaching, etc.) to give and receive feedback on implementation. • Provides to and seeks from individuals, teams, and whole staff constructive feedback on implementation monthly using varied tools and strategies. • Analyzes and shares, with principal, staff, and SLT, feedback data quarterly about implementation.	• Identifies and makes available multiple in-person, blended, and technology-based strategies and tools (e.g., peer coaching, reviewing student work, lesson study, instructional rounds, walk-throughs, peer observation, e-coaching, etc.) to give and receive feedback on implementation. • Provides to and seeks from individuals, teams, and whole staff constructive feedback on implementation quarterly using varied tools and strategies. • Analyzes and shares, with principal and SLT, feedback data quarterly about implementation to improve individual, team,	• Provides to and seeks from individuals, teams, and whole staff constructive feedback on implementation semiannually using varied tools and strategies. • Analyzes and shares, with principal and SLT, feedback data semiannually about implementation to improve individual, team, and schoolwide support.	• Provides to and seeks from individuals, teams, and whole staff constructive feedback on implementation annually using varied tools and strategies.	• Fails to seek and provide input on implementation of professional learning.

7.1 Meet performance standards

Desired outcome 7.1.1: Uses educator performance standards to identify professional learning needs.

Level 1	Level 2	Level 3	Level 4	Level 5	Level 6
• Facilitates individual and team reflection on current practices compared to educator performance standards. • Facilitates individual and team analysis of educator performance standards to identify strengths and areas for growth. • Facilitates colleagues to use the assessment to develop learning goals for individual, team, and schoolwide professional learning.	• Facilitates team reflection on current practices compared to educator performance standards. • Facilitates colleagues' use of educator performance standards to identify strengths and areas for growth. • Facilitates colleagues to use the assessment to develop learning goals for individual and team professional learning.	• Facilitates colleagues' use of educator performance standards to identify strengths and areas for growth. • Facilitates colleagues to use the assessment to develop learning goals for individual professional learning.	• Facilitates reviews of educator performance standards.	• Facilitates colleagues' identification of needs for professional learning based on personal preference.	• Fails to identify needs for professional learning.

7.1 Meet performance standards

Desired outcome 7.1.2: Uses educator performance standards to make decisions about the content of professional learning.

Level 1	Level 2	Level 3	Level 4	Level 5	Level 6
• Links areas for growth to educator performance standards to identify knowledge, skills, practices, and dispositions needed to attain individual, team, and schoolwide goals for professional learning. • Uses educator performance standards to identify the content of schoolwide professional learning. • Supports individuals and teams in using educator performance standards to identify the content of professional learning. • Reviews the content of professional learning for alignment with educator performance standards.	• Links areas for growth to educator performance standards to identify knowledge, skills, and practices needed to attain schoolwide goals for professional learning. • Uses educator performance standards to identify the content of schoolwide professional learning. • Supports individuals and teams in using educator performance standards to identify the content of professional learning.	• Links areas for growth to educator performance standards to identify knowledge and skills needed to attain schoolwide goals for professional learning. • Uses educator performance standards to identify the content of schoolwide professional learning. • Supports individuals in using educator performance standards to identify the content of professional learning.	• Uses educator performance standards to identify the content of schoolwide professional learning.	• Uses colleagues' preferences to identify content for professional learning.	• Selects content for professional learning without analysis of educator performance standards.

7.1 Meet performance standards

Desired outcome 7.1.3: Engages in professional learning to meet coach performance standards.

Level 1	Level 2	Level 3	Level 4	Level 5	Level 6
• Develops research-based knowledge about the role expectations, responsibilities, and coach performance standards. • Engages, with colleagues, in professional learning to develop coaching knowledge, skills, dispositions, and practices reflected in performance standards. • Practices coaching skills until mastery is achieved. • Engages in coaching, feedback, and reflection on own performance.	• Develops knowledge about coach performance standards. • Engages, with colleagues, in professional learning to develop coaching skills reflected in performance standards. • Practices coaching skills until mastery is achieved. • Engages in coaching, feedback, and reflection on own performance.	• Studies coach performance standards. • Engages in professional learning to develop coaching skills reflected in performance standards. • Practices coaching skills until mastery is achieved.	• Reads coach performance standards.	• Fails to engage in professional learning related to performance standards.	

www.learningforward.org   800-727-7288

7.2 Address learning outcomes

Level 1	Level 2	Level 3	Level 4	Level 5	Level 6
Desired outcome 7.2.1: Uses student learning outcomes to identify professional learning needs.					
• Facilitates individual and team reflection on current practices compared to student learning outcomes. • Facilitates individual and team analysis of student learning outcomes to identify strengths and areas of growth. • Facilitates colleagues to use the assessment to develop learning goals for individual, team, and schoolwide professional learning.	• Facilitates team reflection on current practices compared to student learning outcomes. • Facilitates colleagues to use the assessment to develop learning goals for individual and team professional learning.	• Facilitates colleagues' use of student learning outcomes to identify strengths and areas of growth. • Facilitates colleagues to use the assessment to develop learning goals for individual professional learning.	• Facilitates reviews of student learning outcomes.	• Facilitates colleagues' identification of needs for professional learning based on personal preference.	

7.2 Address learning outcomes

	Level 1	Level 2	Level 3	Level 4	Level 5	Level 6

Desired outcome 7.2.2: Uses student learning outcomes to inform decisions about the content of professional learning.

Level 1	Level 2	Level 3	Level 4	Level 5	Level 6
• Links areas for growth to student learning outcomes to identify knowledge, skills, dispositions, and practices needed to attain individual, team, and schoolwide goals for professional learning. • Uses student learning outcomes to select the content of schoolwide professional learning. • Supports individuals and teams in using student learning outcomes to identify the content of professional learning. • Reviews the content of professional learning for alignment with student learning outcomes.	• Links areas for growth to student learning outcomes to identify knowledge, skills, and practices needed to attain schoolwide goals for professional learning. • Uses student learning outcomes to select the content of schoolwide professional learning. • Supports individuals and teams in using student learning outcomes to identify the content of professional learning.	• Links areas for growth to student learning outcomes to identify knowledge and skills needed to attain schoolwide goals for professional learning. • Uses student learning outcomes to select the content of schoolwide professional learning. • Supports individuals in using student learning outcomes to identify the content of professional learning.	• Uses student learning outcomes to select the content of schoolwide professional learning.	• Uses colleagues' preferences to select content for professional learning.	• Identifies content for professional learning without analysis of student learning outcomes or input from colleagues.

Desired outcome 7.2.3: Engages in professional learning to increase student results.

Level 1	Level 2	Level 3	Level 4	Level 5	Level 6
• Engages in professional learning with colleagues to develop content, pedagogy, and pedagogical content related to student learning outcomes. • Engages in coaching, feedback, and reflection on the effects of own performance on student learning.	• Engages in professional learning with colleagues to develop content, pedagogy, and pedagogical content related to student learning outcomes. • Reflects on the effects of own performance on student learning.	• Studies student learning outcomes. • Engages in professional learning to develop content and pedagogy to achieve student learning outcomes.	• Reads about student learning outcomes. • Engages in professional learning on instruction.	• Fails to engage in professional learning related to student learning outcomes.	

7.3 Build coherence

Level 1	Level 2	Level 3	Level 4	Level 5	Level 6
Desired outcome 7.3.1: Builds congruence between professional learning and other school and school system initiatives.					
• Facilitates conversations with individuals and teams to develop understanding of the relationships among school and school system processes and initiatives; the school improvement goals; individual, team, and schoolwide professional learning goals; and professional learning. • Communicates to individuals and teams about the application of professional learning to support multiple school processes and initiatives. • Aligns, with individuals and teams, professional learning with school improvement goals and other school processes and initiatives.	• Facilitates conversations with individuals and teams to develop understanding of the relationships among school and school system processes and initiatives; the school improvement goals; individual, team, and schoolwide professional learning goals; and professional learning. • Communicates to individuals and teams about the application of professional learning to support multiple school processes and initiatives.	• Communicates to individuals and teams about the relationships among the school improvement goals, schoolwide professional learning goals, and professional learning.	• Communicates to individuals about the relationships among the school improvement goals, schoolwide professional learning goals, and professional learning.	• Fails to develop staff understanding of the relationships among the school and school system processes and initiatives, school improvement goals, schoolwide professional learning goals, and professional learning.	

7.3 Build coherence

Desired outcome 7.3.2: Links professional learning with past experiences.

Level 1	Level 2	Level 3	Level 4	Level 5	Level 6
• Contributes to the collection of data about colleagues' past experiences with individual, team, school-wide, and out-of-school professional learning; their experience with the planned content of professional learning; and the school's history with change. • Uses data when planning and implementing professional learning.	• Contributes to the collection of data about colleagues' past experiences with individual, team, and schoolwide professional learning and their experience with the planned content of professional learning. • Uses data when planning professional learning.	• Contributes to the collection of data about colleagues' past experiences with individual, team, and schoolwide professional learning. • Uses data when planning professional learning.	• Forms assumptions about colleagues' past experiences with individual, team, and schoolwide professional learning. • Uses the assumptions when planning professional learning.	• Fails to gather data about colleagues' past experiences with professional learning.	

Innovation
Configuration
Maps

SCHOOL LEADERSHIP TEAM

- **LEARNING COMMUNITIES**
- **LEADERSHIP**
- **RESOURCES**
- **DATA**
- **LEARNING DESIGNS**
- **IMPLEMENTATION**
- **OUTCOMES**

1.1 Engage in continuous improvement

	Level 1	Level 2	Level 3	Level 4	Level 5	Level 6
Desired outcome 1.1.1: Develops own and others' capacity to apply the seven-step cycle of continuous improvement. *						
	• Develops knowledge and skills necessary to use the seven steps of the cycle of continuous improvement. • Contributes to developing colleagues' knowledge and skills about the seven steps of the cycle of continuous improvement.	• Identifies the seven steps of the cycle of continuous improvement. • Contributes to developing colleagues' knowledge and skills about the seven steps of the cycle of continuous improvement.	• Develops understanding of the seven steps of the cycle of continuous improvement. • Shares with colleagues the cycle of continuous improvement.	• Directs staff to use the cycle of continuous improvement.	• Expects staff to use the cycle of continuous improvement.	• Fails to develop own and others' knowledge and skills about the cycle of continuous improvement.
Desired outcome 1.1.2: Applies the cycle of continuous improvement with fidelity to decisions about professional learning.						
	• Uses all seven steps of the cycle of continuous improvement with fidelity in schoolwide professional learning.	• Uses six of the seven steps of the cycle of continuous improvement with fidelity in professional learning.	• Uses five of the seven steps of the cycle of continuous improvement with fidelity in professional learning.	• Uses fewer than five steps of the cycle of continuous improvement about professional learning.	• Fails to use the cycle of continuous improvement about professional learning.	
Desired outcome 1.1.3: Supports application of the cycle of continuous improvement.						
	• Facilitates colleagues' application of the cycle of continuous improvement. • Guides colleagues in applying the cycle with fidelity. • Provides coaching to colleagues to support use of the cycle. • Establishes and maintains a feedback loop with colleagues on the use of the cycle.	• Facilitates colleagues' application of the cycle of continuous improvement. • Guides colleagues in applying the cycle with fidelity. • Establishes and maintains a feedback loop with colleagues on the use of the cycle.	• Guides colleagues in applying the cycle with fidelity. • Establishes and maintains a feedback loop with colleagues on the use of the cycle.	• Guides colleagues in applying some steps of the cycle of continuous improvement.	• Fails to support the implementation of the cycle of continuous improvement.	

*See the Appendix (p. 262) for an explanation of this concept.

1.2 Develop collective responsibility

Level 1	Level 2	Level 3	Level 4	Level 5	Level 6
Desired outcome 1.2.1: Advances collective responsibility.					
• Develops, with principal and colleagues, shared assumptions about and a shared definition of collective responsibility. • Collects from and shares with all staff evidence of collective responsibility. • Challenges, with principal, practices and assumptions that create barriers to collective responsibility. • Takes action, with principal and colleagues, to overcome barriers.	• Develops, with principal, shared assumptions about and a shared definition of collective responsibility. • Collects from and shares with all colleagues evidence of collective responsibility. • Contributes to efforts to identify and overcome barriers to collective responsibility.	• Declares shared assumptions about and a definition of collective responsibility. • Provides evidence of collective responsibility.	• Writes and shares a definition of collective responsibility.	• Fails to address collective responsibility.	
Desired outcome 1.2.2: Fosters engagement of all staff in meeting the needs of all students.					
• Engages colleagues in conversations about the impact of individual and collective decisions about professional learning on student achievement. • Meets with colleagues at least weekly to discuss individual, team, and schoolwide professional learning to address the needs of all students.	• Engages colleagues in conversations about the impact of individual and collective decisions about professional learning on student achievement. • Meets with colleagues every few weeks to discuss individual, team, and schoolwide professional learning to address the needs of all students.	• Shares data with colleagues to learn about the needs of students outside individual classrooms. • Meets with colleagues once a month to discuss individual, team, and schoolwide learning to address the needs of all students.	• Invites colleagues to participate in professional learning to address the needs of students outside individual classrooms.	• Focuses attention only on learning needs of students in individual SLT members' classrooms.	

1.2 Develop collective responsibility

Level 1	Level 2	Level 3	Level 4	Level 5	Level 6
Desired outcome 1.2.3: Models collective responsibility by participating in learning communities.					
• Participates routinely in one or more ongoing learning communities within and beyond the school. • Shares with colleagues own learning as a member of learning communities.	• Participates routinely in one or more school-based learning communities. • Shares with colleagues own learning as a member of learning communities.	• Participates routinely in one school-based learning community.	• Participates occasionally in a school-based learning community.	• Fails to participate in a learning community.	

1.3 Create alignment and accountability

Level 1	Level 2	Level 3	Level 4	Level 5	Level 6
Desired outcome 1.3.1: Aligns professional learning with school and system goals.					
• Facilitates discussion with colleagues to develop understanding of school and system goals and strategies to establish individual, team, and school goals and plans for professional learning that align with school and system goals and strategies. • Aligns SLT professional learning goals with school goals. • Reviews school and team professional learning goals and strategies to check for alignment with system goals and strategies.	• Facilitates discussion with colleagues to develop understanding of school and system goals and strategies to establish individual, team, and school goals and plans for professional learning that align with school and system goals and strategies. • Aligns SLT professional learning goals with school goals. • Reviews school professional learning goals and strategies to check for alignment with system goals and strategies.	• Establishes school professional learning goals and strategies that align with system goals and strategies. • Aligns SLT professional learning goals with school goals.	• Adopts district professional learning goals as school goals.	• Contributes to the development of school professional learning goals and strategies without consideration of system goals and strategies.	• Fails to establish schoolwide professional learning goals.

SCHOOL LEADERSHIP TEAM / **Learning Communities**

1.3 Create alignment and accountability

Desired outcome 1.3.2: Monitors the use of the cycle of continuous improvement to achieve professional learning goals.

Level 1	Level 2	Level 3	Level 4	Level 5	Level 6
• Assesses the fidelity of own and colleagues' use of the cycle of continuous improvement. • Provides constructive feedback to teams and whole staff to improve fidelity of implementation of the cycle. • Provides additional professional learning and support to refine implementation fidelity.	• Assesses the fidelity of own and colleagues' use of the cycle of continuous improvement. • Provides constructive feedback to teams and whole staff to improve fidelity of implementation of the cycle.	• Assesses the fidelity of own and colleagues' use of the cycle of continuous improvement. • Provides constructive feedback to whole staff to improve fidelity of implementation of the cycle.	• Assesses the fidelity of own use of the cycle of continuous improvement.	• Fails to assess the fidelity of implementation of the cycle of continuous improvement.	

2.1 Develop capacity for learning and leading

Level 1	Level 2	Level 3	Level 4	Level 5	Level 6
Desired outcome 2.1.1: Commits to continuous professional learning.					
• States publicly team professional learning goals. • Persists with own professional learning until achieving mastery. • Asks for constructive feedback from principal and staff. • Participates in and models professional learning that occurs over multiple years and includes hands-on and problem-based learning with multiple practice opportunities. • Participates in follow-up and coaching.	• States publicly team professional learning goals. • Persists with own professional learning until achieving mastery. • Participates in and models professional learning that occurs over multiple years and includes hands-on and problem-based learning with multiple practice opportunities. • Participates in follow-up and coaching.	• Participates in professional learning that occurs over a single year and includes hands-on and problem-based learning with multiple practice opportunities. • Participates in follow-up and coaching.	• Participates in a series of short-term learning activities on a variety of topics without ongoing support and assistance to promote implementation of new learning.	• Participates in a variety of disconnected learning activities (e.g. reads articles, attends professional conferences or workshops, participates in webinars, etc.) unrelated to own professional learning goals.	• Fails to participate in continuous professional learning.

2.1 Develop capacity for learning and leading

Desired outcome 2.1.2: Develops own and others' capacity for leadership of professional learning.

Level 1	Level 2	Level 3	Level 4	Level 5	Level 6
• Develops team knowledge and skills related to leadership of professional learning. • Shares with colleagues knowledge and skills related to leadership of professional learning. • Works with principal to create experiences for staff to lead schoolwide and team-based professional learning. • Establishes, with colleagues and principal, transparent and objective guidelines and processes to select and support teacher leaders. • Mentors colleagues to serve as future members of SLT.	• Develops team knowledge and skills related to leadership of professional learning. • Shares with colleagues knowledge and skills related to leadership of professional learning. • Establishes, with colleagues and principal, transparent and objective guidelines and processes to select and support teacher leaders. • Mentors colleagues to serve as future members of SLT.	• Develops team knowledge and skills related to leadership of professional learning. • Shares with colleagues knowledge and skills related to leadership of professional learning. • Encourages staff to lead schoolwide and team-based professional learning.	• Develops team knowledge and skills related to leadership of professional learning. • Shares with colleagues knowledge and skills related to leadership of professional learning.	• Develops team knowledge and skills related to leadership of professional learning.	• Fails to develop team and colleagues' knowledge and skills related to leadership of professional learning.

2.1 Develop capacity for learning and leading

Desired outcome 2.1.3: Understands and uses the Standards for Professional Learning in making decisions about professional learning.

Level 1	Level 2	Level 3	Level 4	Level 5	Level 6
• Studies the Standards for Professional Learning to apply key ideas. • Develops colleagues' understanding of the Standards for Professional Learning. • Accesses and uses new research and information about effective professional learning on an ongoing basis. • Applies the seven Standards for Professional Learning in decision making about professional learning.	• Studies the Standards for Professional Learning to apply key ideas. • Accesses and uses new research and information about effective professional learning on an ongoing basis. • Applies the seven Standards for Professional Learning in decision making about professional learning.	• Studies the Standards for Professional Learning to understand key ideas. • Reviews new research and information about effective professional learning at least annually. • Uses five of the Standards for Professional Learning in decision making about professional learning.	• Names the Standards for Professional Learning.	• Makes decisions about professional learning without reference to the Standards for Professional Learning.	

2.1 Develop capacity for learning and leading

Desired outcome 2.1.4: Serves as a leader of professional learning.

Level 1	Level 2	Level 3	Level 4	Level 5	Level 6
• Articulates the role of the SLT related to professional learning.	• Articulates the role of the SLT related to professional learning.	• Articulates the role of the SLT related to professional learning.	• Articulates the role of the SLT related to professional learning.	• Defers decision-making authority in professional learning to principal or others.	
• Acknowledges responsibility for the quality and results of schoolwide professional learning.	• Acknowledges responsibility for the quality and results of schoolwide professional learning.	• Acknowledges responsibility for the quality and results of schoolwide professional learning.	• Takes an active role in planning individual, team, and schoolwide professional learning.		
• Articulates how decisions about professional learning are made and who is involved.	• Articulates how decisions about professional learning are made and who is involved.	• Articulates how decisions about professional learning are made.	• Oversees or manages less than 80% of SLT's responsibilities for professional learning.		
• Shares leadership for professional learning with others, including principal, teams, coaches, and other learning facilitators.	• Shares leadership for professional learning with principal.	• Takes an active role in planning and evaluating individual, team, and schoolwide professional learning.			
• Takes an active role in planning, implementing, and evaluating individual, team, and schoolwide professional learning.	• Takes an active role in planning, implementing, and evaluating individual, team, and schoolwide professional learning.	• Oversees or manages 80% of SLT's responsibilities for professional learning.			
• Oversees or manages 100% of SLT's responsibilities for professional learning.	• Oversees or manages 90% of SLT's responsibilities for professional learning.				

2.2 Advocate for professional learning

Level 1	Level 2	Level 3	Level 4	Level 5	Level 6
Desired outcome 2.2.1: Articulates the link between student learning and professional learning.					
• Explains the indelible connection between professional learning and student learning to staff, students, parents, system leaders, public officials, and community members. • Provides multiple examples of the link between professional learning and student learning to staff, students, parents, system leaders, public officials, and community members and partners.	• Explains the indelible connection between professional learning and student learning to staff, students, and parents. • Provides multiple examples of the link between professional learning and student learning to staff, students, and parents.	• Explains the indelible connection between professional learning and student learning to staff and parents. • Provides multiple examples of the link between professional learning and student learning to staff and parents.	• Describes the connection between professional learning and student learning.	• Fails to explain the connection between professional learning and student learning.	
Desired outcome 2.2.2: Advocates high-quality professional learning.					
• Promotes high-quality professional learning with staff, students, parents, system leaders, colleagues, public officials, and community members and partners. • Advocates system - and schoolwide conditions and procedures for effective individual, team, and schoolwide professional learning. • Engages and supports colleagues in developing succinct messages about the role of professional learning in student learning.	• Promotes high-quality professional learning with staff, students, parents, system leaders, and colleagues. • Advocates schoolwide conditions and procedures for effective individual, team, and schoolwide professional learning. • Engages colleagues in developing succinct messages about the role of professional learning in student learning.	• Promotes high-quality professional learning with staff and school system leaders. • Advocates schoolwide conditions and procedures for effective schoolwide professional learning.	• Promotes high-quality professional learning with staff.	• Fails to promote high-quality professional learning for staff.	

www.learningforward.org 800-727-7288

2.3 Create support systems and structures

Level 1	Level 2	Level 3	Level 4	Level 5	Level 6
Desired outcome 2.3.1: Establishes systems and structures for effective professional learning.					
• Establishes, with colleagues and principal, schoolwide conditions for effective professional learning (e.g., resources, policies, annual calendars, schedules, procedures, and structures). • Supports colleagues in understanding and implementing conditions for effective schoolwide professional learning. • Solves problems, with principal and colleagues, related to establishing conditions for effective professional learning.	• Establishes, with principal, schoolwide conditions for effective professional learning (e.g., resources, policies, annual calendars, schedules, procedures, and structures). • Solves problems, with principal, related to establishing conditions for effective professional learning.	• Identifies schoolwide conditions necessary for effective professional learning (e.g., resources, policies, annual calendars, schedules, procedures, and structures).	• Fails to establish schoolwide conditions for effective professional learning.		
Desired outcome 2.3.2: Prepares and supports staff for skillful collaboration.					
• Develops, with colleagues, the knowledge and skills to learn and work collaboratively. • Encourages colleagues to use collaboration to achieve individual, team, and schoolwide professional learning goals. • Develops, with colleagues, the capacity to surface assumptions and resolve conflict.	• Develops, with colleagues, the knowledge and skills to learn and work collaboratively. • Encourages colleagues to use collaboration to achieve individual, team, and schoolwide professional learning goals. • Develops, with colleagues, the capacity to resolve conflict.	• Develops, with colleagues, the knowledge and skills to learn and work collaboratively. • Encourages colleagues to use collaboration to achieve individual, team, and schoolwide professional learning goals.	• Encourages colleagues to use collaboration to achieve individual, team, and schoolwide professional learning goals.	• Presumes staff uses collaboration to achieve individual, team, and schoolwide professional learning goals.	

2.3 Create support systems and structures

Level 1	Level 2	Level 3	Level 4	Level 5	Level 6
Desired outcome 2.3.3: Contributes to the development and maintenance of a collaborative culture.					
• Develops and applies research-based knowledge and skills about collaborative cultures to support schoolwide learning and collaborative work. • Models collaboration in interactions with staff, students, parents, community members, and system leaders. • Assesses, with principal and colleagues, the culture to make improvements. • Contributes to the development of the social architecture of a collaborative culture that includes norms for individual, team, and schoolwide interactions; high expectations; collective responsibility; mutual respect; and relational trust. • Identifies and addresses, with principal and staff, assumptions and barriers to collaboration.	• Develops and applies research-based knowledge and skills about collaborative cultures to support schoolwide learning and collaborative work. • Models collaboration in interactions with colleagues, principal, and other school leaders. • Assesses, with principal, the culture to make improvements. • Contributes to the development of the social architecture of a collaborative culture that includes norms for individual, team, and schoolwide interactions; high expectations; collective responsibility; mutual respect; and relational trust.	• Models collaboration in interactions with colleagues, principal, and other school leaders. • Assesses, with principal, the culture to make improvements. • Contributes to the development of the social architecture of a collaborative culture that includes norms for individual, team, and schoolwide interactions; high expectations; and mutual respect.	• Models collaboration in interactions with colleagues, principal, and other school leaders. • Assesses, with principal, the culture to make improvements.	• Accepts the current school culture without making efforts to improve it.	

3.1 Prioritize human, fiscal, material, technology, and time resources

Desired outcome 3.1.1: Defines resources for professional learning.

Level 1	Level 2	Level 3	Level 4	Level 5	Level 6
• Works, with principal and colleagues, to develop a shared definition of resources for professional learning. • Identifies resources for professional learning that include staff, materials, technology, funding, and time.	• Works, with principal, to develop a shared definition of resources for professional learning. • Identifies resources for professional learning that include staff, materials, technology, funding, and time.	• Identifies resources for professional learning that include materials, technology, funding, and time.	• Identifies resources for professional learning that include funding and time.	• Identifies funding as the only resource for professional learning.	• Fails to define resources for professional learning.

3.1 Prioritize human, fiscal, material, technology, and time resources

Desired outcome 3.1.2: Recommends resources to align professional learning with high-priority student and educator learning needs.

Level 1	Level 2	Level 3	Level 4	Level 5	Level 6
• Establishes, with principal and colleagues, criteria for resource allocation for professional learning based on high-priority student learning needs and individual, team, and schoolwide educator learning needs. • Uses consensus to prioritize learning needs in collaboration with principal and staff. • Recommends resources for professional learning to achieve high-priority student and educator learning goals. • Projects and plans for strategic use of resources over multiple years to achieve professional learning goals. • Addresses inequities in student and educator learning through realignment of resources.	• Establishes, with principal, criteria for resource allocation for professional learning based on high-priority student learning needs and individual, team, and schoolwide educator learning needs. • Uses consensus to prioritize learning needs in collaboration with principal. • Recommends resources for professional learning to achieve high-priority student and educator learning goals. • Plans for strategic use of resources over multiple years to achieve professional learning goals. • Addresses inequities in student and educator learning through realignment of resources.	• Establishes criteria for resource allocation for professional learning based on high-priority student learning needs and schoolwide educator learning needs. • Prioritizes learning needs. • Recommends resources for professional learning to achieve high-priority student and educator learning goals.	• Recommends distribution of available resources for professional learning based on individual educator requests.	• Fails to recommend resources for professional learning.	

3.1 Prioritize human, fiscal, material, technology, and time resources

Desired outcome 3.1.3: Allocates time for collaborative professional learning.

Level 1	Level 2	Level 3	Level 4	Level 5	Level 6
• Creates, with principal and colleagues, a daily schedule for learning teams to meet during the school day at least three times per week. • Creates, with principal and staff, an annual schedule for individual, team, and schoolwide professional learning.	• Creates, with principal, a daily schedule for learning teams to meet during the school day at least weekly. • Creates, with principal, an annual schedule for individual, team, and schoolwide professional learning.	• Recommends a daily schedule for learning teams to meet during the school day at least monthly. • Recommends an annual schedule for individual, team, and schoolwide professional learning.	• Recommends a daily schedule for learning teams to meet outside the school day at least monthly. • Recommends an annual schedule for individual, team, and schoolwide professional learning.	• Recommends an annual schedule with days set aside for teams to engage in professional learning.	• Fails to allocate time for professional learning.

3.1 Prioritize human, fiscal, material, technology, and time resources

Desired outcome 3.1.4: Recommends resources to support implementation of professional learning.

Level 1	Level 2	Level 3	Level 4	Level 5	Level 6
• Recognizes the need for long-term investment of resources for full implementation of professional learning. • Provides, with principal and colleagues, sufficient resources over multiple years to support full implementation of professional learning. • Sustains, with principal and colleagues, resources for support until full implementation of professional learning occurs. • Provides with principal and colleagues, resources for differentiated support to all staff for full implementation. • Preserves, with principal and colleagues, time for coaches, other learning facilitators, and peers to work with individuals and teams to support implementation of professional learning.	• Recognizes the need for long-term investment of resources for full implementation of professional learning. • Provides, with principal and colleagues, sufficient resources over multiple years to support full implementation of professional learning. • Sustains, with principal, resources for support until full implementation of professional learning occurs. • Provides, with principal, resources for differentiated support to all staff for full implementation. • Preserves, with principal, time for coaches and other learning facilitators to work with individuals and teams to support implementation of professional learning.	• Recommends sufficient resources over multiple years to support full implementation of professional learning. • Plans for resources for differentiated support to all staff for full implementation of professional learning.	• Recommends resources to support implementation of professional learning for one year.	• Fails to recommend resources to support implementation of professional learning.	

www.learningforward.org   800-727-7288

3.2 Monitor resources

	Level 1	Level 2	Level 3	Level 4	Level 5	Level 6
Desired outcome 3.2.1: Monitors effectiveness of the use of resources for professional learning.	• Establishes, with principal and colleagues, a comprehensive system to track and monitor resources associated with professional learning to ensure equitable distribution of all resources. • Reviews data from quarterly tracking of professional learning resources. • Uses, with principal and colleagues, data from tracking and monitoring quarterly to analyze the effectiveness of resource use and make needed adjustments. • Challenges decisions to divert resources for professional learning to other areas. • Shares responsibility for decisions to redirect resources for professional learning to other areas.	• Establishes a comprehensive system to track and monitor resources associated with professional learning to ensure equitable distribution of all resources. • Reviews data from quarterly tracking of professional learning resources. • Uses, with principal, data from tracking and monitoring quarterly to analyze the effectiveness of resource use and make needed adjustments. • Shares responsibility for decisions to redirect resources for professional learning to other areas.	• Reviews semiannually funding, time, materials, staff, and technology for professional learning. • Uses data from tracking and monitoring semiannually to analyze the effectiveness of resource use and make needed adjustments.	• Reviews annually funding and time for professional learning. • Uses data from tracking and monitoring annually to analyze the effectiveness of resource use and make needed adjustments.	• Reviews funding for professional learning.	• Fails to monitor and/or track resources for professional learning.

3.3 Coordinate resources

Level 1	Level 2	Level 3	Level 4	Level 5	Level 6
Desired outcome 3.3.1: Designs and implements a comprehensive resource plan for professional learning.					
• Analyzes, with principal and colleagues, all possible resources to identify those that can be reallocated for professional learning.	• Analyzes, with principal and colleagues, all possible resources to identify those that can be reallocated for professional learning.	• Contributes to the development of a multi-year resource plan for professional learning based on high-priority needs for student and educator learning.	• Contributes to the development of a multi-year resource plan for professional learning based on high-priority needs for student and educator learning.	• Shares the annual budget for professional learning.	• Fails to develop and implement a resource plan for professional learning.
• Analyzes, with principal, multiple programs, initiatives, improvement efforts, and grants to identify their commonalities with the school's high-priority goals and opportunities to repurpose resources for high-priority professional learning needs.	• Recommends opportunities to repurpose resources for high-priority professional learning needs.	• Supports the implementation of the professional learning resource plan to achieve high-priority student and educator learning goals.			
• Seeks and uses, with colleagues and principal, external resources for professional learning to enhance existing resources to achieve student learning goals.	• Seeks and uses, in collaboration with principal, external resources for professional learning to enhance existing resources to achieve student learning goals.	• Uses resources with consideration of equitable allocation to meet high-priority learning needs for colleagues and students.			
• Develops and builds, with colleagues, principal, and others, consensus about a multiyear resource plan for professional learning based on high-priority needs for student and educator learning.	• Contributes to the development of a multi-year resource plan for professional learning based on high-priority needs for student and educator learning.	• Shares resources with colleagues to increase their effectiveness.			
• Explains to colleagues and others, using data and research, the rationale for the resource allocations in professional learning.	• Explains to colleagues and others the rationale for the resource allocations in professional learning.				
continued…	*continued…*				

www.learningforward.org   800-727-7288

3.3 Coordinate resources

Desired outcome 3.3.1: Designs and implements a comprehensive resource plan for professional learning.

Level 1	Level 2	Level 3	Level 4	Level 5	Level 6
continued… • Supports the implementation of the professional learning resource plan to achieve high-priority student and educator learning goals. • Uses resources with consideration of equitable allocation to meet high-priority learning needs for colleagues and students. • Shares resources with colleagues to increase their effectiveness. • Serves as a resource for staff.	*continued…* • Supports the implementation of the professional learning resource plan to achieve high-priority student and educator learning goals. • Uses resources with consideration of equitable allocation to meet high-priority learning needs for colleagues and students. • Shares resources with colleagues to increase their effectiveness.				

4.1 Analyze student, educator, and system data

Level 1	Level 2	Level 3	Level 4	Level 5	Level 6
Desired outcome 4.1.1: Develops own and colleagues' capacity to analyze and interpret data.					
• Develops own and colleagues' knowledge and skills to access, organize, and display data. • Develops own and colleagues' knowledge and skills to analyze and interpret data from multiple sources to make schoolwide decisions about professional learning.	• Develops own knowledge and skills to access, organize, and display data. • Develops own knowledge and skills to conduct data analysis and interpretation, using multiple sources, to make schoolwide decisions about professional learning.	• Develops own knowledge and skills to access, organize, and display data.	• Fails to develop own or colleagues' knowledge and skills to analyze and interpret data.		
Desired outcome 4.1.2: Analyzes and interprets multiple sources of student data to determine professional learning needs.					
• Analyzes, with colleagues, qualitative and quantitative student data from four or more sources to make predictions, observations, and inferences about the data. • Interprets, with colleagues, qualitative and quantitative student data from four or more sources in to decipher trends, patterns, outliers, and root causes within the data. • Supports colleagues to independently identify findings, trends, patterns, outliers, and root causes from four or more sources of student data.	• Analyzes, with colleagues, qualitative and quantitative student data from three sources to make predictions, observations, and inferences about the data. • Interprets, with colleagues, qualitative and quantitative student data from three sources to decipher trends, patterns, outliers, and root causes within the data.	• Analyzes, with colleagues, qualitative and quantitative student data from two sources to make predictions, observations, and inferences about the data. • Interprets, with colleagues, qualitative and quantitative student data from two sources to decipher trends, patterns, outliers, and root causes within the data.	• Analyzes one source of student data.	• Presents the analysis of schoolwide student data to staff.	• Fails to analyze student data to determine needs for professional learning.

4.1 Analyze student, educator, and system data

Desired outcome 4.1.3: Analyzes and interprets multiple sources of educator data to determine professional learning needs.

Level 1	Level 2	Level 3	Level 4	Level 5	Level 6
• Analyzes, with colleagues, qualitative and quantitative educator data from four or more sources to make predictions, observations, and inferences about the data. • Interprets, with colleagues, qualitative and quantitative educator data from four or more sources to decipher trends, patterns, outliers, and root causes within the data. • Supports colleagues to independently identify findings, trends, patterns, outliers, and root causes from four or more sources of educator data.	• Analyzes, with colleagues, qualitative and quantitative educator data from three sources to make predictions, observations, and inferences about the data. • Interprets, with colleagues, qualitative and quantitative educator data from three sources to decipher trends, patterns, outliers, and root causes within the data.	• Analyzes, with colleagues, qualitative and quantitative educator data from two sources to make predictions, observations, and inferences about the data. • Interprets, with colleagues, qualitative and quantitative educator data from two sources to decipher trends, patterns, outliers, and root causes within the data.	• Analyzes one source of educator data.	• Presents the results of educator data analysis to teachers.	• Fails to analyze educator data to determine needs for professional learning.

4.1 Analyze student, educator, and system data

Level 1	Level 2	Level 3	Level 4	Level 5	Level 6
Desired outcome 4.1.4: Analyzes and interprets multiple sources of school data to determine professional learning needs.					
• Analyzes, with colleagues, qualitative and quantitative school data from four or more sources to make predictions, observations, and inferences about the data. • Interprets, with colleagues, qualitative and quantitative school data from four or more sources to decipher trends, patterns, outliers, and root causes within the data. • Supports colleagues to independently identify findings, trends, patterns, outliers, and root causes from four or more sources of school data.	• Analyzes, with colleagues, qualitative and quantitative school data from three sources to make predictions, observations, and inferences about the data. • Interprets, with colleagues, qualitative and quantitative school data from three sources to decipher trends, patterns, outliers, and root causes within the data.	• Analyzes, with colleagues, qualitative and quantitative school data from two sources to make predictions, observations, and inferences about the data. • Interprets, with colleagues, qualitative and quantitative school data from two sources to decipher trends, patterns, outliers, and root causes within the data.	• Analyzes one source of school data.	• Identifies needs for professional learning without reference to school data.	• Fails to analyze school data to determine needs for professional learning.
Desired outcome 4.1.5: Uses analyzed data to determine professional learning needs.					
• Uses, with colleagues, analyzed data to identify needs for schoolwide professional learning. • Determines, with colleagues, root causes of identified needs.	• Uses analyzed data to identify needs for schoolwide professional learning. • Infers, with colleagues, root causes of identified needs.	• Identifies needs for schoolwide professional learning.	• Fails to use student, educator, or school data to identify needs for schoolwide professional learning.		

4.2 Assess progress

Desired outcome 4.2.1: Determines formative data to assess progress toward professional learning benchmarks and goals.

Level 1	Level 2	Level 3	Level 4	Level 5	Level 6
• Establishes, with principal and colleagues, a systematic process for reviewing progress toward goals for schoolwide professional learning. • Establishes monthly, with principal and colleagues, benchmarks to measure progress toward schoolwide professional learning goals. • Establishes monthly, with principal and colleagues, qualitative and quantitative formative data to measure progress toward schoolwide benchmarks and goals.	• Establishes, with principal, a systematic process for reviewing progress toward goals for schoolwide professional learning. • Establishes quarterly, with principal, benchmarks to measure progress toward for schoolwide professional learning goals. • Identifies quarterly with principal, qualitative and quantitative formative data to measure progress toward schoolwide benchmarks and goals.	• Establishes benchmarks to measure progress toward goals for schoolwide professional learning. • Identifies semiannually either qualitative or quantitative formative data to measure progress toward school-wide professional learning benchmarks and goals.	• Identifies annually either qualitative or quantitative data to measure progress toward professional learning benchmarks and goals.	• Fails to identify data to measure progress toward professional learning benchmarks and goals.	

4.2 Assess progress

Level 1	Level 2	Level 3	Level 4	Level 5	Level 6
Desired outcome 4.2.2: Collects, analyzes, and uses formative data to continuously assess progress toward professional learning benchmarks and goals.					
• Collects, with principal and colleagues, monthly formative data to assess progress toward school-wide professional learning benchmarks and goals. • Analyzes, with principal and colleagues, quarterly formative data to assess progress toward school-wide professional learning benchmarks and goals. • Formulates, in collaboration with principal and colleagues, conclusions about progress toward school-wide professional learning benchmarks and goals.	• Collects, with principal, quarterly formative data to assess progress toward schoolwide professional learning benchmarks and goals. • Analyzes quarterly formative data to assess progress toward school-wide professional learning benchmarks and goals. • Formulates, with principal, conclusions about progress toward schoolwide professional learning benchmarks and goals.	• Collects semiannually formative data to assess progress toward professional learning schoolwide professional learning benchmarks and goals. • Analyzes quarterly formative data to assess progress toward school-wide professional learning benchmarks and goals.	• Collects annually formative data to assess progress toward school-wide professional learning benchmarks and goals.	• Fails to collect and analyze formative data to assess progress toward schoolwide professional learning benchmarks and goals.	

www.learningforward.org   800-727-7288

4.2 Assess progress

Desired outcome 4.2.3: Uses analysis of progress to make adjustments in professional learning.

Level 1	Level 2	Level 3	Level 4	Level 5	Level 6
• Interprets, with principal and colleagues, quarterly analyzed data to identify enhancers of and barriers to progress.	• Interprets, with principal, quarterly analyzed data to identify enhancers of and barriers to progress.	• Interprets quarterly analyzed data to identify enhancers of and barriers to progress.	• Interprets quarterly analyzed data to identify barriers to progress.	• Fails to use analysis of progress to make needed adjustments in professional learning.	
• Solves, with principal and colleagues, problems that create barriers to achieving professional learning benchmarks and goals.	• Solves, with principal, problems that create barriers to achieving professional learning goals.	• Solves problems that create barriers to achieving professional learning goals.			
• Makes, with principal and colleagues, in-process, data-based adjustments in schoolwide professional learning (i.e. learning designs, coaching, and other support systems).	• Makes, with principal, in-process, data-based adjustments in schoolwide professional learning (i.e., learning designs, coaching, and other support systems).	• Makes in-process, data-based adjustments in individual, team, and schoolwide professional learning (i.e., learning designs, coaching, and other support systems).			
• Assists individuals and teams to use formative data to make adjustments to learning designs, coaching activities, and timeframes.	• Celebrates, with principal, progress toward individual, team, and schoolwide professional learning goals.				
• Celebrates, with principal and staff, progress toward individual, team, and schoolwide professional learning benchmarks and goals.					

4.3 Evaluate professional learning

Level 1	Level 2	Level 3	Level 4	Level 5	Level 6
Desired outcome 4.3.1: Contributes to the development of an evaluation plan for professional learning.					
• Develops, with principal and staff, a comprehensive evaluation plan for school-wide professional learning. • Adopts a theory of action detailing the relationship between professional learning and goals for student learning and educator performance. • Develops, with principal and colleagues, a comprehensive evaluation framework (i.ethat specifies SMART goal(s), multiple data sources, data collection methodology, data analysis, interpretation, and dissemination of results to various audiences through various means.	• Develops, with principal, a comprehensive evaluation plan for professional learning. • Develops, with principal, an evaluation framework that specifies SMART goal(s), multiple data sources, data collection methodology, data analysis, interpretation, and dissemination of results to various audiences through various means.	• Develops an evaluation framework that specifies SMART goal(s), multiple data sources, data collection methodology, data analysis, interpretation, and dissemination of results.	• Develops an evaluation framework that specifies SMART goal(s), data sources, data collection methodology, and data analysis.	• Fails to develop a comprehensive school-wide plan to evaluate professional learning.	

4.3 Evaluate professional learning

Desired outcome 4.3.2: Uses a variety of formative and summative data to evaluate the effectiveness and results of professional learning.

Level 1	Level 2	Level 3	Level 4	Level 5	Level 6
• Collects, with principal and colleagues, student data to measure changes in student learning and behaviors associated with professional learning. • Collects, with principal and colleagues, educator data to assess changes in knowledge, skills, dispositions, and practices associated with professional learning. • Collects, with principal and colleagues, school data to assess changes in school culture and organizational structures, policies, and processes associated with professional learning. • Collects reflections from colleagues on the effectiveness of various learning designs used. • Analyzes and interprets, with principal and colleagues, collected data to form conclusions about the effectiveness and results of professional learning.	• Collects, with principal, student data to measure changes in student learning and behaviors associated with professional learning. • Collects, with principal, educator data to assess changes in knowledge, skills, dispositions, and practices associated with professional learning. • Collects, with principal, school data to assess changes in school culture and organizational structures, policies, and processes associated with professional learning. • Analyzes and interprets, with principal, collected data to form conclusions about the effectiveness and results of professional learning.	• Collects student data to measure changes in student learning and behaviors associated with professional learning. • Collects, with colleagues, educator data to assess changes in knowledge, skills, dispositions, and practices associated with professional learning. • Analyzes collected data to form conclusions about the effectiveness and results of professional learning.	• Collects student data to measure changes in student learning and behaviors associated with professional learning.	• Fails to evaluate the effectiveness and results of schoolwide professional learning.	

4.3 Evaluate professional learning

Desired outcome 4.3.3: Supports colleagues in using data to evaluate the effectiveness of schoolwide learning designs, content, and duration.

Level 1	Level 2	Level 3	Level 4	Level 5	Level 6
• Establishes, with principal and colleagues, a regular time for team reflection about attainment of schoolwide professional learning goals. • Facilitates colleagues to analyze and interpret data about schoolwide collaboration, learning, and results. • Facilitates colleagues to form conclusions about the design, content, and duration of schoolwide professional learning.	• Facilitates colleagues to analyze and interpret data about schoolwide collaboration, learning, and results. • Facilitates colleagues to form conclusions about the design, content, and duration of schoolwide professional learning.	• Facilitates colleagues to analyze and interpret data about schoolwide collaboration, learning, and results. • Facilitates colleagues to form conclusions about the design, content, and duration of schoolwide professional learning.	• Identifies data to evaluate the effectiveness of schoolwide learning designs to develop colleagues' knowledge and skills.	• Fails to support colleagues to evaluate the effectiveness of schoolwide professional learning designs, content, and duration.	

4.3 Evaluate professional learning

Desired outcome 4.3.4: Uses evaluation results to improve schoolwide professional learning.

Level 1	Level 2	Level 3	Level 4	Level 5	Level 6
• Uses, with principal and colleagues, evaluation results (i.e., changes in educator practice, student learning, and school culture and practices) to identify strengths and improvements in school-wide professional learning. • Uses evaluation results to identify design elements of professional learning that have a significant impact on teacher practices and student learning. • Applies conclusions to future planning cycles for schoolwide professional learning.	• Uses, with principal, evaluation results (i.e., changes in educator practice, student learning, and school culture and practices) to identify strengths and improvements in schoolwide professional learning. • Uses evaluation results to identify design elements of professional learning that have a significant impact on teacher practices and student learning. • Applies conclusions to future planning cycles for schoolwide professional learning.	• Uses, with principal, evaluation results (i.e., changes in educator practice, student learning, and school culture and practices) to identify strengths and improvements in schoolwide professional learning.	• Uses evaluation results (i.e., changes in educator practice, student learning, and school culture and practices) to identify strengths and improvements in schoolwide professional learning.	• Fails to use evaluation results to improve schoolwide professional learning.	

5.1 Apply learning theories, research, and models

	Level 1	Level 2	Level 3	Level 4	Level 5	Level 6
Desired outcome 5.1.1: Develops and shares a knowledge base about theories, research, and models of adult learning.	• Studies, with principal and colleagues, research, theories, and models of adult learning. • Engages others in developing knowledge and skills related to research, theories, and models of adult learning. • Contributes to a collection of resources on educator learning for personal, individual, team, and whole staff use.	• Studies, with principal, research, theories, and models of adult learning. • Engages others in developing knowledge and skills related to research, theories, and models of adult learning.	• Studies research, theories, and models of adult learning.	• Reads periodically resources about research, theories, and models related to educator learning.	• Accesses resources about educator learning.	• Fails to add to own or others' knowledge base about learning theories, research, and models.
Desired outcome 5.1.2: Acquires and shares knowledge about multiple designs for professional learning. *	• Develops, with colleagues and principal, knowledge about, skills to facilitate, and expertise to implement 12 or more learning designs. • Identifies and discusses essential features of high-quality learning designs (e.g., active engagement, reflection, metacognition, ongoing support, formative assessment). • Shares knowledge, skills, and practices associated with 12 learning designs with coaches, other learning facilitators, and colleagues.	• Develops, with principal, the knowledge about, skills to facilitate, and expertise to implement 10 learning designs. • Identifies and discusses essential features of high-quality learning designs (e.g., active engagement, reflection, metacognition, ongoing support, formative assessment). • Shares knowledge, skills, and practices associated with 10 learning designs with coaches, other learning facilitators, and colleagues.	• Develops knowledge about, skills to facilitate, and expertise to implement eight learning designs. • Identifies and discusses essential features of high-quality learning designs (e.g., active engagement, reflection, metacognition, ongoing support, formative assessment). • Shares knowledge, skills, and practices associated with eight learning designs with coaches, other learning facilitators, and colleagues.	• Develops knowledge about, skills to facilitate, and expertise to implement at least five learning designs.	• Develops knowledge about, skills to facilitate, and expertise to implement fewer than five learning designs.	• Fails to develop knowledge about multiple designs for professional learning.

*See the Appendix (p. 262) for an explanation of this concept.

5.2 Select learning designs

	Level 1	Level 2	Level 3	Level 4	Level 5	Level 6
Desired outcome 5.2.1: Acquires and shares knowledge about the multiple factors influencing the selection of learning designs. *	• Clarifies, with principal and colleagues, the learning outcomes, including knowledge, skills, dispositions, and practices, expected as a result of schoolwide professional learning. • Develops knowledge about factors that influence how adults learn. • Identifies, with principal and colleagues, factors that emerged from analyzed educator and school data to consider in selecting the learning designs. • Supports principal, colleagues, coaches, and other learning facilitators to prioritize the factors, influencing the selection of learning designs.	• Clarifies, with principal and colleagues, the learning outcomes, including knowledge, skills, dispositions, and practices, expected as a result of schoolwide professional learning. • Develops knowledge about factors that influence how adults learn. • Identifies, with principal and colleagues, factors that emerged from analyzed educator and school data to consider in selecting the learning designs.	• Acquires knowledge about factors that influence how adults learn. • Identifies, with principal and colleagues, factors that emerged from analyzed educator and school data to consider in selecting the learning designs.	• Acquires knowledge about factors that influence how adults learn.	• Fails to acquire knowledge about multiple factors influencing the selection of learning designs.	

*See the Appendix (p. 262) for an explanation of this concept.

5.2 Select learning designs

Level 1	Level 2	Level 3	Level 4	Level 5	Level 6
Desired outcome 5.2.2: Applies knowledge about the selection of appropriate learning designs.					
• Confirms the presence of essential features of high-quality learning designs (e.g., active engagement, reflection, metacognition, ongoing support, etc.) in schoolwide professional learning. • Supports colleagues to select appropriate individual and team learning designs.	• Identifies and discusses essential features of high-quality learning designs (e.g., active engagement, reflection, metacognition, ongoing support, etc.) in schoolwide professional learning. • Supports colleagues to select appropriate team learning designs.	• Selects, with principal, learning designs that align with expected outcomes and influencing factors.	• Selects, with principal, learning designs for schoolwide professional learning that align with expected outcomes.	• Fails to select appropriate learning designs for schoolwide professional learning.	
Desired outcome 5.2.3: Develops and shares knowledge about technology-enhanced learning designs.					
• Develops, with colleagues, knowledge about available and emerging technology-enhanced learning designs. • Shares knowledge about technology-enhanced learning designs with colleagues. • Identifies and shares with colleagues benefits and limitations of technology-enhanced learning designs. • Establishes and applies, with principal and colleagues, criteria for selecting technology-enhanced professional learning designs.	• Develops, with colleagues, knowledge about available technology-enhanced learning designs. • Shares knowledge about technology-enhanced learning designs with colleagues. • Identifies the benefits and limitations of technology-enhanced learning designs. • Establishes and applies criteria for selecting technology-enhanced professional learning designs.	• Identifies the benefits and limitations of technology-enhanced learning designs. • Establishes and applies criteria for selecting technology-enhanced professional learning designs.	• Identifies available technology-enhanced learning designs for schoolwide professional learning.	• Fails to develop or share knowledge about how technology contributes to professional learning.	

5.2 Select learning designs

Desired outcome 5.2.4: Implements appropriate learning designs.

Level 1	Level 2	Level 3	Level 4	Level 5	Level 6
• Models appropriate in-person, blended, and online learning designs during meetings and schoolwide and SLT professional learning. • Supports colleagues to implement appropriate in-person, blended, and online learning designs. • Analyzes, with principal, the relationship between learning designs used and results achieved.	• Models appropriate in-person, blended, and online learning designs during meetings and schoolwide and SLT professional learning. • Recommends that learning teams use appropriate in-person, blended, and online learning designs.	• Models appropriate in-person, blended, and online learning designs during schoolwide meetings and professional learning.	• Uses same learning design for schoolwide professional learning.	• Fails to implement appropriate learning designs for schoolwide professional learning.	

5.3 Promote active engagement

Desired outcome 5.3.1: Models active engagement in professional learning.

Level 1	Level 2	Level 3	Level 4	Level 5	Level 6
• Engages actively in team and schoolwide professional learning. • Elicits colleagues' participation in and contribution to discussions in individual, team, and schoolwide professional learning. • Models and shares strategies and protocols for active engagement in individual, team, and schoolwide professional learning. • Assesses, with colleagues, the effectiveness and frequency of active engagement to make improvements.	• Engages actively in team and schoolwide professional learning. • Elicits colleagues' participation in and contribution to discussions in team and schoolwide professional learning. • Models strategies and protocols for active engagement in individual, team, and schoolwide professional learning.	• Engages actively in team and schoolwide professional learning. • Elicits colleagues' participation in and contribution to discussions in team and schoolwide professional learning.	• Engages actively in team and schoolwide professional learning.	• Fails to model and promote active engagement in schoolwide professional learning.	

5.3 Promote active engagement

Desired outcome 5.3.2: Supports colleagues to engage actively in professional learning.

Level 1	Level 2	Level 3	Level 4	Level 5	Level 6
• Establishes an expectation that colleagues participate actively in individual, team, and schoolwide professional learning. • Recommends to and supports colleagues to use active engagement strategies and protocols in individual, team, and schoolwide professional learning. • Supports colleagues in holding each other accountable for active participation in professional learning.	• Establishes an expectation that colleagues participate actively in team and schoolwide professional learning. • Recommends to and supports colleagues to use active engagement strategies and protocols in schoolwide professional learning. • Supports colleagues in holding each other accountable for active participation in professional learning.	• Establishes an expectation that colleagues participate actively in schoolwide professional learning. • Recommends to colleagues active engagement strategies and protocols. • Supports colleagues in holding each other accountable for active participation in professional learning.	• Communicates the expectation that schoolwide professional learning integrates active engagement strategies and protocols.	• Fails to support active engagement strategies in professional learning.	

6.1 Apply change research

Desired outcome 6.1.1: Develops capacity to apply research on change to support implementation of professional learning. *

Level 1	Level 2	Level 3	Level 4	Level 5	Level 6
• Reviews research and examples of exemplary practices about change (IC maps, SoC, LoU, RPLIM, PDSA, etc.) to develop own understanding of and skills needed to lead the change process. • Discusses, with colleagues, information to increase own and others' understanding of and skills needed to lead and participate in the change process. • Participates in, with colleagues, additional professional learning about the change process to address opportunities and problems of practice.	• Reviews research and examples of exemplary practices about change (IC maps, SoC, LoU, RPLIM, PDSA, etc.) to develop own understanding of and skills needed to lead the change process. • Discusses, with colleagues, information to increase their understanding of the change process. • Participates in, with colleagues, additional professional learning about the change process to address opportunities and problems of practice.	• Reviews research and examples of exemplary practices about change (IC maps, SoC, LoU, RPLIM, PDSA, etc.) to develop own understanding of and skills needed to lead the change process. • Discusses, with colleagues, research and exemplary practices on change to support schoolwide change efforts.	• Reads articles, papers, and reports about the change process.	• Fails to engage in ongoing professional learning about the change process.	

*See the Appendix (p. 262) for an explanation of this concept.

6.1 Apply change research

Level 1	Level 2	Level 3	Level 4	Level 5	Level 6
Desired outcome 6.1.2: Applies research on change to plan and lead the implementation of professional learning.					
• Uses, with principal and colleagues, change research, to inform decisions about implementation. • Adopts patience and perseverance to support others throughout the change process. • Interacts with colleagues daily to assess and respond to concerns related to implementation. • Recognizes privately colleagues' implementation efforts and accomplishments.	• Uses, with principal, change research, to inform decisions about implementation. • Adopts patience and perseverance to support others throughout the change process. • Interacts with colleagues weekly to assess and respond to concerns related to implementation. • Recognizes privately colleagues' implementation efforts and accomplishments.	• Uses change research to inform decisions about implementation. • Interacts with colleagues monthly to assess concerns related to implementation. • Recognizes schoolwide efforts and accomplishments in implementation.	• Uses change research to make decisions about implementation.	• Fails to apply change research to plans and actions to support implementation of professional learning.	
Desired outcome 6.1.3: Monitors implementation of professional learning.					
• Develops, with principal and colleagues, guides/tools (e.g., IC maps) to clarify expectations for implementation. • Uses guides/tools to support colleagues' implementation of professional learning. • Meets with principal and colleagues to use guides/tools to assess and refine implementation.	• Develops, with principal and colleagues, guides/tools (e.g., IC maps) to clarify expectations for implementation. • Uses guides/tools to support colleagues' implementation of professional learning. • Meets with principal to use guides/tools to assess and refine implementation.	• Uses guides/tools to monitor progress on implementation.	• States expectation for implementing professional learning.	• Fails to monitor implementation of professional learning.	

6.2 Sustain implementation

Desired outcome 6.2.1: Differentiates support for implementation of professional learning.

Level 1	Level 2	Level 3	Level 4	Level 5	Level 6
• Demonstrates belief in colleagues' ability and willingness to be effective educators. • Embeds differentiated support for implementation into the plan for professional learning. • Uses the Standards for Professional Learning to guide the design and facilitation of ongoing professional learning to deepen understanding, enhance implementation, and refine practice. • Gathers data from colleagues about support needed for full implementation. • Designs and provides differentiated, ongoing professional learning to accelerate and refine implementation based on data gathered. • Employs multiple types of support to address each individual staff member's areas of need related to implementation. • Employs a variety of technology-enhanced implementation supports.	• Embeds differentiated support for implementation into the plan for professional learning. • Uses the Standards for Professional Learning to guide the design and facilitation of ongoing professional learning to deepen understanding, enhance implementation, and refine practice. • Designs and provides differentiated, ongoing professional learning to accelerate and refine implementation based on data gathered. • Employs multiple types of support to address each individual staff member's areas of need related to implementation. • Employs technology-enhanced implementation support.	• Embeds support for implementation of professional learning to achieve schoolwide goals. • Uses the Standards for Professional Learning to guide the design and facilitation of ongoing professional learning to deepen understanding, enhance implementation, and refine practice. • Designs and provides ongoing professional learning.	• Provides implementation support to colleagues when requested.	• Provides implementation support to colleagues when requested.	• Fails to provide differentiated support for implementation.

www.learningforward.org   800-727-7288

6.2 Sustain implementation

Desired outcome 6.2.2: Continues support to reach high-fidelity implementation of professional learning.

Level 1	Level 2	Level 3	Level 4	Level 5	Level 6
• Plans, with principal and colleagues, continuous support for implementation of professional learning for three to five years. • Adjusts, with principal and colleagues, support for implementation of professional learning with the maturity and fidelity of implementation. • Facilitates, with principal and colleagues, easy access to in-person, blended, and technology-enhanced support that individuals, teams, and whole staff can access daily. • Communicates, with principal, expectations that individuals, teams, and whole staff will access support at least weekly to refine and improve implementation.	• Plans, with principal, support for implementation of professional learning for two years. • Adjusts, with principal, support for implementation of professional learning with the maturity and fidelity of implementation. • Facilitates, with principal, easy access to in-person, blended, and technology-enhanced support for implementation that colleagues can access weekly. • Recommends that individuals, teams, and whole staff will access support at least biweekly to refine and improve implementation.	• Plans ongoing support for one year for implementation of professional learning. • Facilitates easy access to in-person, blended, and technology-enhanced support that whole staff can access monthly. • Recommends that individuals, teams, and whole staff will access support at least monthly to refine and improve implementation.	• Plans occasional support for implementation of professional learning. • Facilitates access to support for implementation.	• Facilitates access to support for implementation.	• Fails to provide support for implementation of professional learning.

6.3 Provide constructive feedback

Level 1	Level 2	Level 3	Level 4	Level 5	Level 6
Desired outcome 6.3.1: Develops own and staff's capacity to give and receive constructive feedback.					
• Develops, with colleagues and principal, research-based knowledge and skills to give and receive constructive feedback. • Develops, with principal, colleagues' knowledge and skills to give constructive feedback. • Facilitates, with principal, risk-free opportunities for individuals, teams, and whole staff to practice giving and receiving feedback. • Models giving and receiving constructive feedback. • Provides to and seeks from individuals, teams, and whole staff feedback on use of constructive feedback.	• Develops, with principal, research-based knowledge and skills to give and receive constructive feedback. • Develops, in collaboration with principal, colleagues' knowledge and skills to give constructive feedback. • Models giving and receiving constructive feedback. • Provides to and seeks from whole staff feedback on use of constructive feedback.	• Develops knowledge and skills to give and receive constructive feedback. • Models giving and receiving constructive feedback.	• Develops knowledge and skills to give and receive constructive feedback.	• Fails to develop own and colleagues' knowledge and skills to give and receive constructive feedback.	

6.3 Provide constructive feedback

Desired outcome 6.3.2: Gives and receives constructive feedback to accelerate and refine implementation of professional learning.

Level 1	Level 2	Level 3	Level 4	Level 5	Level 6
• Provides to and seeks from individuals, teams, and whole staff constructive feedback on implementation weekly. • Identifies and makes available, with principal and colleagues, multiple in-person, blended, and technology-based strategies and tools (e.g., peer coaching, reviewing student work, lesson study, instructional rounds, walk-throughs, peer observation, e-coaching, etc.) to give and receive feedback on implementation. • Analyzes and shares, with principal and colleagues, feedback data monthly about implementation to improve individual, team, and schoolwide support.	• Provides to and seeks from individuals, teams, and whole staff constructive feedback on implementation monthly. • Identifies and makes available, with principal and colleagues, and other learning facilitators, multiple in-person, blended, and technology-based strategies and tools (e.g., peer coaching, reviewing student work, lesson study, instructional rounds, walk-throughs, peer observation, e-coaching, etc.) to give and receive feedback on implementation. • Analyzes and shares, with principal and colleagues, feedback data quarterly about implementation to improve individual, team, and schoolwide support.	• Provides to and seeks from individuals, teams, and whole staff constructive feedback on implementation quarterly. • Identifies and makes available, with principal and colleagues, and other learning facilitators, multiple in-person, blended, and technology-based strategies and tools (e.g., peer coaching, reviewing student work, lesson study, instructional rounds, walk-throughs, peer observation, e-coaching, etc.) to give and receive feedback on implementation. • Analyzes and shares, with principal and colleagues, feedback data quarterly about implementation to improve individual, team, and schoolwide support.	• Provides to and seeks from individuals, teams, and whole staff constructive feedback on implementation semiannually. • Analyzes and shares, with principal and colleagues, feedback data semiannually about implementation to improve individual, team, and schoolwide support.	• Provides to and seeks from individuals, teams, and whole staff constructive feedback on implementation annually.	• Fails to seek and provide input on implementation of professional learning.

7.1 Meet performance standards

Level 1	Level 2	Level 3	Level 4	Level 5	Level 6
Desired outcome 7.1.1: Uses educator performance standards to identify professional learning needs.					
• Analyzes, with colleagues, educator performance standards. • Seeks input from colleagues' assessments about strengths and areas for growth based on standards. • Uses reflection on educator performance standards to identify the schoolwide professional learning needs. • Uses the assessment to identify goals for school-wide professional learning.	• Seeks input from colleagues' assessments about strengths and areas for growth. • Uses reflection on educator performance standards to identify the schoolwide professional learning needs. • Reviews the content of schoolwide professional learning for alignment with educator performance standards.	• Collaborates with colleagues about which performance standards to address in schoolwide professional learning.	• Uses educator performance standards to identify schoolwide professional learning needs.	• Identifies needs for schoolwide professional learning based on teacher preference.	• Fails to identify needs for professional learning.
Desired outcome 7.1.2: Uses educator performance standards to make decisions about the content of professional learning.					
• Links areas for growth to educator performance standards to identify knowledge, skills, dispositions, and practices needed to attain school-wide professional learning goals. • Supports individuals and teams in using educator performance standards to identify the content of professional learning. • Monitors the content of schoolwide professional learning for alignment with educator performance standards.	• Reviews educator performance standards to identify knowledge, skills, and practices needed to attain schoolwide goals for professional learning. • Supports teams in using educator performance standards to identify the content of professional learning. • Monitors the content of schoolwide professional learning for alignment with educator performance standards.	• Reviews educator performance standards to identify knowledge and skills needed to attain schoolwide goals for professional learning. • Identifies educator performance standards that become the content for schoolwide professional learning from educator performance standards. • Monitors the content of schoolwide professional learning.	• Identifies educator performance standards that become the content of schoolwide professional learning.	• Identifies content for professional learning based on colleagues' preferences.	• Identifies content for professional learning without reference to educator performance standards.

www.learningforward.org   800-727-7288

7.1 Meet performance standards

	Level 1	Level 2	Level 3	Level 4	Level 5	Level 6
Desired outcome 7.1.3: Engages in professional learning to meet school leadership team performance standards.						
	• Develops research-based knowledge about SLT role expectations, responsibilities, and performance standards. • Engages in professional learning to develop leadership knowledge, skills, dispositions, and practices. • Practices leadership skills until mastery is achieved. • Engages in coaching, feedback, and reflection on own performance.	• Develops knowledge about SLT role expectations, responsibilities, and performance standards. • Engages in professional learning to develop leadership knowledge, skills, dispositions, and practices. • Practices leadership skills until mastery is achieved.	• Studies SLT performance standards. • Engages in professional learning to develop leadership knowledge, skills, practices, and dispositions reflected in performance standards. • Practices leadership skills until mastery is achieved.	• Reads about SLT performance standards.	• Fails to engage in professional learning related to performance standards.	

7.2   Address learning outcomes

Desired outcome 7.2.1: Uses student learning outcomes to identify professional learning needs.

Level 1	Level 2	Level 3	Level 4	Level 5	Level 6
• Collaborates with colleagues to analyze student learning outcomes. • Seeks input from colleagues' assessments about their strengths and areas for growth based on student learning outcomes. • Uses reflection on student learning outcomes to identify schoolwide professional learning needs. • Uses the assessment to identify goals for schoolwide professional learning.	• Seeks input from colleagues' assessments about strengths and areas for growth based on student learning outcomes. • Uses reflection on student learning outcomes to identify schoolwide professional learning needs.	• Seeks input from colleagues about which student learning outcomes they want to address in schoolwide professional learning.	• Uses student learning outcomes to identify schoolwide professional learning needs.	• Uses teacher preferences to identify needs for schoolwide professional learning.	

7.2 Address learning outcomes

	Level 1	Level 2	Level 3	Level 4	Level 5	Level 6
Desired outcome 7.2.2: Uses student learning outcomes to select the content of professional learning.	• Links areas for growth to student learning outcomes to identify knowledge, skills, dispositions, and practices needed to attain schoolwide professional learning goals. • Supports individuals and teams in using student learning outcomes to identify the content of their professional learning. • Monitors the content of schoolwide professional learning for alignment with high-priority student learning outcomes.	• Reviews student learning outcomes to identify knowledge, skills, and practices needed to attain schoolwide goals for professional learning. • Supports teams in using student learning outcomes to identify the content of their professional learning. • Reviews the content of schoolwide professional learning for alignment with high-priority student learning outcomes.	• Reviews student learning outcomes to identify knowledge and skills needed to attain schoolwide goals for professional learning. • Selects student learning outcomes that become the content of schoolwide professional learning. • Reviews the content of schoolwide professional learning.	• Selects student learning outcomes that become the content of schoolwide professional learning.	• Uses colleagues' preferences to select content for professional learning.	• Identifies content for professional learning without reference to student learning outcomes.
Desired outcome 7.2.3: Engages in professional learning to increase student results.	• Engages, with colleagues, in professional learning to develop understanding of the relationship between leadership and student learning. • Engages in coaching, feedback, and reflection to analyze and improve the effects of the SLT's performance on student learning.	• Engages, with colleagues, in professional learning to develop understanding of the relationship between leadership and student learning. • Analyzes the effects of the SLT's performance on student learning.	• Studies effects of leadership on student learning outcomes. • Reflects on the effects of the SLT's performance on student learning.	• Studies effects of leadership on student learning outcomes.	• Fails to engage in professional learning related to leadership and student learning outcomes.	

7.3 Build coherence

Desired outcome 7.3.1: Builds congruence between professional learning and other school and school system initiatives.

Level 1	Level 2	Level 3	Level 4	Level 5	Level 6
• Facilitates conversations among colleagues to develop understanding of the relationships among school and school system processes and initiatives; the school improvement goals; individual, team, and schoolwide professional learning goals; and professional learning. • Emphasizes congruence among multiple initiatives through the use of available resources. • Communicates with colleagues about the application of professional learning to support multiple school processes and initiatives. • Aligns, with principal and colleagues, professional learning with school improvement goals and other school processes and initiatives.	• Facilitates conversations among colleagues to develop understanding of the relationships among school and school system processes and initiatives; the school improvement goals; individual, team, and schoolwide professional learning goals; and professional learning. • Emphasizes congruence among multiple initiatives through the use of available resources. • Communicates with colleagues about the application of professional learning to support multiple school processes and initiatives.	• Facilitates conversations among colleagues to develop understanding of the relationships among the school improvement goals, schoolwide professional learning goals, and professional learning.	• Communicates to colleagues the relationships among the school improvement goals, schoolwide professional learning goals, and professional learning.	• Fails to develop staff's understanding of the relationships among the school and school system processes and initiatives, the school improvement goals, schoolwide professional learning goals, and professional learning.	

7.3 Build coherence

Desired outcome 7.3.2: Links professional learning with past experiences.

Level 1	Level 2	Level 3	Level 4	Level 5	Level 6
• Collects data from colleagues about past experiences with individual, team, school-wide, and out-of-school professional learning; their experience with the planned content of professional learning; and the school's history with change. • Uses the data when planning and implementing professional learning.	• Collects data from colleagues about past experiences with individual, team, and schoolwide professional learning and their experience with the planned content of professional learning. • Uses the data when planning professional learning.	• Collects data from colleagues about past experiences with schoolwide professional learning. • Uses the data when planning professional learning.	• Forms assumptions about colleagues' past experiences with school-wide professional learning. • Uses the assumptions when planning professional learning.	• Fails to consider past experiences in planning and implementing professional learning.	

Innovation Configuration Maps

PRINCIPAL

- **LEARNING COMMUNITIES**
- **LEADERSHIP**
- **RESOURCES**
- **DATA**
- **LEARNING DESIGNS**
- **IMPLEMENTATION**
- **OUTCOMES**

1.1 Engage in continuous improvement

Level 1	Level 2	Level 3	Level 4	Level 5	Level 6
Desired outcome 1.1.1: Develops own and others' capacity to apply the seven-step cycle of continuous improvement.*					
• Develops own knowledge and skills about the seven steps of the cycle of continuous improvement. • Instructs staff and SLT about and models the seven steps of the cycle of continuous improvement.	• Develops own knowledge and skills about the seven steps of the cycle of continuous improvement. • Instructs SLT about and models the seven steps of the cycle of continuous improvement.	• Develops own knowledge and skills about the seven steps of the cycle of continuous improvement. • Instructs the SLT on the cycle of continuous improvement.	• Directs staff to learn about the cycle of continuous improvement.	• Expects staff to learn about the cycle of continuous improvement.	• Fails to develop own and others' knowledge and skills about the cycle of continuous improvement.
Desired outcome 1.1.2: Applies the cycle of continuous improvement with fidelity to lead professional learning.					
• Models the application of the seven-step cycle in schoolwide professional learning. • Facilitates SLT and staff to apply the seven-step cycle of continuous improvement with fidelity in individual, team, and schoolwide professional learning. • Provides SLT and staff coaching to clarify and support faithful use of the cycle.	• Models the application of the seven-step cycle in schoolwide professional learning. • Facilitates SLT to apply the seven-step cycle of continuous improvement with fidelity in schoolwide professional learning. • Guides the SLT in employing the cycle with fidelity.	• Facilitates SLT to apply the seven-step cycle of continuous improvement with fidelity in professional learning related to team and schoolwide professional learning.	• Facilitates SLT to apply some steps of the cycle of continuous improvement schoolwide in professional learning	• Fails to apply the cycle of continuous improvement.	

*See the Appendix (p. 262) for an explanation of this concept.

1.2 Develop collective responsibility

Desired outcome 1.2.1: Advances collective responsibility.

Level 1	Level 2	Level 3	Level 4	Level 5	Level 6
• Develops, with staff and SLT, shared assumptions about and a shared definition of collective responsibility. • Collects from and shares with all staff evidence of practice of collective responsibility. • Identifies and works to overcome, with SLT and staff, barriers to collective responsibility. • Challenges practices and assumptions that create barriers to collective responsibility. • Takes action, with SLT, to overcome barriers.	• Develops, with SLT, shared assumptions about and a shared definition of collective responsibility. • Collects from and shares with all staff evidence of practice of collective responsibility. • Identifies and works to overcome, with SLT, barriers to collective responsibility.	• Declares shared assumptions and the definition of collective responsibility. • Collects evidence of collective responsibility from members of SLT.	• Writes and shares a definition of collective responsibility.	• Fails to address collective responsibility.	

1.2 Develop collective responsibility

Level 1	Level 2	Level 3	Level 4	Level 5	Level 6
Desired outcome 1.2.2: Fosters engagement of all staff in meeting the needs of all students.					
• Engages staff in weekly conversations about the impact of individual and collective decisions about professional learning on student achievement. • Meets with staff weekly to discuss individual, team, and schoolwide professional learning to address the needs of all students. • Shares data with staff to inform them about the needs of students outside individual classrooms.	• Engages staff in monthly conversations about the impact of individual and collective decisions about professional learning on student achievement. • Meets with staff monthly to discuss individual, team, and schoolwide professional learning to address the needs of all students. • Shares data with staff to inform them about the needs of students outside individual classrooms.	• Shares data with staff to inform them about the needs of students outside individual classrooms. • Meets with staff monthly to discuss schoolwide professional learning to address the needs of all students.	• Invites staff to participate in professional learning to address the needs of students outside individual classrooms.	• Focuses attention only on learning needs of students in individual classrooms.	
Desired outcome 1.2.3: Models collective responsibility by participating in learning communities.					
• Participates routinely in one or more learning communities within and beyond the school. • Participates routinely in ongoing learning communities beyond the district. • Shares with staff own learning as a member of learning communities.	• Participates routinely in one or more school-based learning communities. • Shares with staff own learning as a member of learning communities.	• Participates routinely in an ongoing learning community.	• Participates occasionally in an ongoing learning community.	• Fails to participate in a learning community.	

1.3 Create alignment and accountability

Desired outcome 1.3.1: Aligns professional learning with school and system goals.

Level 1	Level 2	Level 3	Level 4	Level 5	Level 6
• Analyzes, with staff and SLT, school and system goals and strategies to establish individual, team, and schoolwide professional learning goals and plans to align with school and system goals and plans. • Monitors individual, team, and schoolwide professional learning goals and plans to check for alignment with school and system goals. • Aligns own professional learning goals with school and system goals.	• Analyzes, with SLT, school and system goals and strategies to establish schoolwide professional learning goals and plans to align with school and system goals and plans. • Monitors individual and team professional learning goals and plans to check for alignment with school and system goals. • Aligns own professional learning goals with school and system goals.	• Analyzes, with SLT, school goals and strategies to establish schoolwide professional learning goals and plans to align with school goals and plans. • Monitors individual professional learning goals and plans to check for alignment with school goals. • Aligns own professional learning goals with school goals.	• Adopts system professional learning goals as schoolwide professional learning goals.	• Establishes schoolwide professional learning goals and plan without consideration of school system goals and plans.	• Fails to create school-wide professional learning goals and plans.

1.3 Create alignment and accountability

Desired outcome 1.3.2: Monitors the use of the cycle of continuous improvement to achieve professional learning goals.

Level 1	Level 2	Level 3	Level 4	Level 5	Level 6
• Sets clear expectations about individual, team, and schoolwide use of the cycle of continuous improvement to achieve professional learning goals. • Sets clear expectations that individual, team, and schoolwide professional learning align with school goals. • Assesses the fidelity of own, staff, and SLT use of the cycle of continuous improvement to achieve professional learning goals. • Provides constructive feedback to individuals, teams, whole staff, and SLT to improve fidelity of implementation of the cycle. • Provides additional professional learning and support to refine implementation fidelity.	• Sets clear expectations about individual, team, and schoolwide use of the cycle of continuous improvement to achieve professional learning goals. • Sets clear expectations that team and schoolwide professional learning align with school goals. • Assesses the fidelity of staff and SLT use of the cycle of continuous improvement to achieve professional learning goals. • Provides constructive feedback to whole staff and SLT to improve fidelity of implementation of the cycle.	• Sets clear expectations about schoolwide use of the cycle of continuous improvement to achieve professional learning goals. • Sets clear expectations that schoolwide professional learning aligns with school goals. • Assesses the fidelity of staff use of the cycle of continuous improvement to achieve professional learning goals. • Provides constructive feedback to whole staff to improve fidelity of implementation of the cycle.	• Sets clear expectations about schoolwide use of the cycle of continuous improvement to achieve professional learning goals.	• Fails to assess the fidelity of implementation of the cycle of continuous improvement.	

2.1 Develop capacity for learning and leading

Desired outcome 2.1.1: Commits to continuous professional learning.

Level 1	Level 2	Level 3	Level 4	Level 5	Level 6
• States publicly own professional learning goals. • Persists with own professional learning until achieving mastery. • Asks for constructive feedback from supervisors, peers, and staff. • Participates in and models professional learning that occurs over multiple years and includes hands-on and problem-based learning with multiple practice opportunities. • Participates in follow-up and coaching.	• States publicly own professional learning goals. • Persists with own professional learning until achieving mastery. • Participates in and models professional learning that occurs over multiple years and includes hands-on and problem-based learning with multiple practice opportunities. • Participates in follow-up and coaching.	• Participates in professional learning that occurs over a single year and includes hands-on and problem-based learning with multiple practice opportunities. • Participates in follow-up and coaching.	• Participates in a series of short-term learning activities on a variety of topics without ongoing support and assistance to promote implementation of new learning.	• Participates in a variety of disconnected learning activities (e.g. reads articles, attends professional conferences or workshops, participates in webinars, etc.) unrelated to own professional learning goals.	• Fails to commit to continuous professional learning.

2.1 Develop capacity for learning and leading

Desired outcome 2.1.2: Develops own and others' capacity for leadership of professional learning.

Level 1	Level 2	Level 3	Level 4	Level 5	Level 6
• Develops own knowledge and skills related to leadership of professional learning. • Develops staff knowledge and skills related to leadership of professional learning. • Creates experiences for staff to lead schoolwide and team-based professional learning. • Establishes transparent and objective guidelines and processes to select and support teacher leaders. • Creates opportunities for staff to serve in formal and informal leadership roles (e.g., mentors, facilitators of collaborative learning teams, master teachers, members of SLT, etc.). • Mentors staff to serve as future members of SLT.	• Develops own knowledge and skills related to leadership of professional learning. • Develops staff knowledge and skills related to leadership of professional learning. • Creates experiences for staff to lead schoolwide and team-based professional learning. • Creates opportunities for staff to serve in formal and informal leadership roles (e.g., mentors, facilitators of collaborative learning teams, master teachers, members of SLT, etc.)	• Develops own knowledge and skills related to leadership of professional learning. • Develops staff knowledge and skills related to leadership of professional learning. • Expects staff to lead schoolwide and team-based professional learning. • Creates opportunities for staff to serve in formal leadership roles (e.g., mentors, facilitators of collaborative learning teams, master teachers, members of SLT, etc.).	• Develops own knowledge and skills related to leadership of professional learning. • Develops staff knowledge and skills related to leadership of professional learning. • Appoints staff to lead schoolwide and team-based professional learning.	• Develops own knowledge and skills related to leadership of professional learning.	• Fails to develop own and staff's knowledge and skills related to leadership of professional learning.

2.1 Develop capacity for learning and leading

Desired outcome 2.1.3: Understands and uses the Standards for Professional Learning in making decisions about professional learning.

Level 1	Level 2	Level 3	Level 4	Level 5	Level 6
• Studies the Standards for Professional Learning to apply key ideas. • Develops staff understanding of the Standards for Professional Learning. • Accesses and uses new research and information about effective professional learning on an ongoing basis. • Applies the seven Standards for Professional Learning in decision making about professional learning.	• Studies the Standards for Professional Learning to apply their key ideas. • Accesses and uses new research and information about effective professional learning on an ongoing basis. • Applies the seven Standards for Professional Learning in decision making about professional learning.	• Studies the Standards for Professional Learning to understand their key ideas. • Applies some but not all of the Standards for Professional Learning in decision making about professional learning. • Reviews new research and information about effective professional learning at least annually.	• Names the Standards for Professional Learning.	• Makes decisions about professional learning without reference to the Standards for Professional Learning.	

2.1 Develop capacity for learning and leading

Desired outcome 2.1.4: Serves as a leader of professional learning.

Level 1	Level 2	Level 3	Level 4	Level 5	Level 6
• Articulates the role of the principal related to professional learning. • Acknowledges responsibility for the quality and results of schoolwide professional learning. • Articulates the process for making decisions about professional learning and who is involved. • Shares leadership for professional learning with others, including SLT, teams, coaches, and other learning facilitators. • Oversees or undertakes 100% of principal's responsibilities for professional learning.	• Articulates the role of the principal related to professional learning. • Acknowledges responsibility for the quality and results of schoolwide professional learning. • Articulates the process for making decisions about professional learning and who is involved. • Shares leadership for professional learning with SLT. • Oversees or undertakes 90% of principal's responsibilities for professional learning.	• Articulates the role of the principal related to professional learning. • Acknowledges responsibility for the quality and results of schoolwide professional learning. • Articulates the process for making decisions about professional learning and who is involved. • Oversees or undertakes 80% of principal's responsibilities for professional learning.	• Articulates the role of the principal related to professional learning. • Acknowledges responsibility for providing professional learning. • Oversees or undertakes less than 80% of principal's responsibilities for professional learning.	• Defers decision-making authority in professional learning to others.	

2.1 Develop capacity for learning and leading

Desired outcome 2.1.5: Coaches and supervises school-based facilitators of professional learning.

Level 1	Level 2	Level 3	Level 4	Level 5	Level 6
• Provides continuous coaching to school-based professional learning facilitators and coaches by providing materials, guidance, feedback, and problem solving. • Monitors and supervises school-based professional learning facilitators' and coaches' work with individuals, teams, and whole staff.	• Provides intermittent coaching to school-based professional learning facilitators and coaches by providing materials, guidance, feedback, and problem solving. • Monitors and supervises school-based professional learning facilitators' and coaches' work with individuals, teams, and whole staff.	• Monitors and supervises school-based professional learning facilitators' and coaches' work with teams and whole staff.	• Supervises school-based professional learning facilitators and coaches.	• Fails to provide coaching or supervision to school-based professional learning facilitators and coaches.	

2.2 Advocate for professional learning

	Level 1	Level 2	Level 3	Level 4	Level 5	Level 6
Desired outcome 2.2.1: Articulates the link between student learning and professional learning.						
	• Explains the indelible connection between professional learning and student learning to staff, students, parents, system leaders, public officials, and community members and partners. • Provides multiple examples of the link between professional learning and student learning to staff, students, parents, system leaders, public officials, and community members and partners.	• Explains the indelible connection between professional learning and student achievement to staff, students, parents, system leaders, and community members and partners. • Provides multiple examples of the link between professional learning and student learning to staff, students, parents, system leaders, and community members and partners.	• Explains the indelible connection between professional learning and student achievement to staff, parents, and system leaders. • Provides multiple examples of the link between professional learning and student learning to staff, parents, and system leaders.	• Describes the connection between professional learning and student learning.	• Fails to explain the connection between professional learning and student learning.	

2.2 Advocate for professional learning

Desired outcome 2.2.2: Advocates high-quality professional learning.

Level 1	Level 2	Level 3	Level 4	Level 5	Level 6
• Promotes high-quality professional learning with staff, students, parents, system leaders, colleagues, public officials, and community members and partners. • Advocates district- and schoolwide conditions and procedures for effective individual, team, and schoolwide professional learning. • Engages staff and SLT in developing and using succinct messages about the role of professional learning in student learning. • Supports collaborative professional learning when challenged by staff, supervisors, colleagues, students, parents, or community members. • Challenges practices, experiences, and designs of ineffective professional learning and advocates improvements.	• Promotes high-quality professional learning with staff, parents, students, system leaders, and colleagues. • Advocates schoolwide conditions and procedures for effective individual, team, and schoolwide professional learning. • Engages SLT in developing and using succinct messages about the role of professional learning in student learning. • Supports collaborative professional learning when challenged by staff, supervisors, colleagues, students, parents, or community members.	• Promotes high-quality professional learning with staff and school system leaders. • Advocates schoolwide conditions and procedures for effective schoolwide professional learning. • Supports collaborative professional learning when challenged by staff, supervisors, colleagues, students, parents, or community members.	• Promotes high-quality professional learning with staff.	• Fails to promote high-quality professional learning for staff.	

2.3 Create support systems and structures

Desired outcome 2.3.1: Establishes systems and structures for effective professional learning.

Level 1	Level 2	Level 3	Level 4	Level 5	Level 6
• Establishes and monitors schoolwide conditions for effective professional learning (e.g., resources, policies, annual calendars, schedules, procedures, and structures). • Supports staff and SLT in understanding and implementing conditions for effective schoolwide professional learning. • Solves problems related to establishing conditions for effective professional learning.	• Establishes and monitors schoolwide conditions for effective professional learning (e.g., resources, policies, annual calendars, schedules, procedures, and structures). • Solves problems related to establishing conditions required for effective professional learning.	• Establishes schoolwide conditions for effective professional learning (e.g., resources, policies, annual calendars, chedules, procedures, and structures). • Solves problems related to establishing conditions required for effective professional learning.	• Fails to establish schoolwide conditions to support effective professional learning.		

2.3 Create support systems and structures

	Level 1	Level 2	Level 3	Level 4	Level 5	Level 6
Desired outcome 2.3.2: Prepares and supports staff for skillful collaboration.						
	• Develops staff knowledge and skills to learn and work collaboratively. • Supports development of facilitation skills to maximize collaboration. • Guides staff in using collaboration to achieve individual, team, and schoolwide professional learning goals. • Provides feedback to improve staff collaboration skills. • Recognizes collaborative behavior of individuals, teams, and whole school staff. • Develops staff capacity to surface assumptions and resolve conflict.	• Develops staff knowledge and skills to learn and work collaboratively. • Supports development of facilitation skills to maximize collaboration. • Guides staff in using collaboration to achieve individual, team, and schoolwide professional learning goals. • Recognizes collaborative behavior of individuals, teams, and whole school staff. • Develops staff capacity to resolve conflict.	• Develops staff knowledge to learn and work collaboratively. • Supports development of facilitation skills to maximize collaboration. • Guides staff in using collaboration to achieve individual, team, and schoolwide professional learning goals.	• Shares the expectation that staff use collaboration to achieve individual, team, and schoolwide professional learning goals.	• Presumes staff uses collaboration to achieve individual, team, and schoolwide professional learning goals.	

2.3 Create support systems and structures

Desired outcome 2.3.3: Cultivates and maintains a collaborative culture.

Level 1	Level 2	Level 3	Level 4	Level 5	Level 6
• Develops and applies research-based knowledge and skills about collaborative cultures to support staff's learning and collaborative work. • Models collaboration in interactions with staff, students, parents, community members, and system leaders. • Assesses the culture. • Constructs social architecture of a collaborative culture that includes norms for individual, team, and schoolwide interactions; high expectations; collective responsibility mutual respect; and relational trust. • Identifies and addresses assumptions and barriers to collaboration.	• Develops and applies research-based knowledge and skills about collaborative cultures to support staff's learning and collaborative work. • Models collaboration in interactions with staff, students, parents, community members, and system leaders. • Assesses the culture. • Constructs social architecture of a collaborative culture that includes norms for individual, team, and schoolwide interactions; high expectations; collective responsibility mutual respect; and relational trust. • Identifies barriers to collaboration.	• Models collaboration in interactions with staff, students, parents, community members, and system leaders. • Defines clear expectations and reinforces staff members' collective responsibility for high levels of learning for all students. • Constructs a collaborative school culture based on norms of high expectations, collective responsibility for high levels of learning for all students, mutual respect, and relational trust.	• Models collaboration in interactions with staff, students, parents, community members, and system leaders. • Reinforces teachers' individual responsibility for high levels of learning for their students.	• Accepts the current school culture without making efforts to improve it.	

2.3 Create support systems and structures

Desired outcome 2.3.4: Creates expectations for collaborative professional learning within the school day.

Level 1	Level 2	Level 3	Level 4	Level 5	Level 6
• Adopts and communicates high expectations for engagement in and implementation of professional learning. • Communicates high expectations and provides ongoing support for staff to achieve individual, team, and schoolwide professional learning goals. • Focuses faculty meeting time on examining progress and results of collaborative professional learning. • Creates guidelines that ensure instructional coaches equitably distribute time among all learning teams. • Advocates coaching as an essential support for high-fidelity implementation of desired practices. • Sets the expectation that all learning teams meet at least three times a week during the workday.	• Adopts and communicates high expectations for engagement in and implementation of professional learning. • Creates guidelines that ensure instructional coaches equitably distribute time among all learning teams. • Advocates coaching as an essential support for high-fidelity implementation of desired practices. • Sets the expectation that all learning teams meet at least two times a week during the workday.	• Communicates expectations for engagement in and implementation of professional learning. • Advocates coaching as an essential support for high-fidelity implementation of desired practices. • Sets the expectation that all learning teams meet once a week during the workday.	• Communicates expectations for engagement in and implementation of professional learning. • Sets the expectation that all learning teams meet once a week during the workday.	• Fails to set expectations or provide support for professional learning within the workday.	

3.1 Prioritize human, fiscal, material, technology, and time resources

Level 1	Level 2	Level 3	Level 4	Level 5	Level 6
Desired outcome 3.1.1: Defines resources for professional learning.					
• Works, with SLT and staff, to develop a shared definition of resources for professional learning. • Identifies resources for professional learning that include staff, materials, technology, funding, and time. • Identifies ongoing school- and classroom-based support for high-fidelity implementation of professional learning.	• Works, with SLT, to develop a shared definition of resources for professional learning. • Identifies resources for professional learning that include staff, materials, technology, funding, and time. • Identifies ongoing school- and classroom-based support for high-fidelity implementation of professional learning.	• Identifies resources for professional learning that include materials, technology, funding, and time. • Identifies ongoing school- based support for high-fidelity implementation of professional learning.	• Identifies resources for professional learning that include funding and time.	• Identifies funding as the only resource for professional learning.	• Fails to define resources for professional learning.

3.1 Prioritize human, fiscal, material, technology, and time resources

Desired outcome 3.1.2: Allocates resources for professional learning to align with high-priority student and educator learning needs.

Level 1	Level 2	Level 3	Level 4	Level 5	Level 6
• Establishes, with SLT and staff, criteria for resource allocation for professional learning based on high-priority student learning needs and individual, team, and schoolwide educator learning needs. • Uses consensus to prioritize learning needs in collaboration with SLT and staff. • Allocates and maintains resources for professional learning as a priority expenditure. • Projects and plans for strategic use of resources over multiple years to achieve professional learning goals. • Addresses inequities in student and educator learning through realignment of resources. • Explains decisions about resource allocation using data and research. • Seeks internal and external resources for professional learning. • Gathers resources for individual, team, and schoolwide professional learning. • Plans for long-range strategic use of professional learning resources.	• Establishes, with SLT, criteria for resource allocation for professional learning based on high-priority student learning needs and individual, team, and schoolwide educator learning needs. • Uses consensus to prioritize learning needs in collaboration with SLT. • Allocates resources for professional learning to achieve high-priority student and educator learning goals. • Plans for strategic use of resources over multiple years to achieve professional learning goals. • Addresses inequities in student and educator learning through realignment of resources. • Gathers resources for individual, team, and schoolwide professional learning. • Explains decisions about resource allocation.	• Establishes criteria for resource allocation for professional learning based on high-priority student learning needs and schoolwide educator learning needs. • Prioritizes learning needs. • Allocates resources for professional learning to achieve high-priority student and educator learning goals. • Gathers resources for individual, team, and schoolwide professional learning. • Communicates decisions about resource allocation for professional learning.	• Distributes available resources for professional learning based on individual educator requests.	• Fails to allocate resources for professional learning.	

3.1 Prioritize human, fiscal, material, technology, and time resources

Desired outcome 3.1.3: Allocates time for collaborative professional learning.

Level 1	Level 2	Level 3	Level 4	Level 5	Level 6
• Creates, with SLT and staff, a daily schedule for learning teams to meet during the school day at least three times per week. • Creates, with SLT and staff, an annual schedule for individual, team, and schoolwide professional learning.	• Establishes, with SLT, a daily schedule for learning teams to meet during the school day at least weekly. • Establishes, with SLT, an annual schedule for individual, team, and schoolwide professional learning.	• Establishes a daily schedule for learning teams to meet during the school day at least monthly. • Establishes an annual schedule for individual, team, and schoolwide professional learning.	• Establishes a daily schedule for learning teams to meet outside the school day at least monthly. • Establishes an annual schedule for individual, team, and schoolwide professional learning.	• Establishes an annual schedule with days set aside for teams to engage in professional learning.	• Fails to allocate time for professional learning.

3.1 Prioritize human, fiscal, material, technology, and time resources

Desired outcome 3.1.4: Allocates resources to support implementation of professional learning.

Level 1	Level 2	Level 3	Level 4	Level 5	Level 6
• Recognizes the need for long-term investment of resources for full implementation of professional learning. • Provides sufficient resources over multiple years to support full implementation of professional learning. • Sustains resources for support until full implementation of professional learning occurs. • Provides resources for differentiated support to all staff for full implementation of professional learning. • Preserves time for coaches, other learning facilitators, and peers to work with individuals and teams to support implementation of professional learning.	• Recognizes the need for long-term investment of resources for full implementation of professional learning. • Provides sufficient resources over multiple years to support full implementation of professional learning. • Sustains resources for support until full implementation of professional learning occurs. • Provides resources for differentiated support to all staff for full implementation of professional learning. • Preserves time for coaches and other learning facilitators to work with individuals and teams to support implementation of professional learning.	• Provides sufficient resources over multiple years to support full implementation of professional learning. • Provides resources for differentiated support to all staff for full implementation of professional learning.	• Allocates resources to support implementation of professional learning for one year.	• Fails to allocate resources to support implementation of professional learning.	

3.2 Monitor resources

Desired outcome 3.2.1: Monitors effectiveness of the use of resources for professional learning.

Level 1	Level 2	Level 3	Level 4	Level 5	Level 6
• Establishes a comprehensive system to track and monitor resources associated with professional learning to ensure equitable distribution of all resources. • Tracks and monitors quarterly funding, time, materials, staff, and technology for professional learning. • Creates guidelines to ensure coaches equitably distribute time among learning teams and staff. • Uses data from tracking and monitoring quarterly to analyze the effectiveness of resource use and make needed adjustments. • Challenges decisions to divert resources for professional learning to other areas. • Assumes responsibility for decisions to redirect resources for professional learning to other areas.	• Establishes a comprehensive system to track and monitor resources associated with professional learning to ensure equitable distribution of all resources. • Tracks and monitors quarterly funding, time, materials, staff, and technology for professional learning. • Uses data from tracking and monitoring quarterly to analyze the effectiveness of resource use and make needed adjustments. • Assumes responsibility for decisions to redirect resources for professional learning to other areas.	• Tracks and monitors semiannually funding, time, materials, staff, and technology for professional learning. • Uses data from tracking and monitoring semiannually to analyze the effectiveness of resource use and make needed adjustments.	• Tracks and monitors annually funding and time for professional learning. • Uses data from tracking and monitoring annually to analyze the effectiveness of resource use and make needed adjustments.	• Tracks funding used for professional learning.	• Fails to monitor and/or track resources for professional learning.

3.3 Coordinate resources

Desired outcome 3.3.1: Designs and implements a comprehensive resource plan for professional learning.

Level 1	Level 2	Level 3	Level 4	Level 5	Level 6
• Analyzes all possible resources to identify those that can be reallocated for professional learning. • Analyzes multiple programs, initiatives, improvement efforts, and grants to identify their commonalities with the school's high-priority goals as well as opportunities to repurpose resources for high-priority professional learning needs. • Directs resources from multiple sources toward professional learning needed to achieve the school's high-priority goals. • Seeks and uses external resources for professional learning to enhance existing resources to achieve student learning goals. • Develops and builds with staff, SLT, and others, consensus about a multi-year resource plan for professional learning based on high-priority needs for student and educator learning. *continued…*	• Analyzes all possible resources to identify those that can be reallocated for professional learning. • Directs resources from multiple sources toward professional learning needed to achieve the school's high-priority goals. • Seeks and uses external resources for professional learning to enhance existing resources to achieve student learning goals. • Develops and shares a multiyear resource plan for professional learning based on high-priority needs for student and educator learning. • Explains, to staff and others, the rationale for the resource allocations in professional learning. • Implements professional learning resource plan to achieve high-priority student and educator learning goals. • Encourages staff to share resources to increase their effectiveness.	• Develops and shares a multiyear resource plan for professional learning based on high-priority needs for student and educator learning. • Implements professional learning resource plan to achieve high-priority student and educator learning goals. • Encourages staff to share resources to increase their effectiveness.	• Develops and shares a multiyear resource plan for professional learning based on high-priority needs for student and educator learning.	• Develops and shares the annual budget for professional learning.	• Fails to develop and implement a resource plan for professional learning.

3.3 Coordinate resources

Level 1	Level 2	Level 3	Level 4	Level 5	Level 6
Desired outcome 3.3.1: Designs and implements a comprehensive resource plan for professional learning.					
continued... • Explains, to staff and others, using data and research, the rationale for the resource allocations in professional learning. • Implements professional learning resource plan to achieve high-priority student and educator learning goals. • Encourages staff to share resources to increase their effectiveness. • Serves as a resource for colleagues.					

4.1 Analyze student, educator, and system data

Level 1	Level 2	Level 3	Level 4	Level 5	Level 6
Desired outcome 4.1.1: Develops own and staff capacity to analyze and interpret data.					
• Develops own and staff knowledge and skills to access, organize, and display schoolwide, grade-level, department, team, and individual data. • Develops own and staff knowledge and skills to analyze and interpret data from multiple sources to make schoolwide, team, grade-level, department, and individual decisions about professional learning.	• Develops own and SLT knowledge and skills to access, organize, and display schoolwide, grade-level, department, team, and individual data. • Develops own and SLT knowledge and skills to analyze and interpret data from multiple sources to make schoolwide, team, grade-level, department, and individual decisions about professional learning.	• Develops own knowledge and skills to access, organize, and display schoolwide, grade-level, department, team, and individual data.	• Develops own knowledge and skills to access, organize, and display data.	• Fails to develop own or staff knowledge and skills to analyze and interpret data.	
Desired outcome 4.1.2: Describes multiple sources of available student, educator, and system data.					
• Identifies quantitative formative and summative student, educator, and system data available to inform decisions about professional learning. • Identifies qualitative student, educator, and system data available to inform decisions about professional learning. • Identifies longitudinal student, educator, and system data to inform decisions about professional learning. • Knows how to access a variety of student, educator, and system data.	• Identifies quantitative formative and summative student, educator, and system data available to inform decisions about professional learning. • Identifies qualitative formative and summative student, educator, and system data available to inform decisions about professional learning. • Identifies available forms of longitudinal student data to inform decisions about professional learning. • Knows how to access multiple types of student, educator, and system data.	• Identifies quantitative formative and summative student data available to inform decisions about professional learning. • Knows how to access multiple types of student, educator, and system data.	• Identifies summative student data available to inform decisions about professional learning.	• Is unfamiliar with available student, educator, and system data to inform decisions about professional learning.	

4.1 Analyze student, educator, and system data

Desired outcome 4.1.3: Analyzes and interprets multiple sources of student data to determine professional learning needs.

Level 1	Level 2	Level 3	Level 4	Level 5	Level 6
• Analyzes, with staff and SLT, qualitative and quantitative student data from four or more sources to make predictions, observations, and inferences about the data. • Interprets, with staff and SLT, qualitative and quantitative student data from four or more sources to decipher trends, patterns, outliers, and root causes within the data. • Supports staff and SLT to independently identify findings, trends, patterns, outliers, and root causes from four or more sources of student data.	• Analyzes, with staff and SLT, qualitative and quantitative student data from three sources to make predictions, observations, and inferences about the data. • Interprets, with staff and SLT, qualitative and quantitative student data from three sources to decipher trends, patterns, outliers, and root causes within the data.	• Analyzes, with staff and SLT, qualitative and quantitative student data from two sources to make predictions, observations, and inferences about the data. • Interprets, with staff and SLT, qualitative and quantitative student data from two sources to decipher trends, patterns, outliers, and root causes within the data.	• Analyzes one source of student data.	• Presents the results of student data analysis to staff or SLT.	• Fails to analyze and interpret student data to determine professional learning needs.

4.1 Analyze student, educator, and system data

Desired outcome 4.1.4: Analyzes and interprets multiple sources of educator data to determine professional learning needs.

Level 1	Level 2	Level 3	Level 4	Level 5	Level 6
• Analyzes, with staff and SLT, qualitative and quantitative educator data from four or more sources to make predictions, observations, and inferences about the data. • Interprets, with staff and SLT, qualitative and quantitative educator data from four or more sources to decipher trends, patterns, outliers, and root causes within the data. • Supports staff and SLT to independently identify findings, trends, patterns, outliers, and root causes from four or more sources of educator data.	• Analyzes, with staff and SLT, qualitative and quantitative educator data from three sources to make predictions, observations, and inferences about the data. • Interprets, with staff and SLT, qualitative and quantitative educator data from three sources to decipher trends, patterns, outliers, and root causes within the data.	• Analyzes, in staff and SLT, qualitative and quantitative educator data from two sources to make predictions, observations, and inferences about the data. • Interprets, with staff and SLT, qualitative and quantitative educator data from two sources to decipher trends, patterns, outliers, and root causes within the data.	• Analyzes one source of educator data.	• Presents the results of educator data analysis to staff or SLT.	• Fails to analyze and interpret educator data to determine professional learning needs.

4.1 Analyze student, educator, and system data

	Level 1	Level 2	Level 3	Level 4	Level 5	Level 6
Desired outcome 4.1.5: Analyzes and interprets multiple sources of school data to determine professional learning needs.	• Analyzes, with staff and SLT, qualitative and quantitative school data from four or more sources to make predictions, observations, and inferences about the data. • Interprets, with staff and SLT, qualitative and quantitative school data from four or more sources to decipher trends, patterns, outliers, and root causes within the data. • Supports staff and SLT to independently identify findings, trends, patterns, outliers, and root causes from four or more sources of school data.	• Analyzes, with staff and SLT, qualitative and quantitative school data from three sources to make predictions, observations, and inferences about the data. • Interprets, with staff and SLT, qualitative and quantitative school data from three sources to decipher trends, patterns, outliers, and root causes within the data.	• Analyzes, with staff and SLT, qualitative and quantitative school data from two sources to make predictions, observations, and inferences about the data. • Interprets, with staff and SLT, qualitative and quantitative school data from two sources to decipher trends, patterns, outliers, and root causes within the data.	• Analyzes one source of school data.	• Presents the results of school data analysis to staff or SLT.	• Fails to analyze and interpret school data to determine professional learning needs.
Desired outcome 4.1.6: Engages in ongoing data analysis and interpretation to support continuous improvement.	• Assists staff, coaches, and other learning facilitators in gathering, analyzing, and interpreting school, classroom, and team data to refine instructional strategies. • Meets with individuals and teams weekly to support analysis and interpretation of student, educator, and system data.	• Assists staff, coaches, and other learning facilitators in gathering, analyzing, and interpreting school, classroom, and team data to refine instructional strategies. • Meets with individuals and teams monthly to support analysis and interpretation of student, educator, and system data.	• Assists staff in gathering and analyzing classroom data to refine instructional strategies. • Meets with individuals and teams quarterly to support analysis and interpretation of student, educator, and system data.	• Meets with individuals and teams once or twice each school year to support analysis and interpretation of student data.	• Fails to support staff in ongoing data use and analysis.	

4.2 Assess progress

Desired outcome 4.2.1: Determines formative data to assess progress toward professional learning benchmarks and goals.

Level 1	Level 2	Level 3	Level 4	Level 5	Level 6
• Establishes, with SLT and staff, a systematic process for reviewing individual, team, and schoolwide progress toward goals for professional learning. • Establishes monthly, with SLT and staff, benchmarks to measure progress toward professional learning goals. • Identifies monthly, with SLT and staff, formative qualitative and quantitative data to measure progress toward professional learning benchmarks and goals.	• Establishes, with SLT, a systematic process for reviewing individual, team, and schoolwide progress toward goals for professional learning. • Establishes quarterly, with SLT, benchmarks to measure progress toward professional learning goals. • Identifies quarterly, with SLT, formative qualitative and quantitative data to measure progress toward professional learning benchmarks and goals.	• Establishes semiannually benchmarks to measure progress toward goals for professional learning. • Identifies semiannually either qualitative or quantitative data to measure progress toward professional learning benchmarks and goals.	• Identifies annually either qualitative or quantitative data to measure progress toward professional learning benchmarks and goals.	• Fails to identify data to measure progress toward professional learning benchmarks and goals.	

4.2 Assess progress

Desired outcome 4.2.2: Collects and analyzes formative data to continuously assess progress toward professional learning benchmarks and goals.

Level 1	Level 2	Level 3	Level 4	Level 5	Level 6
• Collects, with SLT and staff, monthly formative data to measure progress toward individual, team, and schoolwide professional learning benchmarks and goals. • Analyzes, with SLT and staff, quarterly formative data to assess progress toward individual, team, and schoolwide professional learning benchmarks and goals. • Formulates, with SLT and staff, conclusions about progress toward individual, team, and schoolwide professional learning benchmarks and goals.	• Collects, with SLT, quarterly formative data to measure progress toward team and schoolwide professional learning benchmarks and goals. • Analyzes, with SLT, quarterly formative data to assess progress toward team and schoolwide professional learning benchmarks and goals. • Formulates, with SLT, conclusions about progress toward team and school-wide professional learning benchmarks and goals.	• Collects semiannually formative data to measure progress toward school-wide professional learning benchmarks and goals. • Analyzes quarterly formative data to assess progress toward school-wide professional learning benchmarks and goals.	• Collects annually formative data to measure progress toward school-wide professional learning benchmarks and goals.	• Collects annually formative data to measure progress toward school-wide professional learning benchmarks and goals.	• Fails to collect and analyze formative data to measure progress toward professional learning benchmarks and goals.

www.learningforward.org   800-727-7288

4.2 Assess progress

Desired outcome 4.2.3: Uses analysis of progress to make adjustments in professional learning.

Level 1	Level 2	Level 3	Level 4	Level 5	Level 6
• Interprets, with SLT and staff, quarterly analyzed data, to identify enhancers of and barriers to progress. • Solves, with SLT and staff, problems that create barriers to achieving professional learning benchmarks and goals. • Makes, with SLT and staff, in-process, data-based adjustments in schoolwide professional learning (i.e., learning designs, coaching, and other support systems). • Assists individuals and teams to use formative data to make adjustments to learning designs, coaching activities, and timeframes. • Celebrates, with SLT and staff, progress toward individual, team, and schoolwide professional learning benchmarks and goals.	• Interprets, with SLT, quarterly analyzed data to identify enhancers of and barriers to progress. • Solves, with SLT, problems that create barriers to achieving professional learning benchmarks and goals. • Makes, with SLT, in-process, data-based adjustments in schoolwide professional learning (i.e., learning designs, coaching, and other support systems). • Celebrates, with SLT, progress toward individual, team, and schoolwide professional learning benchmarks and goals.	• Interprets quarterly analyzed data to identify enhancers of and barriers to progress. • Solves problems that create barriers to achieving professional learning benchmarks and goals. • Makes in-process, data-based adjustments in individual, team, and schoolwide professional learning (i.e., learning designs, coaching, and other support systems).	• Interprets quarterly analyzed data to identify barriers to progress.	• Fails to use analysis of progress to make needed adjustments in professional learning.	

4.3	Evaluate professional learning					
	Level 1	**Level 2**	**Level 3**	**Level 4**	**Level 5**	**Level 6**
Desired outcome 4.3.1: Develops a comprehensive plan for evaluating the impact of professional learning.						
	• Develops, with staff and SLT, a plan to evaluate the impact of professional learning. • Adopts, with SLT and staff, a theory of change and/or logic model to guide the evaluation of professional learning. • Develops, with SLT and staff, a comprehensive evaluation framework that specifies SMART goal(s), evaluation questions, multiple data sources, data collection methodology, data analysis, interpretation, dissemination of results, and reports to various audiences through various means.	• Develops, with SLT, a plan to evaluate the impact of professional learning. • Adopts, with SLT, a theory of change and/or logic model to guide the evaluation of professional learning. • Develops, with SLT, an evaluation framework that specifies SMART goal(s), evaluation questions, multiple data sources, data collection methodology, data analysis, interpretation, dissemination of results, and reports to various audiences through various means.	• Develops an evaluation framework that specifies SMART goal(s), evaluation questions, data sources, data collection methodology, data analysis, interpretation, and dissemination of results.	• Develops an evaluation framework that specifies SMART goal(s), data sources, and data collection methodology.	• Fails to develop a comprehensive plan to evaluate professional learning.	

4.3 Evaluate professional learning

Desired outcome 4.3.2: Uses a variety of formative and summative data to evaluate the effectiveness and results of professional learning.

Level 1	Level 2	Level 3	Level 4	Level 5	Level 6
• Collects, with SLT and staff, student data to measure changes in student learning and behaviors associated with professional learning. • Collects, with SLT and staff, educator data to assess changes in knowledge, skills, dispositions, and practices associated with professional learning. • Collects, with SLT and staff, school data to assess changes in school culture and organizational structures, policies, and processes associated with professional learning. • Collects staff reflections on the effectiveness of various learning designs used. • Analyzes and interprets data, with SLT and staff, to form conclusions about the effectiveness and results of professional learning.	• Collects, with SLT, student data to measure changes in student learning and behaviors associated with professional learning. • Collects, with SLT, educator data to assess changes in knowledge, skills, dispositions, and practices associated with professional learning. • Collects, with SLT, school data to assess changes in school culture and organizational structures, policies, and processes associated with professional learning. • Analyzes and interprets data, with SLT, to form conclusions about the effectiveness and results of professional learning.	• Collects, with SLT, student data to measure changes in student learning and behaviors associated with professional learning. • Collects, with SLT, educator data to assess changes in knowledge, skills, dispositions, and practices associated with professional learning. • Analyzes, with SLT, collected data.	• Collects student data to measure changes in student learning and behaviors associated with professional learning.	• Fails to evaluate the effectiveness and results of professional learning.	

4.3 Evaluate professional learning

Level 1	Level 2	Level 3	Level 4	Level 5	Level 6
Desired outcome 4.3.3: Supports individuals and learning teams in using data to evaluate the effectiveness of learning designs, content, and duration.					
• Facilitates individuals and learning teams to identify data to evaluate the effectiveness of learning designs to develop their knowledge, skills, dispositions, and practices. • Establishes a consistent time for individual and team reflection about the attainment of goals for professional learning. • Facilitates and supports individuals and learning teams to analyze and interpret data about collaboration, learning, and results. • Supports individuals and learning teams to form conclusions about the design, content, and duration of professional learning. • Provides feedback to individuals and learning teams on use of data to evaluate professional learning.	• Facilitates learning teams to identify data to evaluate the effectiveness of learning designs to develop knowledge, skills, dispositions, and practices. • Facilitates and supports learning teams to analyze and interpret data about collaboration, learning, and results. • Supports learning teams to form conclusions about the design, content, and duration of professional learning. • Provides feedback to learning teams on use of data to evaluate professional learning.	• Facilitates learning teams to identify data to evaluate the effectiveness of learning designs to develop knowledge, skills, and practices. • Facilitates and supports learning teams to analyze and interpret data about collaboration, learning, and results. • Supports learning teams to form conclusions about the design, content, and duration of professional learning.	• Facilitates learning teams to identify data that will determine the effectiveness of learning designs to develop knowledge and skills.	• Fails to support individuals or teams to use data to evaluate the effectiveness of learning designs, content, and duration.	

www.learningforward.org   800-727-7288

4.3 Evaluate professional learning

Desired outcome 4.3.4: Uses evaluation results to improve professional learning.

Level 1	Level 2	Level 3	Level 4	Level 5	Level 6
• Uses, with SLT and staff, evaluation results (i.e., changes in educator practice, student learning, and school culture and practices), to identify strengths and improvements in individual, team, and schoolwide professional learning. • Uses evaluation results to identify design elements of professional learning that have a significant impact on teacher practices and student learning. • Applies conclusions to future planning cycles for professional learning.	• Uses, with SLT, evaluation results (i.e., changes in educator practice, student learning, and school culture and practices), to identify strengths and improvements in individual, team, and schoolwide professional learning. • Uses, with SLT, evaluation results to identify design elements of professional learning that have a significant impact on teacher practices and student learning. • Applies conclusions to future planning cycles for professional learning.	• Uses evaluation results (i.e., changes in educator practice, student learning, and school culture and practices) to identify strengths and improvements in schoolwide professional learning. • Uses evaluation results to identify design elements of professional learning that have a significant impact on teacher practices and student learning. • Applies conclusions to future planning cycles for professional learning.	• Uses evaluation results (i.e., changes in educator practice, student learning, and school culture and practices) to identify strengths and improvements in schoolwide professional learning. • Uses evaluation results to identify design elements of professional learning that have a significant impact on teacher practices and student learning.	• Uses evaluation results (i.e., changes in educator practice, student learning, and school culture and practices) to identify strengths and improvements in schoolwide professional learning.	• Fails to use evaluation results to improve professional learning.

5.1 Apply learning theories, research, and models

Level 1	Level 2	Level 3	Level 4	Level 5	Level 6
Desired outcome 5.1.1: Develops and shares a knowledge base about theories, research, and models of adult learning.					
• Studies, with SLT and staff, research, theories, and models of adult learning. • Engages others in developing knowledge and skills related to research, theories, and models of adult learning. • Creates a collection of resources on educator learning for personal, individual, team, and whole staff use.	• Studies, with SLT, research, theories, and models of adult learning. • Engages others in developing knowledge and skills related to research, theories, and models of adult learning.	• Studies research, theories, and models of adult learning.	• Reads periodically resources about research, theories, and models related to educator learning.	• Accesses resources about educator learning.	• Fails to add to own or others' knowledge base about learning theories, research, and models.
Desired outcome 5.1.2: Acquires and shares knowledge about multiple designs for professional learning. *					
• Develops knowledge about, skills to facilitate, and expertise to implement 12 or more learning designs. • Identifies and discusses essential features of high-quality learning designs (e.g., active engagement, reflection, metacognition, ongoing support, etc.). • Shares knowledge, skills, and practices associated with 12 or more learning designs with SLT, coaches, other learning facilitators, and whole staff.	• Develops knowledge about, skills to facilitate, and expertise to implement 10 learning designs. • Identifies and discusses common features of high-quality learning designs (e.g., active engagement, reflection, metacognition, ongoing support, etc.). • Shares knowledge, skills, and practices associated with 10 learning designs with SLT, coaches, other learning facilitators, and whole staff.	• Develops knowledge about, skills to facilitate, and expertise to implement eight to nine learning designs. • Identifies and discusses common features of high-quality learning designs (e.g., active engagement, reflection, metacognition, ongoing support, etc.). • Shares knowledge, skills, and practices associated with eight to nine learning designs with SLT, coaches, other learning facilitators, and whole staff.	• Develops knowledge about, skills to facilitate, and expertise to implement at least five to seven learning designs.	• Develops knowledge about, skills to facilitate, and expertise to implement fewer than five learning designs.	• Fails to develop knowledge about multiple designs for professional learning.

*See the Appendix (p. 262) for an explanation of this concept.

5.2 Select learning designs

Desired outcome 5.2.1: Acquires and shares knowledge about the multiple factors influencing the selection of learning designs. *

Level 1	Level 2	Level 3	Level 4	Level 5	Level 6
• Clarifies the learning outcomes, including knowledge, skills, dispositions, and practices, expected as a result of professional learning. • Develops knowledge about factors that influence how adults learn. • Identifies, with staff and SLT, factors that emerged from analyzed educator and school data to consider in selecting the learning designs. • Supports staff, SLT, coaches, and other learning facilitators to identify and prioritize factors influencing the selection of learning designs.	• Clarifies the learning outcomes, including knowledge, skills, dispositions, and practices, expected as a result of professional learning. • Acquires knowledge about factors that influence how adults learn. • Identifies factors, in collaboration with SLT, that emerged from analyzed educator and school data to consider in selecting the learning designs. • Prioritizes factors influencing the selection of learning designs.	• Acquires knowledge about factors that influence how adults learn. • Identifies factors that emerged from analyzed educator and school data to consider in selecting the learning designs. • Shares factors with SLT, coaches, and other learning facilitators.	• Acquires knowledge about factors that influence how adults learn.	• Fails to acquire knowledge about multiple factors influencing the selection of learning designs.	

*See the Appendix (p. 262) for an explanation of this concept.

5.2 Select learning designs

Desired outcome 5.2.2: Applies knowledge to the selection of appropriate learning designs.

Level 1	Level 2	Level 3	Level 4	Level 5	Level 6
• Confirms the presence of essential features of high-quality learning designs (e.g., active engagement, reflection, metacognition, ongoing support, etc.). • Selects in-person, blended, and online learning designs to achieve professional learning goals. • Supports individuals, teams, coaches, SLT, and other learning facilitators to select appropriate learning designs for individual, team, and schoolwide professional learning.	• Identifies and discusses essential features of high-quality learning designs (e.g., active engagement, reflection, metacognition, ongoing support, etc.). • Selects in-person, blended, and online learning designs to achieve professional learning goals. • Supports teams, coaches, and other learning facilitators to select appropriate learning designs for individual, team, and schoolwide professional learning.	• Selects in-person, blended, and online learning designs to achieve professional learning goals. • Supports teams to select appropriate learning designs for individual, team, and schoolwide professional learning.	• Selects learning designs that align with expected outcomes.	• Fails to select appropriate learning designs in professional learning.	

5.2 Select learning designs

Desired outcome 5.2.3: Develops and shares knowledge about technology-enhanced learning designs.

Level 1	Level 2	Level 3	Level 4	Level 5	Level 6
• Develops knowledge about available and emerging technology-enhanced learning designs. • Shares knowledge about technology-enhanced learning designs with staff, SLT, coaches, and other learning facilitators. • Identifies and shares, with SLT, coaches, and other learning facilitators, the benefits and limitations of technology-enhanced learning designs. • Establishes and applies, with staff, SLT, coaches, and other learning facilitators, criteria for selecting technology-enhanced professional learning designs. • Advocates the use of technology-enhanced learning designs to increase the efficiency and effectiveness of professional learning.	• Develops knowledge about available technology-enhanced learning designs. • Shares knowledge about technology-enhanced learning designs with SLT, coaches, and other learning facilitators. • Identifies and shares, with SLT, coaches, and other learning facilitators, the benefits and limitations of technology-enhanced learning designs. • Establishes and applies, with SLT, coaches, and other learning facilitators, the criteria for selecting technology-enhanced professional learning designs. • Advocates the use of technology-enhanced learning designs to increase the efficiency and effectiveness of professional learning.	• Identifies and shares with learning facilitators available technology-enhanced learning designs. • Identifies and shares benefits and limitations of technology-enhanced learning designs. • Establishes and applies criteria for selecting technology-enhanced professional learning designs.	• Identifies available technology-enhanced learning designs.	• Fails to develop or share knowledge about technology-enhanced professional learning designs.	

5.2 Select learning designs

Desired outcome 5.2.4: Implements appropriate learning designs.

Level 1	Level 2	Level 3	Level 4	Level 5	Level 6
• Models appropriate in-person, blended, and online learning designs during meetings and professional learning with individuals, teams, whole staff, and SLT. • Establishes expectations that learning teams use appropriate in-person, blended, and online learning designs. • Supports coaches and other learning facilitators to implement appropriate in-person, blended, and online learning designs to enhance and differentiate professional learning. • Analyzes the relationship between learning designs used and results achieved.	• Models appropriate in-person, blended, and online learning designs during meetings and professional learning with individuals, teams, whole staff, and SLT. • Establishes expectations that learning teams use appropriate in-person, blended, and online learning designs. • Supports coaches and other learning facilitators to implement appropriate in-person, blended, and online learning designs to enhance and differentiate professional learning.	• Models appropriate in-person, blended, and online learning designs during professional learning with individuals, teams, whole staff, and SLT. • Establishes expectations that learning teams use appropriate in-person, blended, and online learning designs. • Supports coaches and other learning facilitators to implement appropriate in-person, blended, and online learning designs to enhance and differentiate professional learning.	• Models appropriate in-person, blended, and online learning designs during schoolwide professional learning. • Supports coaches and other learning facilitators to implement appropriate in-person, blended, and online learning designs.	• Models appropriate in-person, blended, and online learning designs during schoolwide professional learning.	• Fails to implement appropriate learning designs for professional learning.

5.2 Select learning designs

Desired outcome 5.2.5: Aligns professional learning designs with desired changes in classroom instruction.

Level 1	Level 2	Level 3	Level 4	Level 5	Level 6
• Identifies, with staff, SLT, coaches, and other learning facilitators, the changes in classroom instruction required to achieve professional learning goals. • Selects designs for individual, team, and schoolwide professional learning that model and align with the desired changes in instructional practice. • Implements the learning designs with fidelity. • Analyzes, with staff, SLT, coaches, and other learning facilitators, the effectiveness of the selected learning designs to produce changes in classroom practice.	• Identifies, with SLT, coaches, and other learning facilitators, the changes in classroom instruction desired to achieve professional learning goals. • Selects designs for individual, team, and schoolwide professional learning that model and align with the desired changes in instructional practice. • Implements the learning designs with fidelity.	• Identifies changes in classroom instruction desired to achieve professional learning goals. • Selects designs for individual, team, and schoolwide professional learning that model and align with the desired changes in instructional practice. • Implements the learning designs with fidelity.	• Selects designs for individual professional learning that model and align with the desired changes in instructional practice.	• Fails to align professional learning designs with desired changes in classroom instruction.	

5.3 Promote active engagement

Desired outcome 5.3.1: Models active engagement in professional learning.

Level 1	Level 2	Level 3	Level 4	Level 5	Level 6
• Engages actively as a participant in individual, team, and schoolwide professional learning. • Elicits staff members' participation and contribution to discussions during individual, team, and schoolwide professional learning. • Models and shares strategies and protocols for active engagement in individual, team, and schoolwide professional learning. • Provides self-assessment tools about active engagement. • Assesses, with staff, the effectiveness and frequency of active engagement.to make improvements.	• Engages actively as a participant in individual, team, and schoolwide professional learning. • Elicits staff members' participation and contribution to discussions in individual, team, and schoolwide professional learning. • Models strategies and protocols for active engagement in individual, team, and schoolwide professional learning. • Provides self-assessment tools about active engagement.	• Engages actively as a participant in individual, team, and schoolwide professional learning. • Elicits staff members' participation and contribution to discussions in individual, team, and schoolwide professional learning. • Models strategies and protocols for active engagement in individual, team, and schoolwide professional learning.	• Engages actively as a participant in individual, team, and schoolwide professional learning. • Elicits staff members' participation and contribution to discussions in individual, team, and schoolwide professional learning.	• Engages actively as a participant in individual, team, and schoolwide professional learning.	• Fails to model and promote active engagement in professional learning.

5.3 Promote active engagement

Desired outcome 5.3.2: Promotes active engagement in the learning process.

Level 1	Level 2	Level 3	Level 4	Level 5	Level 6
• Establishes an expectation that individual, team, and schoolwide professional learning integrates active engagement strategies and protocols. • Recommends to and supports SLT, coaches, and other learning facilitators to use active engagement strategies and protocols in professional learning. • Supports staff to engage actively in learning processes. • Supports staff in holding each other accountable for active participation in professional learning. • Monitors active engagement in individual, team, and schoolwide learning.	• Establishes an expectation that individual, team, and schoolwide professional learning integrates active engagement strategies and protocols. • Recommends to and supports SLT, coaches, and other learning facilitators to use strategies and protocols for active engagement in professional learning. • Supports staff to engage actively in learning processes. • Supports staff in holding each other accountable for active participation in professional learning. • Monitors active engagement in team and schoolwide learning.	• Establishes an expectation that individual, team, and schoolwide professional learning integrates active engagement strategies and protocols. • Supports staff to engage actively in learning processes. • Supports staff in holding each other accountable for active participation in professional learning. • Monitors active engagement in schoolwide learning.	• Establishes an expectation that individual, team, and schoolwide professional learning integrates active engagement strategies and protocols.	• Fails to promote or support active engagement in professional learning.	

6.1 Apply change research

Desired outcome 6.1.1: Develops own and staff's capacity to apply research on change to support implementation of professional learning. *

Level 1	Level 2	Level 3	Level 4	Level 5	Level 6
• Reviews research studies and examples of exemplary change practices (IC maps, SoC, LoU, RPLIM, PDSA, etc.) to develop own understanding of and skills needed to lead the change process. • Participates, with colleagues and staff, in professional learning about the change process to address opportunities and problems of practice. • Develops SLT, individual, team, and whole staff understanding of and skills needed to lead, facilitate, and participate in the change process. • Demonstrates the value of research by sharing and citing relevant studies and reports when discussing change.	• Reviews research studies and examples of exemplary change practices (IC maps, SoC, LoU, RPLIM, PDSA, etc.) to develop own understanding of and skills needed to lead the change process. • Participates in professional learning about the change process to address opportunities and problems of practice. • Discusses information with SLT to increase its understanding of the change process. • Demonstrates the value of research by sharing and citing relevant studies and reports when discussing change.	• Reviews research studies and examples of exemplary practice (IC maps, SoC, LoU, RPLIM, PDSA, etc.) to develop own understanding of and skills needed to lead the change process. • Participates in professional learning about the change process to address opportunities and problems of practice.	• Reads articles, papers, and reports about the change process.	• Fails to engage in ongoing professional learning about the change process.	

*See the Appendix (p. 262) for an explanation of this concept.

6.1 Apply change research

Desired outcome 6.1.2: Applies research on change to plan and lead the implementation of professional learning.

Level 1	Level 2	Level 3	Level 4	Level 5	Level 6
• Uses, with SLT, individuals, teams, and whole staff, change research to make decisions about implementation. • Adopts patience and perseverance to support staff throughout the change process. • Interacts monthly with each staff member to assess and respond to concerns related to implementation. • Recognizes staff members' efforts and accomplishments in implementation with public and private acknowledgment.	• Uses, with SLT, change research to make decisions about implementation. • Adopts patience and perseverance to support staff throughout the change process. • Interacts quarterly with each staff member to assess and respond to concerns related to implementation. • Recognizes staff members' efforts and accomplishments in implementation with private acknowledgment.	• Uses change research to make decisions about implementation. • Interacts semiannually with each staff member to assess and respond to concerns related to implementation. • Recognizes schoolwide efforts and accomplishments in implementation.	• Uses change research to make decisions about implementation.	• Fails to apply change research to plans and actions to support implementation of professional learning.	

Desired outcome 6.1.3: Monitors implementation of professional learning.

Level 1	Level 2	Level 3	Level 4	Level 5	Level 6
• Develops, with staff, coaches, other learning facilitators, and SLT, guides/tools (e.g., IC maps) to clarify expectations for implementation. • Uses guides/tools to support staff implementation of professional learning. • Meets with individuals, teams, whole staff, and SLT to use guides/tools to assess and refine implementation.	• Develops, with SLT, coaches, and other learning facilitators, guides/tools (e.g., IC maps) to clarify expectations. • Uses guides/tools to observe staff use of professional learning. • Meets with individuals and SLT to use guides/tools to assess and refine implementation.	• Uses guides/tools to observe staff use of professional learning. • Meets with individuals to discuss use of guides/tools to assess and refine implementation.	• States expectation for implementing professional learning.	• Fails to monitor implementation of professional learning.	

6.2 Sustain implementation

	Level 1	Level 2	Level 3	Level 4	Level 5	Level 6
Desired outcome 6.2.1: Differentiates support for implementation of professional learning.						
	• Demonstrates belief in colleagues' ability and willingness to be effective educators. • Embeds differentiated support for implementation into the plan for professional learning. • Uses the Standards for Professional Learning to guide the design and facilitation of ongoing professional learning to deepen understanding, enhance implementation, and refine practice. • Gathers data from colleagues about support needed for full implementation. • Designs and provides differentiated, ongoing professional learning to accelerate and refine implementation based on data gathered. • Employs multiple types of support to address each individual staff member's areas of need related to implementation. • Employs a variety of technology-enhanced implementation supports.	• Embeds differentiated support for implementation into the plan for professional learning. • Uses the Standards for Professional Learning to guide the design and facilitation of ongoing professional learning to deepen understanding, enhance implementation, and refine practice. • Designs and provides differentiated, ongoing professional learning to accelerate and refine implementation based on data gathered. • Employs multiple types of support to address each individual staff member's areas of need related to implementation. • Employs technology-enhanced implementation support.	• Embeds support for implementation into the plan for professional learning. • Uses the Standards for Professional Learning to guide the design and facilitation of ongoing professional learning to deepen understanding, enhance implementation, and refine practice. • Employs multiple types of support to address each individual staff member's areas of need related to implementation.	• Provides implementation support to individuals and teams when requested.	• Provides implementation support to individuals when requested.	• Fails to provide differentiated support for implementation.

6.2 Sustain implementation

Desired outcome 6.2.2: Continues support to reach high-fidelity implementation of professional learning.

Level 1	Level 2	Level 3	Level 4	Level 5	Level 6
• Plans, with SLT, staff, coaches, and other learning facilitators, continuous support for three to five years for implementation of professional learning. • Adjusts, with SLT and staff, support for implementation of professional learning with the maturity and fidelity of implementation. • Provides easily accessible in-person, blended, and technology-enhanced support that individuals, teams, and whole staff can access daily. • Communicates, with SLT and staff, expectations that individuals, teams, and whole staff will access support at least weekly to refine and improve implementation.	• Plans, with SLT, coaches, and other learning facilitators, continuous support for two years for implementation of professional learning. • Adjusts, with SLT, support for implementation of professional learning with the maturity and fidelity of implementation. • Provides easily accessible in-person, blended, and technology-enhanced support that teams and whole staff can access weekly. • Communicates, with SLT, expectations that individuals, teams, and whole staff will access support at least biweekly to refine and improve implementation.	• Plans ongoing support for one year for implementation of professional learning. • Provides easily accessible in-person, blended, and technology-enhanced support that whole staff can access monthly. • Communicates expectations that individuals, teams, and whole staff will access support at least monthly to refine and improve implementation.	• Provides easily accessible support that staff can access quarterly.	• Facilitates access to support for implementation.	• Fails to provide support for implementation of professional learning.

6.3 Provide constructive feedback

Desired outcome 6.3.1: Develops own and staff's capacity to give and receive constructive feedback.

Level 1	Level 2	Level 3	Level 4	Level 5	Level 6
• Develops, with staff and SLT, research-based knowledge and skills to give and receive constructive feedback. • Provides risk-free opportunities for individuals, teams, and whole staff to practice giving and receiving feedback. • Models giving and receiving constructive feedback.	• Develops, with staff and SLT, research-based knowledge and skills to give and receive constructive feedback. • Models giving and receiving constructive feedback.	• Develops, with SLT, knowledge and skills to give and receive constructive feedback.	• Develops knowledge and skills to give and receive constructive feedback.	• Fails to develop own and staff knowledge and skills in giving and receiving constructive feedback.	

6.3 Provide constructive feedback

Desired outcome 6.3.2: Gives and receives constructive feedback to accelerate and refine implementation of professional learning.

Level 1	Level 2	Level 3	Level 4	Level 5	Level 6
• Identifies and makes available, with staff, SLT, coach, and other learning facilitators, multiple in-person, blended, and technology-based strategies and tools (e.g., peer coaching, reviewing student work, lesson study, instructional rounds, walk-throughs, peer observation, e-coaching, etc.) to give and receive feedback on implementation. • Provides to and seeks from individuals, teams, and whole staff constructive feedback on implementation weekly using varied tools and strategies. • Analyzes and shares, with staff and SLT, feedback data monthly about implementation to improve individual, team, and schoolwide support.	• Identifies and makes available, with staff, SLT, coach, and other learning facilitators, multiple in-person, blended, and technology-based strategies and tools (e.g., peer coaching, reviewing student work, lesson study, instructional rounds, walk-throughs, peer observation, e-coaching, etc.) to give and receive feedback on implementation. • Provides to and seeks from individuals, teams, and whole staff constructive feedback on implementation monthly using varied tools and strategies. • Analyzes and shares, with staff and SLT, feedback data quarterly about implementation to improve individual, team, and schoolwide support.	• Identifies and makes available, with staff, SLT, coach, and other learning facilitators, multiple in-person, blended, and technology-based strategies and tools (e.g., peer coaching, reviewing student work, lesson study, instructional rounds, walk-throughs, peer observation, e-coaching, etc.) to give and receive feedback on implementation. • Provides to and seeks from individuals, teams, and whole staff constructive feedback on implementation quarterly using varied tools and strategies. • Analyzes and shares, with staff and SLT, feedback data quarterly about implementation to improve individual, team, and schoolwide support.	• Provides to and seeks from individuals, teams, and whole staff constructive feedback on implementation semiannually using varied tools and strategies. • Analyzes and shares, with staff and SLT, feedback data semiannually about implementation to improve individual, team, and schoolwide support.	• Provides to and seeks from individuals, teams, and whole staff constructive feedback on implementation annually using varied tools and strategies.	• Fails to seek and provide input on implementation of professional learning.

7.1 Meet performance standards

Desired outcome 7.1.1: Uses educator performance standards to identify professional learning needs.

Level 1	Level 2	Level 3	Level 4	Level 5	Level 6
• Analyzes, with individuals, teams, and whole staff, educator performance standards. • Assesses staff practice based on performance standards. • Facilitates individual, team, and whole staff reflection on current practices compared to educator performance standards. • Uses the assessment, reflection, and standards to promote individual, team, and whole staff identification of strengths, areas for growth, needs, and goals for professional learning.	• Assesses staff practice based on performance standards. • Uses the assessment and standards to promote individual, team, and whole staff identification of strengths, areas for growth, needs, and goals for professional learning.	• Assesses staff practice based on performance standards. • Uses the assessment to promote individual, team, and whole staff identification of strengths, areas for growth, needs, and goals for professional learning.	• Identifies staff strengths, areas for growth, needs, and goals for professional learning without reference to performance standards.	• Identifies needs for professional learning without considering staff performance standards.	• Fails to identify needs for professional learning.

www.learningforward.org   800-727-7288

7.1 Meet performance standards

Desired outcome 7.1.2: Uses educator performance standards to make decisions about the content of professional learning.

Level 1	Level 2	Level 3	Level 4	Level 5	Level 6
• Links areas for growth to educator performance standards to identify knowledge, skills, dispositions, and practices needed to attain individual, team, and schoolwide professional learning goals. • Monitors content of individual, team, and schoolwide professional learning for alignment with educator performance standards. • Supports individuals and teams in using educator performance standards to identify the content of professional learning.	• Links areas for growth to educator performance standards to identify knowledge, skills, and practices needed to attain individual, team, and schoolwide professional learning goals. • Monitors content of individual, team, and schoolwide professional learning for alignment with educator performance standards.	• Links areas for growth to educator performance standards to identify knowledge and skills needed to attain schoolwide professional learning goals. • Monitors content of schoolwide professional learning for alignment with educator performance standards.	• Identifies the content for professional learning based on educator performance standards.	• Identifies the content for professional learning without reference to educator performance standards.	

7.1 Meet performance standards

Desired outcome 7.1.3: Engages in professional learning to meet principal performance standards.

Level 1	Level 2	Level 3	Level 4	Level 5	Level 6
• Develops research-based knowledge about principal role expectations, responsibilities, and performance standards. • Engages in professional learning to develop leadership knowledge, skills, dispositions, and practices reflected in performance standards. • Practices leadership skills until mastery is achieved. • Engages in coaching, feedback, and reflection on own leadership performance.	• Develops knowledge about principal performance standards. • Engages in professional learning to develop leadership knowledge, skills, practices, and dispositions reflected in performance standards. • Practices leadership skills until mastery is achieved. • Engages in coaching, feedback, and reflection on own leadership performance.	• Studies principal performance standards. • Engages in professional learning to develop leadership skills reflected in performance standards. • Practices leadership skills until mastery is achieved.	• Reads principal performance standards.	• Fails to engage in professional learning related to performance standards.	

7.2 Address learning outcomes

Desired outcome 7.2.1: Uses student learning outcomes to identify professional learning needs.

Level 1	Level 2	Level 3	Level 4	Level 5	Level 6
• Analyzes, with colleagues, student learning outcomes. • Facilitates individual, team, and schoolwide assessment of current practice based on student learning outcomes. • Assesses staff practice based on student learning outcomes. • Prepares and models for individuals, teams, and whole staff how to derive professional learning needs from high-priority student learning outcomes. • Uses the assessment, reflection, and standards to promote individual, team, and whole staff reflection on strengths, areas for growth, and needs and goals for professional learning.	• Assesses staff's practice based on student learning outcomes. • Prepares and models for individuals, teams, and whole staff how to derive professional learning needs from high-priority student learning outcomes. • Uses the assessment and standards to promote individual, team, and whole staff reflection on strengths, areas for growth, and needs and goals for professional learning.	• Assesses staff's practice based on student learning outcomes. • Uses the assessment to promote individual, team, and whole staff reflection on strengths, areas for growth, and needs and goals for professional learning.	• Identifies needs and goals for professional learning without reference to student learning outcomes.	• Identifies needs for professional learning without reference to student learning outcomes.	

7.2 Address learning outcomes

	Level 1	Level 2	Level 3	Level 4	Level 5	Level 6
Desired outcome 7.2.2: Uses student learning outcomes to make decisions about the content of professional learning.						
	• Links student learning outcomes to areas for growth to identify knowledge, skills, dispositions, and practices needed to attain individual, team, and schoolwide professional learning goals. • Monitors content of individual, team, and schoolwide professional learning for alignment with high-priority student learning outcomes. • Uses student learning outcomes to identify the learning designs needed to attain individual, team, and schoolwide professional learning goals.	• Links student learning outcomes to areas for growth to identify knowledge, skills, and practices needed to attain individual, team, and schoolwide professional learning goals. • Uses student learning outcomes to identify the learning designs needed to attain individual, team, and schoolwide professional learning goals.	• Links student learning outcomes to areas for growth to identify knowledge and skills needed to attain schoolwide professional learning goals. • Uses student learning outcomes to identify the learning designs needed to attain schoolwide professional learning goals.	• Selects the content for professional learning from student learning outcomes.	• Identifies the content for professional learning without reference to student learning outcomes.	
Desired outcome 7.2.3: Engages in professional learning to increase student results.						
	• Engages, with colleagues, in professional learning to develop understanding of the relationship between leadership and student learning outcomes. • Engages in coaching, feedback, and reflection to analyze and improve the effects of own performance on student learning outcomes.	• Engages in professional learning to develop understanding of the relationship between leadership and student learning. • Analyzes the effects of own performance on student learning outcomes.	• Studies effects of leadership on student learning outcomes. • Reflects on the effects of own performance on student learning.	• Studies effects of leadership on student learning outcomes.	• Fails to engage in professional learning related to leadership and student learning outcomes.	

7.3 Build coherence

Desired outcome 7.3.1: Builds congruence between professional learning and other school and school system initiatives.

Level 1	Level 2	Level 3	Level 4	Level 5	Level 6
• Develops staff understanding of the relationships among school and system initiatives; school improvement goals; their individual, team, and schoolwide professional learning goals; and professional learning. • Emphasizes congruence among multiple initiatives through the use of available resources. • Leverages expectations and school improvement goals to reinforce how professional learning applies across multiple other school and system processes and initiatives. • Aligns professional learning with school improvement goals and other school and system processes and initiatives.	• Develops staff understanding of the relationships among school and system initiatives, the school improvement goals, schoolwide professional learning goals, and professional learning. • Emphasizes congruence among multiple initiatives through the use of available resources. • Leverages expectations and school improvement goals to reinforce how professional learning applies across multiple other school and system processes and initiatives.	• Develops staff understanding of the relationships among the school improvement goals, schoolwide professional learning goals, and professional learning.	• Communicates to staff the relationships among the school improvement goals, schoolwide professional learning goals, and professional learning.	• Fails to develop staff understanding of the relationships among the school and system initiatives and processes, the school improvement goals, schoolwide professional learning goals, and professional learning.	

7.3 Build coherence

	Level 1	Level 2	Level 3	Level 4	Level 5	Level 6
Desired outcome 7.3.2: Links professional learning with past experiences.						
	• Collects data about staff's past experiences with individual, team, schoolwide, and out-of-school professional learning; experience with the planned content of professional learning; and the school's history with change. • Uses the data when planning and implementing professional learning.	• Collects data about staff's past experiences with individual, team, and schoolwide professional learning and experience with the planned content of professional learning. • Uses the data when planning professional learning.	• Collects data about staff's past experiences with individual, team, and schoolwide professional learning. • Uses the data when planning professional learning.	• Forms assumptions about staff's past experiences with individual, team, schoolwide, and out-of-school professional learning. • Uses the assumptions when planning professional learning.	• Fails to gather data about staff's past experiences with professional learning.	

Crosswalk

Use the crosswalk on the following pages to compare desired outcomes across the four school-based roles.

The crosswalk is useful in considering how educators in different roles have different responsibilities in standards implementation.

1.0 Learning Communities

TEACHER	COACH	SCHOOL LEADERSHIP TEAM	PRINCIPAL
1.1 Engage in continuous improvement			
Desired outcome 1.1.1: Develops capacity to apply the seven-step cycle of continuous improvement.	**Desired outcome 1.1.1:** Develops own and others' capacity to apply the seven-step cycle of continuous improvement.	**Desired outcome 1.1.1:** Develops own and others' capacity to apply the seven-step cycle of continuous improvement.	**Desired outcome 1.1.1:** Develops own and others' capacity to apply the seven-step cycle of continuous improvement.
Desired outcome 1.1.2: Applies the cycle of continuous improvement with fidelity in professional learning.	**Desired outcome 1.1.2:** Applies the cycle of continuous improvement with fidelity to facilitate professional learning.	**Desired outcome 1.1.2:** Applies the cycle of continuous improvement with fidelity to decisions about professional learning.	**Desired outcome 1.1.2:** Applies the cycle of continuous improvement with fidelity to lead professional learning.
		Desired outcome 1.1.3: Supports application of the cycle of continuous improvement.	
1.2 Develop collective responsibility			
Desired outcome 1.2.1: Advances collective responsibility.	**Desired outcome 1.2.1:** Advances collective responsibility.	**Desired outcome 1.2.1:** Advances collective responsibility.	**Desired outcome 1.2.1:** Advances collective responsibility.
Desired outcome 1.2.2: Engages with colleagues to meet the needs of all students.	**Desired outcome 1.2.2:** Fosters engagement of all colleagues in meeting the needs of all students.	**Desired outcome 1.2.2:** Fosters engagement of all staff in meeting the needs of all students.	**Desired outcome 1.2.2:** Fosters engagement of all staff in meeting the needs of all students.
Desired outcome 1.2.3: Models collective responsibility by participating in learning communities.	**Desired outcome 1.2.3:** Models collective responsibility by participating in learning communities.	**Desired outcome 1.2.3:** Models collective responsibility by participating in learning communities.	**Desired outcome 1.2.3:** Models collective responsibility by participating in learning communities.
1.3 Create alignment and accountability			
Desired outcome 1.3.1: Aligns professional learning with school goals.	**Desired outcome 1.3.1:** Aligns professional learning with school goals.	**Desired outcome 1.3.1:** Aligns professional learning with school and system goals.	**Desired outcome 1.3.1:** Aligns professional learning with school and system goals.
	Desired outcome 1.3.2: Supports colleagues to use the cycle of continuous improvement to achieve professional learning goals.	**Desired outcome 1.3.2:** Monitors the use of the cycle of continuous improvement to achieve professional learning goals.	**Desired outcome 1.3.2:** Monitors the use of the cycle of continuous improvement to achieve professional learning goals.

www.learningforward.org   800-727-7288

2.0 Leadership

TEACHER	COACH	SCHOOL LEADERSHIP TEAM	PRINCIPAL
2.1 Develop capacity for learning and leading			
Desired outcome 2.1.1: Commits to continuous professional learning.	**Desired outcome 2.1.1:** Commits to continuous professional learning.	**Desired outcome 2.1.1:** Commits to continuous professional learning.	**Desired outcome 2.1.1:** Commits to continuous professional learning.
Desired outcome 2.1.2: Develops capacity for leadership of professional learning.	**Desired outcome 2.1.2:** Develops own and others' capacity for leadership of professional learning.	**Desired outcome 2.1.2:** Develops own and others' capacity for leadership of professional learning.	**Desired outcome 2.1.2:** Develops own and others' capacity for leadership of professional learning.
Desired outcome 2.1.3: Understands and uses the Standards for Professional Learning in decisions about professional learning.	**Desired outcome 2.1.3:** Understands and uses the Standards for Professional Learning in making decisions about professional learning.	**Desired outcome 2.1.3:** Understands and uses the Standards for Professional Learning in making decisions about professional learning.	**Desired outcome 2.1.3:** Understands and uses the Standards for Professional Learning in making decisions about professional learning.
Desired outcome 2.1.4: Serves as a leader of professional learning.	**Desired outcome 2.1.4:** Serves as a leader of professional learning.	**Desired outcome 2.1.4:** Serves as a leader of professional learning.	**Desired outcome 2.1.4:** Serves as a leader of professional learning.
			Desired outcome 2.1.5: Coaches and supervises school-based facilitators of professional learning.
2.2 Advocate for professional learning			
Desired outcome 2.2.1: Articulates the link between student learning and professional learning.	**Desired outcome 2.2.1:** Articulates the link between student learning and professional learning.	**Desired outcome 2.2.1:** Articulates the link between student learning and professional learning.	**Desired outcome 2.2.1:** Articulates the link between student learning and professional learning.
Desired outcome 2.2.2: Advocates high-quality professional learning.	**Desired outcome 2.2.2:** Advocates high-quality professional learning.	**Desired outcome 2.2.2:** Advocates high-quality professional learning.	**Desired outcome 2.2.2:** Advocates high-quality professional learning.

2.0 Leadership

TEACHER	COACH	SCHOOL LEADERSHIP TEAM	PRINCIPAL
2.3 Create support systems and structures			
Desired outcome 2.3.1: Contributes to systems and structures for effective professional learning.	**Desired outcome 2.3.1:** Contributes to establishing systems and structures for effective professional learning.	**Desired outcome 2.3.1:** Establishes systems and structures for effective professional learning.	**Desired outcome 2.3.1:** Establishes systems and structures for effective professional learning.
Desired outcome 2.3.2: Develops capacity for skillful collaboration.	**Desired outcome 2.3.2:** Prepares and supports colleagues to develop collaboration skills.	**Desired outcome 2.3.2:** Prepares and supports staff for skillful collaboration.	**Desired outcome 2.3.2:** Prepares and supports staff for skillful collaboration.
Desired outcome 2.3.3: Contributes to the development and maintenance of a collaborative culture.	**Desired outcome 2.3.3:** Contributes to the development and maintenance of a collaborative culture.	**Desired outcome 2.3.3:** Contributes to the development and maintenance of a collaborative culture.	**Desired outcome 2.3.3:** Cultivates and maintains a collaborative culture.
			Desired outcome 2.3.4: Creates expectations for collaborative professional learning within the school day.

3.0 Resources

3.1 Prioritize human, fiscal, material, technology, and time resources

TEACHER	COACH	SCHOOL LEADERSHIP TEAM	PRINCIPAL
Desired outcome 3.1.1: Contributes to definition of resources for professional learning.	**Desired outcome 3.1.1:** Defines resources for professional learning.	**Desired outcome 3.1.1:** Defines resources for professional learning.	**Desired outcome 3.1.1:** Defines resources for professional learning.
Desired outcome 3.1.2: Recommends resources to align professional learning with high-priority student and educator learning needs.	**Desired outcome 3.1.2:** Recommends resources to align professional learning with high-priority student and educator learning needs.	**Desired outcome 3.1.2:** Recommends resources to align professional learning with high-priority student and educator learning needs.	**Desired outcome 3.1.2:** Allocates resources for professional learning to align with high-priority student and educator learning needs.
Desired outcome 3.1.3: Selects appropriate resources for professional learning.	**Desired outcome 3.1.3:** Develops internal resources to support professional learning.	**Desired outcome 3.1.3:** Allocates time for collaborative professional learning.	**Desired outcome 3.1.3:** Allocates time for collaborative professional learning.
	Desired outcome 3.1.4: Recommends resources to support implementation of professional learning.	**Desired outcome 3.1.4:** Recommends resources to support implementation of professional learning.	**Desired outcome 3.1.4:** Allocates resources to support implementation of professional learning.
	Desired outcome 3.1.5: Serves as a resource for professional learning.		

3.2 Monitor resources

TEACHER	COACH	SCHOOL LEADERSHIP TEAM	PRINCIPAL
Desired outcome 3.2.1: Monitors effectiveness of the use of resources for professional learning.	**Desired outcome 3.2.1:** Monitors effectiveness of the use of resources for professional learning.	**Desired outcome 3.2.1:** Monitors effectiveness of the use of resources for professional learning.	**Desired outcome 3.2.1:** Monitors effectiveness of the use of resources for professional learning.

3.3 Coordinate resources

TEACHER	COACH	SCHOOL LEADERSHIP TEAM	PRINCIPAL
Desired outcome 3.3.1: Implements a comprehensive resource plan for professional learning.	**Desired outcome 3.3.1:** Contributes to a comprehensive resource plan for professional learning.	**Desired outcome 3.3.1:** Designs and implements a comprehensive resource plan for professional learning.	**Desired outcome 3.3.1:** Designs and implements a comprehensive resource plan for professional learning.

4.0 Data

TEACHER	COACH	SCHOOL LEADERSHIP TEAM	PRINCIPAL
4.1 Analyze student, educator, and system data			
Desired outcome 4.1.1: Develops capacity to analyze and interpret data.	**Desired outcome 4.1.1:** Develops own and colleagues' capacity to analyze and interpret data.	**Desired outcome 4.1.1:** Develops own and colleagues' capacity to analyze and interpret data.	**Desired outcome 4.1.1:** Develops own and staff capacity to analyze and interpret data.
Desired outcome 4.1.2: Analyzes and interprets multiple sources of student data to determine professional learning needs.	**Desired outcome 4.1.2:** Engages colleagues in analyzing and interpreting multiple sources of student data to determine professional learning needs.	**Desired outcome 4.1.2:** Analyzes and interprets multiple sources of student data to determine professional learning needs.	**Desired outcome 4.1.2:** Describes multiple sources of available student, educator, and system data.
Desired outcome 4.1.3: Analyzes and interprets educator data to determine professional learning needs.	**Desired outcome 4.1.3:** Engages colleagues in analyzing and interpreting multiple sources of educator data to determine professional learning needs.	**Desired outcome 4.1.3:** Analyzes and interprets multiple sources of educator data to determine professional learning needs.	**Desired outcome 4.1.3:** Analyzes and interprets multiple sources of student data to determine professional learning needs.
Desired outcome 4.1.4: Analyzes and interprets school data to determine professional learning needs.	**Desired outcome 4.1.4:** Engages colleagues in analyzing and interpreting multiple sources of school data to determine professional learning needs.	**Desired outcome 4.1.4:** Analyzes and interprets multiple sources of school data to determine professional learning needs.	**Desired outcome 4.1.4:** Analyzes and interprets multiple sources of educator data to determine professional learning needs.
Desired outcome 4.1.5: Uses analyzed data to determine professional learning needs.	**Desired outcome 4.1.5:** Supports colleagues to use analyzed data to determine professional learning needs.	**Desired outcome 4.1.5:** Uses analyzed data to determine professional learning needs.	**Desired outcome 4.1.5:** Analyzes and interprets multiple sources of school data to determine professional learning needs.
	Desired outcome 4.1.6: Supports colleagues in ongoing data analysis and interpretation to support continuous improvement.		**Desired outcome 4.1.6:** Engages in ongoing data analysis and interpretation to support continuous improvement.

4.0 Data

TEACHER	COACH	SCHOOL LEADERSHIP TEAM	PRINCIPAL
4.2 Assess progress			
Desired outcome 4.2.1: Determines formative data to assess progress toward professional learning benchmarks and goals.	**Desired outcome 4.2.1:** Determines formative data to assess progress toward professional learning benchmarks and goals.	**Desired outcome 4.2.1:** Determines formative data to assess progress toward professional learning benchmarks and goals.	**Desired outcome 4.2.1:** Determines formative data to assess progress toward professional learning benchmarks and goals.
Desired outcome 4.2.2: Collects, analyzes, and uses data to continuously assess progress toward professional learning benchmarks and goals.	**Desired outcome 4.2.2:** Supports colleagues in collecting, analyzing, and using formative data to continuously assess progress toward professional learning benchmarks and goals.	**Desired outcome 4.2.2:** Collects, analyzes, and uses formative data to continuously assess progress toward professional learning benchmarks and goals.	**Desired outcome 4.2.2:** Collects and analyzes formative data to continuously assess progress toward professional learning benchmarks and goals.
Desired outcome 4.2.3: Uses analysis of progress to make adjustments in professional learning.	**Desired outcome 4.2.3:** Supports colleagues to use analysis of progress to make adjustments in professional learning.	**Desired outcome 4.2.3:** Uses analysis of progress to make adjustments in professional learning.	**Desired outcome 4.2.3:** Uses analysis of progress to make adjustments in professional learning.
4.3 Evaluate professional learning			
Desired outcome 4.3.1: Contributes to the development of an evaluation plan for professional learning.	**Desired outcome 4.3.1:** Contributes to the development of an evaluation plan for professional learning.	**Desired outcome 4.3.1:** Contributes to the development of an evaluation plan for professional learning.	**Desired outcome 4.3.1:** Develops a comprehensive plan for evaluating the impact of professional learning.
Desired outcome 4.3.2: Uses a variety of formative and summative data to evaluate the effectiveness and results of professional learning.	**Desired outcome 4.3.2:** Uses a variety of formative and summative data to evaluate the effectiveness and results of professional learning.	**Desired outcome 4.3.2:** Uses a variety of formative and summative data to evaluate the effectiveness and results of professional learning.	**Desired outcome 4.3.2:** Uses a variety of formative and summative data to evaluate the effectiveness and results of professional learning.
Desired outcome 4.3.3: Uses data to evaluate the effectiveness of professional learning designs, content, and duration.	**Desired outcome 4.3.3:** Supports colleagues to use data to evaluate the effectiveness of professional learning designs, content, and duration.	**Desired outcome 4.3.3:** Supports colleagues in using data to evaluate the effectiveness of schoolwide learning designs, content, and duration.	**Desired outcome 4.3.3:** Supports individuals and learning teams in using data to evaluate the effectiveness of learning designs, content, and duration.
	Desired outcome 4.3.4: Supports colleagues to use evaluation results to improve individual and team professional learning.	**Desired outcome 4.3.4:** Uses evaluation results to improve schoolwide professional learning.	**Desired outcome 4.3.4:** Uses evaluation results to improve professional learning.
	Desired outcome 4.3.5: Uses evaluation results to improve coaching.		

5.0 Learning Designs

TEACHER	COACH	SCHOOL LEADERSHIP TEAM	PRINCIPAL
5.1 Apply learning theories, research, and models			
Desired outcome 5.1.1: Develops a knowledge base about theories, research, and models of adult learning.	**Desired outcome 5.1.1:** Develops and shares a knowledge base about theories, research, and models of adult learning.	**Desired outcome 5.1.1:** Develops and shares a knowledge base about theories, research, and models of adult learning.	**Desired outcome 5.1.1:** Develops and shares a knowledge base about theories, research, and models of adult learning.
Desired outcome 5.1.2: Develops a knowledge base about multiple designs for professional learning.	**Desired outcome 5.1.2:** Builds colleagues' knowledge base about multiple designs for professional learning.	**Desired outcome 5.1.2:** Acquires and shares knowledge about multiple designs for professional learning.	**Desired outcome 5.1.2:** Acquires and shares knowledge about multiple designs for professional learning.
	Desired outcome 5.1.3: Implements multiple learning designs to facilitate professional learning.		
5.2 Select learning designs			
Desired outcome 5.2.1: Acquires and shares knowledge about the multiple factors influencing the selection of learning designs.	**Desired outcome 5.2.1:** Acquires and shares knowledge about the multiple factors influencing the selection of learning designs.	**Desired outcome 5.2.1:** Acquires and shares knowledge about the multiple factors influencing the selection of learning designs.	**Desired outcome 5.2.1:** Acquires and shares knowledge about the multiple factors influencing the selection of learning designs.
Desired outcome 5.2.2: Applies knowledge to the selection of appropriate learning designs.	**Desired outcome 5.2.2:** Applies knowledge to the selection of appropriate learning designs.	**Desired outcome 5.2.2:** Applies knowledge about the selection of appropriate learning designs.	**Desired outcome 5.2.2:** Applies knowledge to the selection of appropriate learning designs.
Desired outcome 5.2.3: Uses appropriate technology to enhance and extend professional learning.	**Desired outcome 5.2.3:** Develops and shares knowledge about technology-enhanced learning designs.	**Desired outcome 5.2.3:** Develops and shares knowledge about technology-enhanced learning designs.	**Desired outcome 5.2.3:** Develops and shares knowledge about technology-enhanced learning designs.
Desired outcome 5.2.4: Implements appropriate learning designs	**Desired outcome 5.2.4:** Implements appropriate learning designs.	**Desired outcome 5.2.4:** Implements appropriate learning designs.	**Desired outcome 5.2.4:** Implements appropriate learning designs.
Desired outcome 5.2.5: Aligns professional learning designs with desired changes in classroom instruction.	**Desired outcome 5.2.5:** Aligns professional learning designs with desired changes in classroom instruction.		**Desired outcome 5.2.5:** Aligns professional learning designs with desired changes in classroom instruction.

5.0 Learning Designs

5.3 Promote active engagement

TEACHER	COACH	SCHOOL LEADERSHIP TEAM	PRINCIPAL
Desired outcome 5.3.1: Engages with colleagues during professional learning.	**Desired outcome 5.3.1:** Models active engagement in professional learning.	**Desired outcome 5.3.1:** Models active engagement in professional learning.	**Desired outcome 5.3.1:** Models active engagement in professional learning.
Desired outcome 5.3.2: Supports colleagues to engage actively in professional learning.	**Desired outcome 5.3.2:** Supports colleagues to engage actively in professional learning.	**Desired outcome 5.3.2:** Supports colleagues to engage actively in professional learning.	**Desired outcome 5.3.2:** Promotes active engagement in the learning process.
	Desired outcome 5.3.3: Incorporates strategies to promote active engagement in professional learning.		

6.0 Implementation

	TEACHER	COACH	SCHOOL LEADERSHIP TEAM	PRINCIPAL
6.1 Apply change research				
	Desired outcome 6.1.1: Develops capacity to apply research on change to support implementation of professional learning.	**Desired outcome 6.1.1:** Develops capacity to apply research on change to support implementation of professional learning.	**Desired outcome 6.1.1:** Develops capacity to apply research on change to support implementation of professional learning.	**Desired outcome 6.1.1:** Develops own and staff's capacity to apply research on change to support implementation of professional learning.
	Desired outcome 6.1.2: Applies research on change when making decisions about professional learning.	**Desired outcome 6.1.2:** Applies research on change to facilitate the implementation of professional learning.	**Desired outcome 6.1.2:** Applies research on change to plan and lead the implementation of professional learning.	**Desired outcome 6.1.2:** Applies research on change to plan and lead the implementation of professional learning.
	Desired outcome 6.1.3: Monitors implementation of professional learning.	**Desired outcome 6.1.3:** Supports monitoring of the progress of implementation of professional learning.	**Desired outcome 6.1.3:** Monitors implementation of professional learning.	**Desired outcome 6.1.3:** Monitors implementation of professional learning.
6.2 Sustain implementation				
	Desired outcome 6.2.1: Participates in differentiated support for implementation of professional learning.	**Desired outcome 6.2.1:** Differentiates support for implementation of professional learning.	**Desired outcome 6.2.1:** Differentiates support for implementation of professional learning.	**Desired outcome 6.2.1:** Differentiates support for implementation of professional learning.
	Desired outcome 6.2.2: Continues support to reach high-fidelity implementation of professional learning.	**Desired outcome 6.2.2:** Continues support to reach high-fidelity implementation of professional learning.	**Desired outcome 6.2.2:** Continues support to reach high-fidelity implementation of professional learning.	**Desired outcome 6.2.2:** Continues support to reach high-fidelity implementation of professional learning.
6.3 Provide constructive feedback				
	Desired outcome 6.3.1: Develops capacity to give and receive constructive feedback.	**Desired outcome 6.3.1:** Develops capacity to give and receive constructive feedback.	**Desired outcome 6.3.1:** Develops own and staff's capacity to give and receive constructive feedback.	**Desired outcome 6.3.1:** Develops own and staff's capacity to give and receive constructive feedback.
	Desired outcome 6.3.2: Gives and receives constructive feedback to accelerate and refine implementation of professional learning.	**Desired outcome 6.3.2:** Gives and receives constructive feedback to accelerate and refine implementation of professional learning.	**Desired outcome 6.3.2:** Gives and receives constructive feedback to accelerate and refine implementation of professional learning.	**Desired outcome 6.3.2:** Gives and receives constructive feedback to accelerate and refine implementation of professional learning.

7.0 Outcomes

TEACHER	COACH	SCHOOL LEADERSHIP TEAM	PRINCIPAL
7.1 Meet performance standards			
Desired outcome 7.1.1: Uses educator performance standards to identify professional learning needs.	**Desired outcome 7.1.1:** Uses educator performance standards to identify professional learning needs.	**Desired outcome 7.1.1:** Uses educator performance standards to identify professional learning needs.	**Desired outcome 7.1.1:** Uses educator performance standards to identify professional learning needs.
Desired outcome 7.1.2: Uses educator performance standards to make decisions about the content of professional learning.	**Desired outcome 7.1.2:** Uses educator performance standards to make decisions about the content of professional learning.	**Desired outcome 7.1.2:** Uses educator performance standards to make decisions about the content of professional learning.	**Desired outcome 7.1.2:** Uses educator performance standards to make decisions about the content of professional learning.
Desired outcome 7.1.3: Engages in professional learning to meet teacher performance standards.	**Desired outcome 7.1.3:** Engages in professional learning to meet coach performance standards.	**Desired outcome 7.1.3:** Engages in professional learning to meet school leadership team performance standards.	**Desired outcome 7.1.3:** Engages in professional learning to meet principal performance standards.
7.2 Address learning outcomes			
Desired outcome 7.2.1: Uses student learning outcomes to identify professional learning needs.	**Desired outcome 7.2.1:** Uses student learning outcomes to identify professional learning needs.	**Desired outcome 7.2.1:** Uses student learning outcomes to identify professional learning needs.	**Desired outcome 7.2.1:** Uses student learning outcomes to identify professional learning needs.
Desired outcome 7.2.2: Uses student learning outcomes to make decisions about the content of professional learning.	**Desired outcome 7.2.2:** Uses student learning outcomes to inform decisions about the content of professional learning.	**Desired outcome 7.2.2:** Uses student learning outcomes to select the content of professional learning.	**Desired outcome 7.2.2:** Uses student learning outcomes to make decisions about the content of professional learning.
Desired outcome 7.2.3: Engages in professional learning to increase student results.	**Desired outcome 7.2.3:** Engages in professional learning to increase student results.	**Desired outcome 7.2.3:** Engages in professional learning to increase student results.	**Desired outcome 7.2.3:** Engages in professional learning to increase student results.
7.3 Build coherence			
Desired outcome 7.3.1: Develops an understanding of the congruence between professional learning and other school and school system initiatives.	**Desired outcome 7.3.1:** Builds congruence between professional learning and other school and school system initiatives.	**Desired outcome 7.3.1:** Builds congruence between professional learning and other school and school system initiatives.	**Desired outcome 7.3.1:** Builds congruence between professional learning and other school and school system initiatives.
	Desired outcome 7.3.2: Links professional learning with past experiences.	**Desired outcome 7.3.2:** Links professional learning with past experiences.	**Desired outcome 7.3.2:** Links professional learning with past experiences.

Appendix:
Selected terms and concepts

The Innovation Configuration maps include several concepts for which readers may need more information to advance their work in standards implementation. A few are included here, listed in order by the standard where they are primarily referenced. Learning Forward's website (www.learningforward.org) is also useful for finding articles and tools on specific concepts included in this book.

LEARNING COMMUNITIES
Seven-step cycle of continuous improvement

This concept is referenced in the desired outcomes for the Learning Communities standard across all school-based roles. Educators undertaking the seven steps:

1. Analyze educator, student, and school data to identify student learning needs.
2. Define educator professional learning goals based on student learning needs.
3. Select and implement evidence-based designs for professional learning to achieve professional learning goals.
4. Provide job-embedded coaching and other forms of assistance to support transfer of learning.
5. Assess and evaluate the effectiveness of professional learning.
6. Inform ongoing improvement in teaching, leadership, and learning.
7. Tap external assistance when necessary.

LEARNING DESIGNS
What are high-quality learning designs?

An understanding of this concept is useful for readers studying all roles as they work to implement the Learning Designs standard. Learning designs that align with the standards share the following features:
- Outcomes aligned with performance standards and student learning outcomes;
- Active engagement;
- Reflection;
- Metacognition; and
- Ongoing support.

Learning environments

A range of learning environments are possible for high-quality learning designs;
- Online (dynamic, i.e., social networking, and static, i.e., online courses, repositories of information, video cases, etc.);
- In-person (or face-to-face); and
- Hybrid (or blended).

Types of learning designs

(Note: Frequently multiple designs are coupled together in a single learning experience)
- Peer coaching
- Coaching
- Collaborative learning communities
- Action research

- Examining student work, e.g., assessment results, work products, assignments, etc.
- Examining educator work, e.g., assignments, assessments, communications, learning tools, etc.
- Co-construction of learning tools, i.e., lesson plans, common assessments, units, etc.
- Participating in online communities and networks
- Courses (online, in-person, hybrid)
- Workshops (usually shorter in length than courses)
- Instructional rounds
- Walk-throughs
- Co-teaching
- Lesson study
- Video reviews and critiques
- Observing or presenting demonstrations
- Observing peers and/or students
- Discussion/Dialogue groups
- Socratic seminars
- Cooperative learning
- Data analysis
- Reading research and scholarly papers, books, etc.
- Attending conferences
- Writing papers for publication
- Case studies

Factors that influence the selection of learning designs

While the standards call for high-quality learning designs as described above, educators must consider a range of factors when they decide which learning designs to use for a given situation. This concept is referenced in the desired outcomes for all roles under the concept **Select learning designs**.

Individual factors

- Learning preference
- Experiences in education
- Experiences outside of education
- Personal background and beliefs (beliefs, attitudes about learning and change, culture, language, etc.)
- Previous experience with the content
- Experience with change
- Initial level of understanding and use of the content
- Perceived need and urgency
- Perceived value and purpose
- Opportunity to contribute to design and content of learning
- Experience with learning designs employed

School and system factors

- Established need and urgency
- Clear, consistent, and shared vision and goals
- Experience with previous change efforts
- Culture for risk-taking and learning
- School's and system's experience with past change efforts

- Stability of leadership
- Time available for professional learning
- Availability and opportunities for sustained support, practice, coaching, and feedback
- Expectation about the degree of fidelity of implementation
- Monitoring system
- Sufficiency of resources (staff, time, materials, technology, and funds) to support learning

Content-related
- Complexity of the learning outcomes
- Degree of change expected
- Type of learning outcomes (e.g., awareness, application, mastery, etc.)

IMPLEMENTATION
Change theories, research, models, and tools

In the **Apply change research** concept for all roles, the Innovation Configuration maps reference these change theories and models:

IC maps: Innovation Configuration maps are tools to support the implementation of new programs, practices, or skills, referred to here as innovations. They describe the behaviors associated with the innovation in degrees of variation beginning with the ideal to emerging levels. These levels are useful in assisting implementers to know how to strengthen their practice to achieve full implementation of the innovation.

SoC: Stages of Concern describe seven types or stages of reactions, feelings, perceptions, or attitudes implementers experience as they proceed through change. Stages of Concern address the affective dimensions of change. Knowing implementers' stage of concern allows those responsible for facilitating implementation to tailor personalized support for each implementer in a way that provides each implementer with the support needed to move to full implementation. The stages encompass 0=Awareness and 6=Refocus.

LoU: Levels of Use delineates the degree or level of use of the change. Levels of Use are behaviors of people who are engaged in the change. Knowing the level of use for individuals and teams helps those facilitating implementation provide supports to overcome barriers to implementation and increase the level of use. The levels encompass Non-use at Level 0 and Renewal at Level VI.

RPLIM: RPLIM is a process for planning, implementing, and assessing change that guides those facilitating change in the process and helps them plan for, assess, and monitor their work as change leaders. R=Readiness; P=Planning; L=Learning; I=Implementation; and M=Monitoring. Each phase requires specific actions to prepare for the next phase.

PDSA: PDSA is another version of a cycle for planning and implementing change. Like RPLIM, it helps those facilitating change understand how to lead change. P=Plan; D=Do; S=Study; A=Act.

User Guide

Standards for Professional Learning describe the attributes of effective professional learning. Yet, the standards alone will not be sufficient to improve the quality and results of professional learning unless they are used to guide the planning, implementation, and evaluation of professional learning that occurs in teams, schools, school systems, regional agencies, state and provincial agencies, and national and international settings. To advance implementation of the standards and use them as a lever for excellence in all forms of professional learning, Learning Forward developed Innovation Configuration (IC) maps for those who work in schools and have a role in professional learning. Other volumes address roles in school systems and roles outside of schools.

IC maps paint a picture of what an innovation looks like in practice because change is not a light-switch operation. Change is a process that is simultaneously personal and developmental. In the IC maps for the standards, descriptions of ideal or high-fidelity practices accompany descriptions of practices at the opposite end of the spectrum (nonuse of the standard) as well as a range of variations in between the ideal and nonuse. The ideal variations help to clarify what full implementation of a standard looks like. Leading up to the ideal variations, from the right, are multiple variations that describe how one progresses from nonuse to ideal use. These intermediate variations provide guidance to someone who wishes to move from his or her current level of use to the ideal.

USING THE IC MAPS

In *The Knowing-Doing Gap*, Jeffrey Pfeffer and Robert Sutton (2000) acknowledge that hundreds of books offer useful and proven ideas to improve practice in many businesses; however, most of these ideas remain unimplemented. The authors argue that knowing is not the same as doing. They conclude that simply reading books and articles will not shrink the knowing-doing gap. Reducing the gap requires moving into action, applying what is known, and maintaining momentum. Pfeffer and Sutton describe the world of business. Their message, however, resonates with educators. New programs, curricula, professional learning, and initiatives abound, yet educators' best efforts to implement them fully often do little more than build awareness and simultaneously hope for sustainability. Little effort goes into implementation, a prerequisite for results and sustainability.

The IC maps for Standards for Professional Learning are tools that bridge the knowing-doing gap, the gap between knowing about the standards and using them to increase the quality and effectiveness of professional learning. This user guide for the IC maps offers some ideas for engaging stakeholders in using the standards and creating the changes necessary for effective professional learning. Edward Tobia and Shirley Hord (2002) in a review of literature about change in education, identified six strategies to help schools navigate the labyrinth of change and successfully implement innovation. While these strategies are common sense, they are not always common practice. The six strategies necessary to move from knowing to doing are:

1. Creating an atmosphere and context for change. Leadership recognizes that creating an atmosphere that encourages and supports change is one of its primary goals. Taking risks is encouraged and supported.

2. Developing and communicating a shared vision. Clear vision is the mental picture of what any change might look like when fully implemented—a preferred image of the future.

3. Planning and providing resources. Leaders, working with staff, create implementation plans and discuss how to best use people, time, and money to support a new program.

4. Investing in professional learning. Change efforts usually involve learning new information, skills, and attitudes. Professional learning also includes the support structures necessary for consistent implementation.

5. Checking progress. There is a need to monitor progress, identify challenges to implementation, and seek input about needs related to the change. This is a check of current performance against the vision.

6. Continuing to give assistance. Assistance needs to be provided as practices change over time. It also needs to be differentiated according to individual and organizational needs. This strategy is coupled with the checking progress strategy.

IC maps give educators the resources for several of these strategies. They communicate a shared vision, identify what key educators do to be successful, provide a resource for monitoring progress, and specify what the outcomes of assistance are. The tools that follow identify specific ways that educators who lead, facilitate, support, and engage in professional learning can work together to implement the standards. The chart on the following page aligns steps in standards implementation with related uses of IC maps and tools in this guide to help learners on this journey.

REFERENCES

Pfeffer, J. & Sutton, R. (2000). *The knowing-doing gap.* Cambridge, MA: Harvard Business School Press.

Tobia, E., & Hord, S. (2002, March). Making the leap: Leadership, learning, and successful program implementation. *Instructional Leader.* Austin, TX: Texas Elementary Principals and Supervisors Association.

Steps to implementing Standards for Professional Learning	Innovation Configuration map benefits	Tools to accomplish
Define the standards	• Describes the standards in practice by roles. • Describes best practices associated with the standards. • Provides a common vocabulary for dialogue about the standards. • Provides the text for conversations to promote understanding of the standards. • Promotes buy-in to the standards.	Tool 1: Developing a Shared Vision
Monitor implementation of the standards	• Gauges level of implementation of the standards within various contexts (teams, grades, departments, schools, school systems, etc.) and by various roles (teacher, coach, school leadership team, principal). • Sets expectations for high-fidelity implementation. • Informs goal setting to move the bar over time for continuous improvement. • Refines understanding of the standards.	Tool 2: Checking Progress
Self-assess or reflect on practice	• Promotes individual reflection and assessment of practice. • Continues to refine understanding of the standards.	Tool 3: Using the IC Maps as a Self-Assessment
Support implementation	• Enables the identification of resources and support for implementation of the standards. • Informs goal setting to move the bar over time for continuous improvement.	Tool 4: Determining Support Strategies
Guide professional learning	• Provides support for the planning, implementation, and evaluation of professional learning.	Tool 5: Backmapping Model

TOOL 1:
Developing a Shared Vision

A key concept undergirding the creation of a shared vision is a mental picture, held by those who implement the change, that describes what the change will look like when it is fully implemented. Every educator in a school can use the IC maps to create a mental picture of what he or she will be doing when each of the standards is fully implemented.

Purpose: Develop a shared vision about the implementation of one of the Standards for Professional Learning.

Group Size: 4 people

Time: 50–60 minutes

Materials: Copies of the IC maps for each of the role groups for one standard (group decides which standard to work on) and the explanation for the selected standard. Educators within a school have permission to copy the IC maps after purchasing at least one school copy for the purpose of using the maps to improve professional learning. The explanations for all standards are included in the front of this volume.

DIRECTIONS

1. Each team selects one of the seven standards to study in greater depth. Teams may want to divide the standards among the teams.

2. Team members read the explanation for the selected standard and divide up the IC maps for all of the roles among the team. For example:
   a. Person 1 reads the Teacher IC map—Learning Communities
   b. Person 2 reads the Coach IC map—Learning Communities
   c. Person 3 reads the School Leadership Team IC map—Learning Communities
   d. Person 4 reads the Principal IC map—Learning Communities

3. Each person reads the desired outcome statements and the corresponding Level 1 description and prepares to explain the tasks and responsibilities required of the role group assigned.

4. Team members reconvene and share the information from their individual reading within the group and use the note-taking guide to record their findings.

TOOL: Developing a Shared Vision

TEACHER			COACH
_____	STANDARD		_____
_____	_____		_____
_____	_____		_____
_____	_____		_____
	_____		
	_____		
SCHOOL LEADERSHIP TEAM	_____		PRINCIPAL
_____	_____		_____
_____			_____
_____			_____
_____			_____
			_____

NOTES:

_____

_____

_____

_____

_____

_____

_____

_____

TOOL 2:
Checking Progress

The activity described in this tool models how to use the IC maps to check progress and conduct a self-assessment. The key concepts behind checking progress on taking steps to standards implementation are monitoring progress, identifying challenges to implementation, and seeking input about needs related to the change. Checking progress provides an opportunity to assess current practice and compare it to the ideal. Members of each role group can use the IC map to determine their current practices and how close or far away those practices are from ideal practice.

Purpose: Check progress toward full implementation of one standard using the IC maps.

Group Size: 2–3 people

Time: 30 minutes

Materials: Descriptions of a school leadership team's current practice related to the Implementation standard; one copy of the School Leadership Team IC map for the Implementation standard for each person; one copy of the scoring sheet for each person.

DIRECTIONS

1. Team members read descriptions of a school leadership team's actions in the vignettes below and score them using the IC map. Team members will determine whether the actions best match Level 1, Level 2, or Level 3 descriptions. There are two options to accomplish this step:

   A. Each member reads the descriptions and scores them individually. The group discusses each description and reaches a consensus on the level that is the best match.

   B. Each member reads one description, scores it individually, and shares rationale for his or her scores.

   Note: The first option takes more time to complete because the team members are striving for consensus about the meaning of the IC map description.

Sample Scoring Sheet

Implementation Standard Desired Outcomes	SLT A	SLT B	SLT C	SLT D
Desired outcome 6.1.1: Develops capacity to apply research on change to support implementation of professional learning.	Level 2	Level 1	Level 3	Level 2

Score Sheet

Implementation Standard Desired Outcomes	SLT A	SLT B	SLT C	SLT D
Desired outcome 6.1.1: Develops capacity to apply research on change to support implementation of professional learning.				
Desired outcome 6.1.2: Applies research about change to plan and lead the implementation of professional learning.				
Desired outcome 6.1.3: Monitors implementation of professional learning.				
Desired outcome 6.2.1: Differentiates support for implementation of professional learning.				
Desired outcome 6.2.2: Continues support to reach high-fidelity implementation of professional learning.				
Desired outcome 6.3.1: Develops own and staff's capacity to give and receive constructive feedback.				
Desired outcome 6.3.2: Gives and receives frequent constructive feedback based on data to accelerate and refine implementation of professional learning.				

School Leadership Team Vignettes

SCHOOL LEADERSHIP TEAM A

Jensen Park Middle School's leadership team has responsibility for the entire school improvement plan. Elected by their peers, the team is cofacilitated by the principal and a teacher leader who also serves as a member of the team. The team acknowledges that it has significant responsibilities for setting goals and identifying the processes to accomplish the goal of improving reading of all students by implementing the balanced literacy program.

Members of the SLT suggest that the school's coach provide the support needed for professional learning. They write into their plan that he will meet with the whole staff and teams throughout the year to check if they are implementing the reading program and to provide resources they need. In addition, he will summarize the status of the reading program at the end of both the semester and the year to report back to the SLT.

The team members are not very knowledgeable about professional learning and have expressed several times that they wish the principal would appoint a separate group to handle whatever professional learning is needed in the school. They also believe the coach is responsible for any professional learning associated with the new literacy program. The principal has offered several times to provide information about how school improvement and professional learning are so interconnected that it would be difficult to separate the responsibilities; professional learning is the means through which the school improves. The principal has also offered to ask the district coordinator of professional learning to provide some background knowledge on effective professional learning to help the SLT members plan for long-term change and to build in the support needed to move their goals into results.

The SLT members believe that their responsibility is developing the plan and that others are responsible for putting the plan into action and making sure it works. They will do their part to contribute in their individual classrooms. They are uncomfortable taking any monitoring role because they do not feel prepared to deal with the resistance they know will arise with the new program.

SCHOOL LEADERSHIP TEAM B

The school leadership team at Marion Elementary School has been frustrated with its past professional learning plan. The members can't seem to meet everyone's needs and keep a schoolwide focus on the school's goals with everyone doing individual professional learning. To correct that problem, they study how to promote school change by engaging in a series of webinars with several leading authorities on school change. They also participate in a total of two days of professional learning with the whole staff over three months to describe what their new Thinking Math program looks like in practice at each grade level. This leads to a good deal of discussion about how difficult it is to implement the program effectively.

The SLT meets with the staff to talk about the support they want to refine implementation and remove inconsistencies that exist across the grades. Teachers agree to observe at least three other teachers, one at their own grade level, one at the grade level above, and one at the grade level below. Kindergarten teachers observe third- and fourth-grade teachers, and sixth-grade teachers visit classrooms at two middle schools. They agree to provide feedback to the teachers they observe using the cross-grade level Thinking Math implementation rubric as a guide. They plan to find examples of the behaviors specified on the rubric.

At the end of each quarter, the SLT reviews the math benchmark scores, surveys teachers about their perceptions of successes and challenges with implementation, and prepares a brief summary report to share with the staff. Following their second report, SLT members discuss with the principal how to provide extra support to the new teachers and to a few teachers who have requested additional support. Their goal, they say, is to be sure everyone has an opportunity to succeed with the program.

SCHOOL LEADERSHIP TEAM C

Friar's Point High School's school leadership team is composed of teachers, parents, students, and administrators. They are responsible for developing, monitoring, and evaluating the school's annual improvement plan. As part of a school that has been "in need of improvement" for two years, their plans are focused on professional learning that builds the capacity of all staff. Their goal for the last three years has been to increase students' academic achievement and engagement by implementing high-yield instructional strategies and personalizing learning. They have seen some small improvements in student achievement, but not enough. The SLT recommends organizing teachers into communities of practice within the school for their professional learning and collaborative work. Because staff members are unfamiliar with how to work together collaboratively, the SLT works with the principal to allot time for communities to meet at least twice a month; reads several articles on how to implement change; sets an action plan; seeks volunteer teacher leaders to participate in district training on facilitation; and identifies several benchmarks to serve as indicators of success throughout the year. The SLT knows it has a significant responsibility to provide leadership, support, and guidance to teams as they learn to become communities of practice focused on improving instruction and student learning.

The team members agree to take an active role in supporting their plan. Each agrees to talk with small groups of staff members several times per year to get input about what is working and what isn't. The principal, according to the plan, will meet with each community at least three times during the year. Throughout the year, they identify challenges that occur and meet to discuss how to address them in an expedient manner. Individually, they have conversations with peers to talk about the role of collaboration and listen to the concerns being raised. They gather feedback by survey three times during the year to assess the quality and progress of communities of practice. They invite facilitators to meet with the SLT several times during the year to listen to discussions of successes and challenges. They devote two faculty meetings during the year to considering how communities of practice are working and what can improve them.

SCHOOL LEADERSHIP TEAM D

Booker T. Washington K–8 School staff have been proud of their students' substantial improvements in literacy and math achievement over the last three years. Teachers want to incorporate science, so the school leadership team agrees to write a grant to participate in the scientist-in-residence program available through the local college. The SLT members admit that they know little about how to implement a science program, but they have experience with success in math and literacy. They spend one meeting doing a journey map process to look back over all they have done as a school to achieve improvements. They study past school improvement plans, look over minutes of meetings, gather information from staff, compile a history of what they have done in the past five years to improve student achievement, and examine the information for leverage points for their new plan.

Using the information they gather, they plan the science program implementation. Their grant proposal calls for a series of whole-school learning experiences with the scientist-in-residence. They receive notice about a month after submitting the proposal that they have been selected, and Dr. Kyle Jankowski from the Physical Science Department—or Dr. J, as he asks to be called—is their scientist-in-residence. He arranges to come to the school six times during the year to model lessons for teachers and to work with teachers in small groups by grade level to adjust the lessons he models to each grade level. He even brings equipment that is unavailable in the school for teachers to use.

Teachers are excited about their learning and most try the lessons Dr. J models. Students also seem excited about science and ask for more opportunities to engage in science lessons. Teachers frequently remark that they would like to do more science, but literacy and math continue to be their priority areas, so it is difficult to do less in those areas. When the school year is over, teachers all agree that it was a great opportunity to have the scientist-in-residence in their school.

TOOL 3:
Using the IC Maps as a Self-Assessment

IC maps can be used as a self-assessment tool. Similar to the process described in Tool 2, Checking Progress, an individual (or even a team) can use the same process to conduct a self-assessment.

Purpose: Conduct a self-assessment to check implementation progress of one or more standards and compare current behaviors to the descriptions in the IC maps.

Group Size: 1 (or more, if conducting team assessments)

Time: 10 minutes (longer if more than one person is involved)

Materials: IC map for one standard for the appropriate role group.

DIRECTIONS

1. The individual identifies one or more standards to self-assess. If the school or a team has a goal for improvement in one standard area, everyone might use the same standard with the appropriate role group IC map to conduct periodic self-assessments.

2. The individual reads the desired outcomes and all the variations and determines the level that best matches his or her current practice. He or she should record those levels on a separate sheet and include the date.

3. The individual can use this information to identify next steps or assistance necessary for improvement. More information on next steps is included in Tool 4.

TOOL 4:
Determining Support Strategies

Purpose: Determine assistance and support needed to strengthen implementation based on the data from Tool 2, Checking Progress, or Tool 3, Self-Assessment.

Group Size: 4–5 people

Time: 30 minutes

Materials:
- List of individuals' current levels of practice—Teachers/Learning Community
- Group summary—Teachers/Learning Community
- Copy of Teacher IC maps for the Learning Community standard
- Questions for Analysis, Teams and Individuals

DIRECTIONS

This activity has two parts. First, a small group will use Questions for Analysis—Individuals to recommend support for individual teachers related to the Learning Community standard. Second, the group will use Questions for Analysis—Teams to identify support for groups of teachers related to the Learning Community standard.

1. Review the list of individuals' current levels of practice that is provided below. This is an anonymous summary of how individual teachers responded to the self-assessment on the Learning Community standard (Tool 4.1.1 and 4.1.2).

2. Review the Teacher IC map for the Learning Community standard to ensure everyone has a common understanding of what each level means. See pp. 46-48.

3. Answer the analysis questions as a group. These questions will help the group recommend assistance for individuals (Tool 4.2).

4. Repeat the process, following the same procedure, using the Team Summary data (Tool 4.3.1 and 4.3.2). Answer the analysis questions based on this data (Tool 4.4).

5. Discuss the advantages and disadvantages of each kind of data display and analysis.

TOOL 4.1.1: SCORING SHEET FOR INDIVIDUALS—Teacher/Learning Community

This table represents the anonymous self-assessment scores from individual teachers.
Means are rounded up.

Teacher	Desired outcome 1.1.1: Develops capacity to apply the seven-step cycle of continuous improvement.	Desired outcome 1.1.2: Applies the cycle of continuous improvement with fidelity in professional learning.	Desired outcome 1.2.1: Advances collective responsibility.	Desired outcome 1.2.2: Engages with colleagues to meet the needs of all students.	Desired outcome 1.2.3: Models collective responsibility by participating in learning communities.	Desired outcome 1.3.1: Aligns professional learning with school goals.
A	1	1	2	2	2	1
B	5	5	5	5	5	5
C	2	4	2	3	3	2
D	3	3	4	3	4	3
E	5	5	5	4	5	4
F	2	1	1	2	1	2
G	5	5	5	5	4	5
H	3	2	1	2	2	2
I	4	3	5	4	5	4
J	1	2	1	1	2	2
K	3	4	3	2	3	2
L	2	3	2	3	3	2
M	3	4	2	3	4	4
MEAN*	**3.00**	**3.23**	**3.00**	**3.00**	**2.92**	**3.00**

*Lower score indicates higher implementation.

TOOL 4.1.2: INDIVIDUAL SUMMARY DATA

This table summarizes the percentage of teachers scoring at each level based on the data in Tool 4.1.1. Percentages are rounded.

Desired Outcome	Level 1	Level 2	Level 3	Level 4	Level 5
Desired outcome 1.1.1: Develops capacity to apply the seven-step cycle of continuous improvement.	15%	23%	31%	8%	23%
Desired outcome 1.1.2: Applies the cycle of continuous improvement with fidelity in professional learning.	15%	15%	23%	23%	23%
Desired outcome 1.2.1: Advances collective responsibility.	23%	31%	8%	8%	31%
Desired outcome 1.2.2: Engages with colleagues to meet the needs of all students.	8%	31%	31%	15%	15%
Desired outcome 1.2.3: Models collective responsibility by participating in learning communities.	8%	23%	23%	23%	23%
Desired outcome 1.3.1: Aligns professional learning with school goals.	8%	46%	8%	23%	15%

TOOL 4.2: QUESTIONS FOR ANALYSIS—INDIVIDUALS

1. Which teacher(s) seem to have the highest degree of implementation?

_____

_____

2. Which teacher(s) seem to have the lowest degree of implementation?

_____

_____

3. What additional resources or information would be of assistance to individual or groups of teachers?

_____

_____

4. What recommendations do you have for providing support or assistance? Who might provide the support?

_____

_____

5. Would some training help some of these teachers? If so, what would the content of the training be? Who might provide the training for teachers? What other kind of learning experience might be appropriate?

_____

_____

6. What other strategies could be used to increase implementation by individual teachers?

_____

_____

TOOL 4.3.1: SCORING SHEET FOR TEAMS—Teacher/Learning Community

This table represents the anonymous self-assessment scores from teams of teachers. Means are rounded up.

TEAM	Desired outcome 1.1.1: Develops capacity to apply the seven-step cycle of continuous improvement.	Desired outcome 1.1.2: Applies the cycle of continuous improvement with fidelity in professional learning.	Desired outcome 1.2.1: Advances collective responsibility.	Desired outcome 1.2.2: Engages with colleagues to meet the needs of all students.	Desired outcome 1.2.3: Models collective responsibility by participating in learning communities.	Desired outcome 1.3.1: Aligns professional learning with school goals.
A	1	2	2	2	2	1
B	5	5	5	5	5	5
C	2	2	2	3	3	2
D	3	4	4	4	4	3
E	2	1	2	2	1	2
F	4	3	3	3	4	3
G	3	1	2	1	2	2
H	4	5	5	5	5	4
MEAN*	3.00	2.88	3.13	3.13	3.25	2.75

*Lower score indicates higher implementation.

TOOL 4.3.2: TEAM SUMMARY DATA—Teacher/Learning Community

This table summarizes the percentage of teams scoring at each level based on the data in Tool 4.3.1. Percentages are rounded.

Desired Outcome	Level 1	Level 2	Level 3	Level 4	Level 5
Desired outcome 1.1.1: Develops capacity to apply the seven-step cycle of continuous improvement.	13%	25%	25%	25%	13%
Desired outcome 1.1.2: Applies the cycle of continuous improvement with fidelity in professional learning.	25%	25%	13%	13%	25%
Desired outcome 1.2.1: Advances collective responsibility.	0%	38%	13%	13%	38%
Desired outcome 1.2.2: Engages with colleagues to meet the needs of all students.	13%	25%	25%	13%	25%
Desired outcome 1.2.3: Models collective responsibility by participating in learning communities.	13%	25%	13%	25%	25%
Desired outcome 1.3.1: Aligns professional learning with school goals.	13%	38%	25%	13%	13%

TOOL 4.4: QUESTIONS FOR ANALYSIS—TEAMS

1. Which desired outcome(s) seem to have the highest degree of implementation?

_____

_____

2. Which desired outcome(s) seem to have the lowest degree of implementation?

_____

_____

3. What additional resources or information would be of assistance to most teachers?

_____

_____

4. What interventions could principals, coaches, school leadership teams, or central office offer?

_____

_____

5. Which of the desired outcomes require special attention because of the overall implementation level? How does this area affect success in other areas?

_____

_____

6. What strategies might increase implementation of this desired outcome?

_____

_____

TOOL 5:
Backmapping Model for Planning Professional Learning

The Backmapping Model for Planning Professional Learning describes a seven-step process for planning professional development (Killion, 1999). A district, school, department, or grade-level can use this process, but when analysis and planning take place at the school and/or department level, a closer alignment with student learning needs is more likely to occur.

Some of these steps may seem familiar for they are similar to most school improvement planning models. In fact, school improvement and professional development should complement and be aligned with each other. School improvement identifies student learning goals while professional development assists educators to acquire new knowledge and skills in order to accomplish those same student learning needs. Depending on the current school/district improvement process, this planning model may suggest a few additional steps to add to established processes.

Purpose: To guide the planning of professional learning that improves student learning/achievement.

Group Size: May vary – this process is valuable for school leadership teams, department level teams, whole-school faculties.

Time: Several sessions for teams or faculties.

Materials: Copy of diagram and steps with questions for all participants.

DIRECTIONS

This planning process requires several steps for teams and will guide data analysis and discussion for several meeting periods. Determine which elements of this process will require larger group discussions and which will benefit from smaller group discussions and plan individual sessions accordingly.

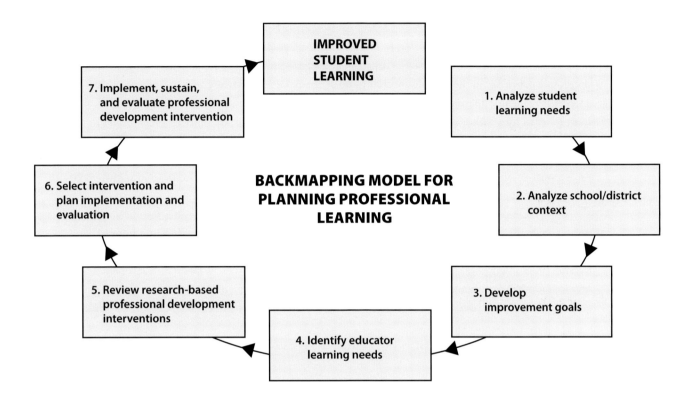

BACKMAPPING MODEL FOR PLANNING PROFESSIONAL LEARNING

IMPROVED STUDENT LEARNING

7. Implement, sustain, and evaluate professional development intervention

1. Analyze student learning needs

6. Select intervention and plan implementation and evaluation

2. Analyze school/district context

5. Review research-based professional development interventions

3. Develop improvement goals

4. Identify educator learning needs

STEP 1: ANALYZE STUDENT LEARNING NEEDS.

To produce results, professional development must be directly tied to student learning needs. Before selecting or designing professional development, a careful and thorough analysis of student achievement data occurs. This analysis will help identify specific student achievement strengths and areas of need and will guide decisions about the format of professional development.

Key questions to answer during this step include:
- What assessment data are available?
- What is being measured in each assessment?
- What areas of student performance are meeting or exceeding expectations?
- What areas of student performance are below expectations?
- What patterns exist within the data? How are the data similar or different in various grade levels, content areas, and individual classes?
- How did various subpopulations of student perform? (Consider gender, race, and socio-economic status.)
- What are other data telling us about student performance?
- What surprises us?
- What confirms what we already know?

The data analysis process results in staff knowing or identifying:
- Specific areas of student need;
- Specific knowledge and skills that students need in order to improve achievement results; and
- Specific students or groups of students for whom the need is most prevalent or pronounced.

For example, assume a school's scores on a state assessment are below the expected or desired level in mathematics. *These scores are insufficient by themselves to use for planning professional development interventions.* Now assume that the mathematics department analyzes subtest and subpopulation scores. Perhaps they find a deficiency in the area of probability and statistics for a particular group of students. This analysis may include a review of the curriculum to determine which standards or learning objectives are most essential for students to achieve and what fundamental knowledge and skills are prerequisites to these standards. This type of information can be used to establish schoolwide and/or department improvement goals, identify specific actions necessary to achieve those goals, and guide the selection and/or design of a professional development intervention to address the need of increasing the probability and statistic skills of the identified group of students.

In the example above, to simply identify *mathematics* as the area of focus provides insufficient information to guide the design and/or selection of a professional development program. The latter information, in contrast, is actionable — that is, it is specific enough to identify what teachers need to know and be able to do in order to improve student performance in probability and statistics. While state assessment data is important, other data should be included in this analysis. District or school formative assessments, grades, attendance, discipline issues, graduation rates, demographics, and other student data need to be considered.

STEP 2: IDENTIFY UNIQUE CHARACTERISTICS OF COMMUNITY, DISTRICT, SCHOOL, DEPARTMENT, AND STAFF.

When school leaders and teachers understand the unique characteristics of students, they can use this information to make appropriate instructional and program decisions. The parallel is true for professional development leaders. Knowing the unique characteristics of the adults who will participate in the professional development will influence the design of the learning experience and the nature of the follow-up support.

Understanding the conditions under which the professional development will be implemented also helps inform the selection and/or design of professional development. For example, professional development for experienced teachers may be different from professional development for novices. Likewise, professional development that is intended to enable staff to meet the needs of urban, disadvantaged students may be different from professional development for rural schools. Additionally, professional development in a district or school setting with limited resources and/or time for professional learning will be different than in settings where time and resources are available.

Districts, schools, and/or departments develop profiles that provide information about the school environment and conditions. Detailing the context helps professional development leaders make informed decisions about appropriate professional development strategies and interventions.

Key questions to answer in this step include: What are the characteristics of our students? Some characteristics to consider include:

- Ethnicity/race;
- Gender;
- Socioeconomic status;
- Mobility;
- Family support;
- Motivation;
- Attitude toward school;
- Experience in school;
- Academic performance;
- Retention rates;
- Parents' education level; and
- Sibling data.

What are the characteristics of staff? Some characteristics to consider include:

- Years of experience;
- Years at grade level;
- Years in the school;
- Past experience with professional development;
- Motivation;
- Performance/ability;
- Attitude;
- Sense of efficacy;
- Response to change;
- Collegiality;
- Extent to which teachers' preparation aligns with teaching assignments; and
- Level of education.

What are some characteristics of our formal and informal leadership for both teachers and administrators? Some characteristics to consider include:

- Leadership style;
- Roles of formal and informal leaders;
- Level of participation in leadership activities;
- Opportunities to be involved in leadership roles/activities;
- Trust in leadership;
- Support by leadership;
- Support for leadership; and
- Level of communication.

What are some characteristics of our community? Some characteristics to consider include:

- Support for education;
- Support for the school;
- Involvement in school activities;
- Support for students; and
- Support for professional development.

What resources are available to support professional development? Some considerations include:
- Budget;
- Time;
- Support personnel in the building;
- Support personnel outside the building;
- Union contract; and
- Incentives.

A variety of job-embedded professional development strategies can be used to develop awareness of new instructional strategies, build knowledge, translate new knowledge into practice, practice using new strategies, and reflect on new practice. Each job-embedded strategy needs to be matched to its most appropriate use. For example, if the school/district has an experienced staff and one of the intended outcomes is to build more collaborative professional relationships, then Study Groups, Critical Friends Groups, Lesson Study, Peer Coaching, and Tuning Protocol would be appropriate strategies to use. If, on the other hand, there are many new educators in the building and there is a need to build the instructional capacity of staff, then Critical Friends Groups, Case Discussions, Curriculum Designers, Journaling, Mentoring, Peer Coaching, and Standards in Practice would be appropriate.

Questions to consider in addition to the ones identified above include:
- What are the characteristics of the context of the school or district?
- What do teachers already know and what do they need to know next?
- What practices are being used in the classroom currently? How different are desired practices from current practice?
- What is the school culture? Does it embrace new practices or resist change?
- What are teachers' current levels of understanding of content related to state standards?
- What support do teachers need in order to implement new strategies?

STEP 3: ESTABLISH CLEAR, MEASURABLE OUTCOMES FOR THE PROFESSIONAL DEVELOPMENT.

Educators need to understand the goals for both student and teacher learning that are intended to result from their professional development efforts. Missing the mark is easy if you don't have a clear goal and specific target.

Key questions about outcomes include:
- What results do we seek for students?
- What new practices do we expect from staff?

The intended results of professional development are stated primarily in terms of student achievement. Actions or changes that occur for teachers and principals are means to achieve the goal of increased student achievement and are best stated as objectives rather than outcomes or goals. In other words, expected outcomes are stated in terms that allow the school to know if it has or has not achieved the intended results.

For example, a goal that states, "100% of the staff will participate in training in brain-based learning" does not include the intended student impact because of this training. Too often, professional development goals are stated as activities that will be conducted rather than results that will be accomplished.

A preferable goal would be this: "In three years, 90% of students will read on grade level as a result of teachers learning and implementing new brain-based instructional strategies." The latter goal is focused on the end result of professional development rather than on what occurs in the process. These goals might include a statement that most teachers will use new practices routinely and with high quality or high fidelity. Student learning will only be impacted when teachers *implement* new strategies well — not just *know* them.

STEP 4: IDENTIFY TEACHER AND PRINCIPAL LEARNING NEEDS.

Professional development frequently begins with needs assessments that ask adult learners to identify what they want to learn. This common practice often leaves a gap between what educators *want to learn* and what they may *need to learn* to address the identified, student learning goals. For example, teachers are often eager to learn about new educational innovations, and principals may want to learn how to shortcut nagging managerial tasks. However, if the goal is to increase student reading performance and comprehension and interpretation of nonfiction text were identified as the area of great deficit, both teachers and principals have a specific need to develop their skills and knowledge in this area in order to teach and support classroom instruction in reading nonfiction text. Professional development on topics other than these areas may deflect time and resources from the established school improvement goals.

Classroom walkthroughs are helpful when determining teacher learning needs. Classroom walkthroughs help administrators and teams of teachers gather information about instructional strengths and needs, provide a framework for using that information to discuss instruction, monitor the implementation of professional development, and measure the impact of professional development to enhance classroom practices. Classroom walkthroughs can provide administrators with clear information about current practices in the building. They help administrators identify trends and patterns of practice within a school/ district. This information informs the conversation between administration and faculty about effective classroom practices. It also assists the administrator and faculty to determine appropriate learning needs to accomplish their student learning and professional development goals.

After educators' learning needs are identified, professional development leaders consider specific actions for meeting the identified learning needs. The scope and content of the necessary professional development will be clearer when the district, school, or department team has a clear understanding of student learning needs, the context and characteristics of the school or district, the specific goal, and the learning needs of educators.

STEP 5: STUDY THE RESEARCH EVIDENCE FOR SPECIFIC PROFESSIONAL DEVELOPMENT PROGRAMS/ INTERVENTIONS.

After establishing teacher/educator learning goals, professional development leaders examine the research for specific professional development practices to ensure they are supported with evidence of impact on student learning. Too often, this important step is overlooked. District, school, and/or grade-level staffs often fail to conduct a critical review of the programs and practices that are available and determine whether those new practices have proven successful. In their urgency and enthusiasm to improve student performance, school staffs may pass over this critical step and select or adapt programs with which they are unfamiliar.

The following questions are helpful when examining professional development options:

- Which professional development addresses the skills and knowledge we have identified as educator learning needs?
- Which professional development is being used by schools with similar student demographics?
- If our school's characteristics do not match those of schools in which the professional development was successful, what are the key differences? How likely are those differences to interfere with our success?
- What changes could be implemented to increase the likelihood of success?
- What aspects of the professional development (if any) might need to be modified to accommodate the unique features of our school?
- What are the strengths and weaknesses of the professional development?
- What school, district, and community support was required to make the professional development successful?

After examining research-based evidence, the district, school, and/or department team may decide to either adopt/adapt an existing professional development program **or** create its own. This is a significant decision that needs to be made with careful thought and thorough discussion. When making this decision, members are deciding where to place their energy and resources for the long run. Too often schools fail to achieve success because they use a revolving door approach to innovations — that is, a series of experts pop in to prescribe the best treatment for the problem. Sometimes, professional development or improvement efforts are viewed as temporary intrusions that staff can wait out. In fact, any professional development intervention requires a new way of doing business, one that the district, school, and/or grade level will fully commit to and one that they fully expect to become a routine part of their everyday practice. Without this level of commitment, no staff development intervention holds promise for improving student and teacher learning.

STEP 6: PLAN INTERVENTION, IMPLEMENTATION, AND EVALUATION.

Initiating new professional development takes times and energy. To implement new professional development strategies requires that leaders or faculty plan follow-up or long-term support beyond the immediate school year. A professional development intervention needs to be carefully selected to match teacher learning needs. There are many questions to ask and answer to get the best fit between educator needs and appropriate professional development design. Many job-embedded professional development strategies can be used in combination to help educators learn about new practices, begin implementing new practices, and consistently use new practices. Each of these three aspects of learning new classroom strategies requires different kinds of professional development experiences. The ultimate goal is to enhance the instructional practices used in the classroom so that student learning is enhanced.

After a professional development program has been selected, adapted, or designed and before implementing it, these questions should be considered:

- How will we assess initiating, implementing, and sustaining the professional development?
- What kind of support is necessary for this professional development to be successful?
- How will we support the individuals involved?
- What are we equipped to do ourselves to support and implement the professional development, and what external resources will we need?

- What resources are we dedicating to the professional development?
- What is our timeline for full implementation by all faculty members?
- What benchmarks along the way will help us know if we are being successful?
- Are we willing to commit time, energy, and financial resources to this effort for the long term?
- How will we align this new initiative with existing ones? What might we need to eliminate to make resources available for this program?
- How closely do the goals of the program align with our school improvement goals and the district's strategic goals?

When planning the evaluation of a professional development program, leaders will:

1) Assess the design of the professional development program to determine if it is thorough, well-conceived, and able to be implemented;
2) Identify the key questions they hope to answer; and
3) Design the evaluation framework, which is the plan for conducting the evaluation.

An evaluation framework includes data collection methodology, data sources, personnel to conduct the evaluation, and a timeline (Killion, 2002). Plans for both formative and summative evaluation are also necessary. A formative assessment allows professional development leaders to know how well the program is being implemented, provides opportunities to take corrective actions, and answers questions such as:

- Are the professional development experiences being implemented as planned?
- Are resources adequate to implement the professional development as planned?
- To what degree are differences occurring in implementation that may influence the results of the professional development?
- A summative evaluation allows professional development leaders to know the program's impact and answers questions such as:
- Have the intended results been achieved?
- What changes for teachers have resulted from the professional development?
- What changes for students have resulted from the professional development
- What changes in the organization have resulted from the professional development?

Planning the evaluation, at the same time as planning the professional development and its implementation, provides greater options for evaluation. Dual planning of professional development and evaluation helps identify important baseline data to collect, which may be necessary for determining the impact of the professional development. Dual planning gives professional development leaders and the evaluator greater clarity about how the professional development is intended to work, thus increasing the likelihood that the professional development will be implemented as designed and that the intended results will be realized.

STEP 7: IMPLEMENT, SUSTAIN, AND EVALUATE THE PROFESSIONAL DEVELOPMENT.

To secure high-quality implementation, participants require constant nurturing and support. In order to continuously improve professional development, the district, school, and/or department team will use data from formative assessments to make continuous adjustments and refinements to strengthen the results. This nurturing is the primary responsibility of the staff development leaders including the principal and teacher leaders. With a long-term commitment, a focus on results for students, and clear indicators of success, a school team has the necessary resources to monitor and make adjustments, strengthening the results of the professional development and ensuring success.

Engaging teachers in professional development requires that those responsible for implementation have a clear understanding of what high-quality performance means and looks like. The IC maps in this volume are valuable tools for reaching agreement on the acceptable level of implementation. Attention to setting expectations and standards for acceptable implementation will make a significant difference in the quality of implementation.

Once the professional development is implemented, attention can turn toward sustaining it. In other words, "How will district, school, and/or department teams keep the focus on the results, provide the necessary resources to continue the professional development, and use data about what teachers have learned in order to continually improve it?" If professional development is fully implemented, sustaining the learning becomes easier yet requires constant attention and resources.

Summative evaluation provides information about the impact of professional development and valuable data to improve its results. Using both formative and summative evaluation processes will provide the best data for district, school, and/or grade-level teams to use to continually improve the professional development and increase the likelihood that it will achieve the results it was designed to achieve (Killion, 2002).

REFERENCES

Killion, J. (1999). *What works in the middle: Results-based staff development*. Oxford: OH: National Staff Development Council.

Killion, J. (2008). *Assessing impact: Evaluating staff development*, 2nd edition. Thousand Oaks: Corwin & NSDC.

Source: Tool 5 adapted from Roy, P. (2007). *A tool kit for quality professional development in Arkansas*. Oxford, OH: NSDC & Arkansas Dept. of Education.

REFLECTIONS

Considering the backmapping model, which of these steps are you using?

_____

_____

Do you need to refine these activities to bring them into line with the model?

_____

_____

Where can you go to find research to support the adoption of new professional development?

_____

_____

Does the school or district have a committee that is assigned to design professional development?

_____

_____

How well prepared is that committee to plan professional development as described in this chapter?

_____

_____

If committee members do not feel ready, who can help increase their capacity?

_____

_____

Is there a variety of student data available for analysis?

_____

_____

Are staff members comfortable conducting their own analysis of student data?

_____

_____

What could be done to help them become more comfortable?

_____

_____